The
EVERYTHING.
Holiday Cookbook

Dear Reader:

Everyone has a favorite holiday, and, inevitably that holiday revolves around food. It might be the memory of a special birthday cake or the traditional Thanksgiving turkey being displayed before it is carved. Maybe it's grandma's not-so-wonderful cheese ball or the first time you sneaked a sip of the spiked Yuletide punch. (My cousin Paula and I romped through snowbanks without our coats on that Christmas Eve!)

Today, our lives are so busy that we turn to holidays as one of the few times in the year that we can gather with family and friends. We now use food as a celebration of our extended lives. We celebrate bonds that are stretched by distance, time, and diverse interests as we gather at the family dining table. The act of eating and enjoying food gives us the common element to tighten those bonds for a few short moments.

For most of us, the holidays incorporate traditional foods. "It wouldn't be the same without Dad's cheese soufflé," my girls complain when we try to suggest a different Christmas Eve meal. And while nobody ever eats the fresh-cooked cranberries, it simply wouldn't be Thanksgiving without sticky red blotches dotting the kitchen floor.

Still, there is room to experiment. Perhaps a new dessert is in order. Or maybe you need to celebrate a new event—Memorial Day and Labor Day deserve their special dishes, too. Possibly you could start a tradition of trying a new dish on every holiday. You might find a new memory.

However you decide to use this cookbook, I know you will have fun with it. Whether you're on the verge of starting new traditions, looking for old favorites, or hunting for something different, you are sure to find it in this wonderful collection.

Margaret Kaeter

The EVERYTHING® Series

Editorial

Publishing Director	Gary M. Krebs
Managing Editor	Kate McBride
Copy Chief	Laura MacLaughlin
Acquisitions Editor	Kate Burgo
Development Editor	Karen Johnson Jacot
Production Editor	Jamie Wielgus

Production

Production Director	Susan Beale
Production Manager	Michelle Roy Kelly
Series Designers	Daria Perreault
	Colleen Cunningham
Cover Design	Paul Beatrice
	Frank Rivera
Layout and Graphics	Colleen Cunningham
	Rachael Eiben
	Michelle Roy Kelly
	John Paulhus
	Daria Perreault
	Erin Ring
Series Cover Artist	Barry Littmann

Visit the entire Everything® Series at www.everything.com

THE

EVERYTHING®

HOLIDAY
COOKBOOK

300 treasured favorites—
all in one collection

Margaret Kaeter

Adams Media
Avon, Massachusetts

To my mother, Dorothy Kaeter,
for making every celebration truly wonderful.

An Everything® Series Book.
Everything® and everything.com® are registered trademarks of F+W Publications, Inc.

Published by Adams Media, an F+W Publications Company
57 Littlefield Street, Avon, MA 02322 U.S.A.
www.adamsmedia.com

ISBN: 1-59337-129-2
Printed in the United States of America.

J I H G F E D C B A

Library of Congress Cataloging-in-Publication Data
Kaeter, Margaret.
The everything holiday cookbook / Margaret Kaeter.
p.   cm.
ISBN 1-59337-129-2
1. Cookery. 2. Holidays. I. Title. II. Series: Everything series.
TX739.K26 2004
641.5'68–dc22
                                                            2004001789

This book is available at quantity discounts for bulk purchases.
For information, call 1-800-872-5627.

Contents

Acknowledgments

To Michael Olesen, for his patience and help; to Emma and Gretchen Olesen, for their inspiration; to Benjamin Heigl, for his sense of humor; and to everyone everywhere who knows that it's impossible to celebrate without food.

Introduction

▶ TO CELEBRATE IS TO EAT; TO EAT IS TO CELEBRATE. It may not be the most profound statement in the world, but it does sum up the way life should be. Every celebration I can think of, from a wedding to a job well done, includes a morsel of food or, at least, a glass of wine. And, on the other side of the equation, we really should celebrate every bite we eat. It is a sign that we are vital human beings enjoying the most fundamental aspect of life. We eat, thus we celebrate. We celebrate, thus we eat.

As you peruse this book, you will find that statement imbedded in the very essence of all the recipes. Some are simple. Some are old favorites. Some are exotic and complicated. But all of them are worthy of celebrations and celebrating.

However, before you embark on this celebratory journey, it's important to keep a few things in mind. Follow good cooking practices and you will have the best celebration possible.

Before You Plan the Meal

Before you even page through the book, think about what you want to achieve with your celebration. Keep these things in mind:

• **Will children be present?** You don't want a lengthy meal with foods that are difficult to eat if there will be young children at the party. Unless you know the children are adventurous, you also likely want to stay away from new foods with exotic spices.

- **How many will be attending?** If you don't have an exact number, you want to stay away from meals with individual servings. There's nothing worse than having one steak too few or an entire lobster too many. If you don't know the exact number, make items that are flexible. Or, make too many if you know the leftover dishes can be frozen.

- **Does anyone have food allergies or other special needs?** Keep these in mind as you plan your menu. There are plenty of wonderful dishes for people on low-salt, low-carb, and low-fat diets.

Planning the Meal

As you look at the recipes, determine which ones will work best for your celebration. Keep these things in mind:

- **What will the weather be like?** If you live in a northern climate, don't plan a meal that must be served outdoors in the spring or fall. You never know if you will have super-cold weather. Likewise, you might not want to be outdoors at 110° during a Southern summer.

- **How much experience do you have as a cook?** Realistically, do you know what you're in for? Most of the recipes in this book are easy, but a few require precise cooking methods. Are you confident enough in your cooking abilities to know you can handle them?

- **Do you have the utensils?** Read each of the recipes thoroughly and determine if you have the right pots and pans as well as miscellaneous utensils. Remember that you will be making all of the recipes at the same time; so, if something is being chilled in a bowl, that bowl won't be usable for another recipe.

- **How much time do you have?** Again, read the recipes and determine how long it will take you to make the meal. If the event is on a Thursday night and you have an evening class on Wednesdays, you need to plan accordingly.

- **How big is your kitchen?** Be realistic, again. If you live in a small apartment, you likely don't have room to make meals that require a lot of dishes. Go with something simpler such as a pasta dish, salad, and easy dessert.

- **Are the ingredients available?** A few of the recipes in this book call for some exotic ingredients. Most are available in big-city grocery stores, but if you live in a small town, they might be impossible to find. If you have time, you could plan a trip to a larger town or you could get the spices via mail order, but you'll need to plan for it.

- **Do you have the money?** There is nothing worse than planning a celebration that depletes your bank account. It becomes less of a celebration and more of a burden for you. Don't overextend your budget. Instead, make a wonderful-tasting meal, perhaps accented with extra attention to presentation; add fresh garnishes to a plate of simple chops, for example.

Making the Meal

Keep the elements of good cooking in mind as you start to make your meal. These things are most important:

- **Try a new dish beforehand.** If you're at all concerned about something turning out right, make it for yourself a few days ahead of time. That way you can tweak the ingredients or your technique when it really counts.

- **Cut corners where you can.** Did we really say that? Yes, there is no harm in using a good-quality store-bought French bread if you don't have the time, space, or pans to make the real thing. Buy precleaned veggies or even precut salad greens. This will give you more time to attend to the important aspects of the meal.

- **Follow directions.** You may have cooked many complicated meals before, but if you haven't cooked these dishes, follow the directions carefully. Timing and temperature are especially important when cooking, because various spices and ingredients react differently at different temperatures and over different amounts of time.

- **Plan ahead.** Know which items you will make first, which can be made a day ahead, and which must be served fresh. Plan your cooking schedule just as you would the other aspects of a big celebration.

Pay Attention to Details

Good cooking is in the details. Follow these guidelines to make sure your meal turns out perfect:

- **Measure correctly.** Some ingredients aren't important, such as spices. The amounts can be altered according to taste. However, the main ingredients, such as flour, liquids, and sugars, should be measured exactly. There is no room for spillage or "good enough," especially in a celebration. You don't want a gooey cake or a runny stew.
- **Preheat.** If the recipe says to preheat, allow at least 15 minutes to get the oven up to the correct temperature. This is important; otherwise, the food will start cooking at the lower temperature, which could completely alter the chemistry of the baking.
- **Know what slicing means**. Become familiar with the various terms for cutting something:

Zesting: Making small grated pieces from the thin, colored part of a citrus fruit's peel
Bias slice: To cut at a 45° angle
Chop: To cut into small irregular pieces
Core: To remove the center of a fruit or vegetable
Crush: To smash seasonings to release their flavor
Cube: To cut food into squares about ½-inch on each side
Cut up: To cut into small irregular pieces

Diagonal slice: To cut at a 45° angle
Dice: To cut into fairly uniform pieces about ¼-inch square
Grate: To rub food against a sharp-edged tool called a grater, making small or fine particles
Julienne: To cut into thin strips about 2 inches long
Mince: To chop into very small bits
Score: To cut through the surface about ¼-inch deep
Section: To cut the pulp of a peeled citrus fruit away from the membranes, separating its segments
Shred: To cut in narrow, thin strips
Slice: To cut into flat pieces that are usually thin and even
Snip: To cut herbs or other food into small pieces using scissors
Tear: To break into pieces using your hands

- **Know how to mix it.** Become familiar with the various terms for mixing ingredients:

Beat: To stir briskly with a spoon, whisk, egg beater, or electric mixer
Blend: To mix two or more ingredients until they make a uniform mixture
Cream: To beat a fat until it is light and fluffy, often in combination with other ingredients
Cut in: To combine a solid fat with dry ingredients until the fat is in very small pieces, about the size of small peas, by using a pastry blender or a fork
Fold: To combine ingredients gently, using a spatula or spoon to lift ingredients from the bottom of the bowl and "fold" them over the top
Knead: To work dough by continuous folding over and pressing down until it is smooth and elastic (Dough can also be kneaded with an electric mixer attachment called a dough hook.)
Stir: To mix ingredients at a moderate pace to combine
Toss: To mix ingredients by gently lifting them from the bottom of the bowl and allowing them to tumble, usually using two forks or other utensils

Whip: To beat rapidly with a wire whisk, hand beater, or electric mixer (Whipping increases volume because it adds air to the ingredients.)

• **Know how to prepare it.** Become familiar with the various terms for preparing the meal:

Baste: To spoon or pour broth, sauce, or other liquid over food while cooking to prevent dryness or add flavor

Blacken: To cook Cajun-seasoned foods over a very high heat

Bread: To coat foods before cooking in bread or cracker crumbs

Caramelize: To coat the top of a food with sugar and then broil quickly until the sugar is melted; or, to melt sugar in a saucepan over a low heat until it turns into a golden syrup

Deglaze: To add liquid to a skillet in which meat has been cooked, stirring to loosen meat bits and make a broth (The broth can be used to make a sauce.)

Dot: To place pieces of butter randomly on top of a food

Drizzle: To pour a liquid topping in thin, irregular lines over a food

Dust: To sprinkle a dry ingredient lightly and fairly evenly over a food

Glaze: To spread a thin coating such as jelly on food, making it appear glossy

Grease: To coat the surface of a pan with shortening, oil, or cooking spray to prevent foods from sticking while they bake; to "grease and flour" is to dust the plan lightly with flour after applying the shortening

Marinate: To let food stand in a special liquid to flavor it or tenderize it (The liquid is called a marinade.)

Purée: To process ingredients into a thick liquid, usually by using a blender or food processor

Reduce: To boil a liquid until some of it evaporates, thus concentrating the flavor

Roux, to make: To combine melted butter, flour, and seasonings over heat to use as a thickening base for sauces

Sift: To process dry ingredients through a kitchen sifter (Sifting adds air to dry ingredients that have been compressed in storage and also removes any lumps.)

Skim: To remove fat or foam that has accumulated on the surface of a liquid, usually using a spoon

- **Know how to cook it.** Become familiar with the various terms for cooking the meal:

Bake: To cook food with the indirect dry heat of an oven (Covering food while baking it preserves moistness. Leaving food uncovered results in a drier or crisp surface.)

Barbecue: To cook with barbecue sauce or spices, or to cook slowly on a grill or spit, usually outdoors

Blanch: To cook fruits, vegetables, or nuts very briefly in boiling water or steam, usually to preserve the color or nutritional value or remove the skin; also called *Parboil.*

Boil: To cook a liquid at a temperature at which bubbles rise and break on the surface ("Bring to a boil" means to heat just until bubbling begins. In a full, or rolling, boil, the bubbles are larger and form quickly and continuously.)

Braise: To cook food slowly in a tightly covered pan in a small amount of liquid (Usually, food is first browned in a small amount of fat. Braising tenderizes food and can be done on either the stovetop or in the oven.)

Broil: To cook food under a direct source of intense heat or flame, producing a browned or crisp exterior and a less well-done interior

Deep-fry: To cook food in hot, liquefied fat, usually 350° to 375°, deep enough to cover and surround the food completely

Fry: To cook in hot fat or oil, producing a crisp exterior

Grill: To cook foods directly above a source of intense heat flame (Foods can be pan-grilled on a stovetop by using a specially designed pan with raised grill ridges.)

Oven-fry: To cook food, usually breaded, in a hot oven with a small amount of fat, usually dotted or drizzled on top of the food

Pan-fry: To fry with little or no added fat, using only the fat that accumulates during cooking

Parboil: See *Blanch*

Poach: To cook in a simmering, not boiling, liquid

Roast: To cook meat or poultry in the indirect heat of the oven, uncovered (Roasted foods are not cooked in added liquid but are often basted with liquids for flavor and moistness.)

Sauté: To cook in a small amount of fat over high heat

Scald: To heat a liquid to just below the boiling point, when small bubbles begin to appear around the edges of the pan (When milk is scalded, a film will form on the surface.)

Sear: To brown on all sides over high heat to preserve juiciness

Simmer: To keep a liquid just below the boiling point (A few bubbles will rise and break on the surface.)

Steam: To cook food above, not in, boiling or simmering water

Stew: To cook food, covered, very slowly in liquid

Stir-fry: To cook small pieces of food in a hot wok or skillet, using a small amount of fat and a constant stirring motion.

Have Fun!

You are celebrating. Have fun with the event. Enjoy the food, the people, and the surroundings.

- **Create a theme.** Give your celebration an added lift with place cards, decorations, and other thematic elements. These can make an ordinary dinner a truly special event.

- **Present it beautifully.** This is the time to unpack Mom's china and Grandma's silver. Serve the meal on a beautiful platter. Even if you can't afford luxurious, you can have fun with brightly colored paper tablecloths and napkins.

- **Finally, don't worry.** You have done the best you could. So the meal wasn't perfect, but the celebration is what really matters.

CHAPTER 1
THANKSGIVING

ROASTED GARLIC MASHED POTATOES

Serves 4

These potatoes are excellent without gravy. For even more flavor, sprinkle with crumbled blue cheese or grated Parmesan.

4 garlic cloves
¼ teaspoon olive oil
¾ pound potatoes
½ teaspoon salt
1 small head cauliflower
1 small yellow onion

¼ cup buttermilk
⅛ cup nonfat cottage cheese
2 teaspoons butter
¼ teaspoon freshly ground
    black pepper

1. Preheat oven to 350°. Brush the garlic cloves with the olive oil and place in a shallow baking pan. Bake for 1 hour or until the cloves are soft. Remove the skin and cut the cloves into fourths.
2. Peel the potatoes and cut them into quarters. Place in a large pot and cover with water. Add the salt and boil for 10 to 20 minutes or until the potatoes are tender. Drain.
3. Break the cauliflower into small pieces and place in a large pot. Cover with water and boil for about 10 minutes or until the cauliflower is tender. Drain.
4. Remove the skin from the onion and chop into ¼-inch pieces.
5. Combine all the ingredients and whip until fluffy. If the mixture is too thin, add the buttermilk gradually until the whipped mixture reaches the desired consistency.

Defatting Meat

To remove most of the fat from ground beef or bacon, cook it in the microwave, then lay it on several paper towels to drain. Lay a paper towel on top of the meat and pat it lightly before adding it to the dish you are making.

ROAST TURKEY WITH FRUIT STUFFING

1 (10- to 15-pound) turkey
1 small white onion
¾ pound prunes
6 dried apricots
2 large Granny Smith apples
5 tablespoons margarine

2 quarts cubed toast
1 cup apple juice
2 teaspoons dried sage
1 teaspoon dried basil
2¼ teaspoons salt
¼ teaspoon pepper

Serves 8

Serve as the center-piece for a traditional Thanksgiving turkey dinner. It is excellent with Roasted Garlic Mashed Potatoes (page 2).

1. Preheat oven to 375°.
2. Peel the onion and chop it into ¼-inch pieces. Slice the prunes into ½-inch pieces. Chop the apricots into ¼-inch pieces. Peel the apples and cut into 1-inch chunks.
3. In a medium-sized frying pan over medium heat, melt the margarine; sauté the onions until golden brown.
4. In a mixing bowl, toss the toast chunks with the onions, prunes, apples, apricots, apple juice, and seasonings.
5. Spoon the stuffing into the turkey. Fasten with poultry pins if necessary.
6. Place the turkey in a pan and roast in the oven for 25 minutes per pound. Scoop out the fat from the pan as it gathers. Check regularly the last 30 minutes of cooking. The juices should run clear when the bird is done. Do not overcook.

Low-Fat Sautéing

For a fat-free alternative, add flavored vinegars when sautéing meats and vegetables. They will add a light flavor to the dish and tend to blend well with almost any recipe.

TURKEY AND CRANBERRY ON BUTTERNUT SQUASH

1 butternut squash
1 teaspoon salt
½ teaspoon nutmeg
12 ounces fresh-roasted turkey
6 ounces precooked cranberries

2 tablespoons extra-virgin olive oil
3 tablespoons orange juice
1 teaspoon fresh-cracked black pepper

1. Preheat oven to 250°.
2. Peel the butternut squash and cut in half lengthwise. Remove and rinse the seeds, and place the seeds on a baking sheet. Toast for 5 to 10 minutes, until golden. Sprinkle lightly with salt when done.
3. Thinly slice the butternut squash lengthwise. Brush another baking sheet with oil and lay out the squash slices. Sprinkle with nutmeg. Roast the squash for 20 to 30 minutes or until the squash is tender when pierced with a fork. Let cool, then place the cooled squash on serving plates.
4. Thinly slice the turkey. Arrange the turkey slices on top of the squash and sprinkle cranberries over the turkey. Drizzle with the olive oil and orange juice. Sprinkle the squash seeds on top. Season with salt and pepper.

Cooking Fresh Cranberries

While many people shy away from fresh cranberries, they are very easy to cook. Simply steam them and sprinkle lightly with sugar until they are slightly soft.

FRUIT-STEWED TURKEY

4 cups precooked turkey meat
1 small red onion
1 cup pineapple chunks,
    drained
6 pitted prunes
¼ cup dried apricots

1 tablespoon olive oil
½ cup fresh raspberries
1 teaspoon salt
1 teaspoon ground white
    pepper

Serves 4

Serve over white rice
or fettucine noodles
for a day-after-
Thanksgiving treat.

1. Cut the turkey into 1-inch chunks. Remove the skin from the onion
   and cut the onion into quarters. Cut the pineapple into 1-inch chunks,
   if necessary. Cut the prunes and apricots in half.
2. In a large frying pan, preheat the olive oil to medium temperature.
   Add the turkey chunks and fry until lightly browned on all sides.
3. Drain off the oil and add the onion, pineapple, apricots, prunes, raspberries, salt, and pepper to the pan. Turn heat to low and cook for
   1 hour, stirring periodically.

Mushrooms for Meat

*To turn any meat dish into an instant vegetarian entrée, substitute
morel mushrooms for the meat. Be sure to substitute by volume, not
weight, because even these heavier mushrooms weigh less than meat.*

WARM SWEET POTATO AND APPLE SALAD

Serves 12

This is the perfect complement to a traditional holiday turkey.

2½ pounds sweet potatoes
2 medium-sized Granny Smith
   apples
1 (20-ounce) can pineapple
   chunks

¾ cup mayonnaise
¾ cup plain yogurt
1½ tablespoons curry powder
½ teaspoon salt
½ cup golden raisins

1. Cook the sweet potatoes in boiling water. Drain and let cool. Peel the potatoes and cut into ¾-inch pieces. Peel the apples and cut into ½-inch pieces. Drain the pineapple.
2. In a large saucepan, whisk together the mayonnaise, yogurt, curry powder, and salt over low heat until well blended.
3. Stir in the potatoes, apples, pineapples, and raisins. Toss gently to mix and coat evenly.
4. Cover and continue to cook over low heat for 7 to 10 minutes, until the potatoes are heated through.

Seasonal Best

Because there are so many types of apples available year-round, you should always inquire about which ones are in season. This will ensure that you are using the tastiest ones in the bunch. Also, try combining different kinds for added flavor and variety.

OVEN-ROASTED ASPARAGUS

1 pound fresh asparagus
2 garlic cloves
1 teaspoon fresh parsley
2 tablespoons water
2 tablespoons dry white wine

2 teaspoons lemon juice
1 teaspoon olive oil
¼ teaspoon salt
⅛ teaspoon freshly ground
* black pepper*

Serves 4

This is the perfect simple-yet-elegant accompaniment to any holiday meal.

1. Preheat oven to 400°.
2. Break off the tough ends of the asparagus spears. With a vegetable peeler, peel the bottom half of the asparagus stalks. Peel the garlic and cut into slivers. Roughly chop the parsley.
3. Scatter the garlic and parsley in a 13" × 9" baking dish. Arrange the asparagus spears in a single layer.
4. In a small bowl, combine the water, wine, lemon juice, oil, salt, and pepper; pour over the asparagus.
5. Bake for 10 minutes. Turn the asparagus over and bake for 10 more minutes, or until the asparagus stalks are tender but slightly crisp and the liquid is almost gone.

Asparagus Knowledge

Although it is a popular belief, thick asparagus is not always woody and tough. In fact, it can have much more natural juiciness, sweetness, and silky texture than the pencil-thin variety. Check the cut bottoms of asparagus for freshness, making sure they are plump, moist, and recently cut.

SWEET POTATO–GINGER SOUP

Serves 6

Serve as a first course
to a large holiday meal.

1½ pounds butternut squash
4 large sweet potatoes
1 large russet potato
1 tablespoon olive oil
1 small yellow onion

2 tablespoons fresh minced
  ginger
8 cups chicken broth
½ cup plain yogurt

1. Peel, seed, and dice the squash. Peel and dice the sweet potatoes. Peel and dice the potato. Peel and chop the onion.
2. In a soup pot, heat the oil on medium for 30 seconds. Add the onion and sauté until translucent, about 5 minutes.
3. Add the ginger and cook for about 1 minute. Add the squash, sweet potatoes, russet potato, and broth. Bring to a boil, reduce heat to low, and cover; cook until the vegetables are tender, about 30 minutes.
4. Remove from heat and allow to cool slightly. Working in 1-cup batches, purée in a food processor or blender until smooth.
5. Pour into a clean pot, stir in the yogurt, and reheat gently. Ladle into bowls and serve.

The Squash Bowl

Use squash as a soup bowl. Many small squash make excellent complements to soups and stews. Cut them in half, remove the seeds, and prebake in the microwave or oven. Ladle your soup or stew into the squash for a festive look.

CRANBERRY SHERBET

1½ teaspoons unflavored gelatin
2 cups cranberry juice
½ cup granulated sugar
⅛ teaspoon salt

2 tablespoons nonfat dry milk
  powder
½ cup corn syrup
3 tablespoons lemon juice

Serves 4

This is a perfect end-of-meal treat for any large holiday feast. Nearly any flavor can be created by simply changing the juice used.

1. In a small saucepan, sprinkle the gelatin over ½ cup of the juice. Let stand for a few minutes to allow the gelatin to soften.
2. Place over low heat and stir until dissolved. Stir in the sugar and salt until dissolved.
3. Pour the remaining 1½ cups juice into a bowl. Sprinkle the milk powder over the top and beat with a fork to dissolve. Add the gelatin mixture to the milk-juice mixture, then add all the remaining ingredients. Stir until well mixed.
4. Pour into a metal ice cube train or loaf pan and freeze until almost firm. Beat until fluffy. Refreeze until firm, then serve.

Use Good Pans

Thin, flimsy stainless steel pans don't conduct heat well, resulting in hot spots where foods burn and cold spots where they don't cook at all. Better pans have a thick core of highly conductive aluminum or even copper bonded to their bottoms.

CRANBERRY SCONES

Makes 1 dozen

Serve as an early-morning treat before holiday festivities or as a breakfast treat throughout the holiday weeks.

1 cup dairy sour cream
1½ teaspoons fresh-grated
orange peel
2 cups sifted all-purpose flour
½ cup granulated sugar

2 teaspoons baking powder
½ teaspoon salt
¼ cup butter, softened
1 large egg, at room temperature
¼ cup dried cranberries

1. Preheat oven to 375°.
2. In a small bowl, combine the sour cream and grated orange peel. Set aside.
3. In a large bowl, mix together the flour, sugar, baking powder, and salt.
4. Using a pastry blender or 2 knives, cut the butter into the flour mixture until coarse crumbs form.
5. Break the egg into a small dish and beat well with a fork. Add the egg to the flour mixture and beat together until blended. Add the sour cream and orange peel mixture and beat just until blended.
6. Prepare a smooth surface by sprinkling it lightly with flour. Turn the dough out of the bowl. Using floured hands, knead the dough for about 30 seconds, or until smooth. Taking only ½ the dough at a time, roll it out with a floured rolling pin until it is about ½-inch thick. Using a 3-inch round cookie cutter or the mouth of an empty can or drinking glass, cut out rounds of dough.
7. Place the rounds 1 inch apart on a greased or nonstick cookie sheet. Before putting them in the oven, push 5 dried cranberries into the top of each scone. Bake until the tops are just barely browned, 12 to 18 minutes. Let cool on wire racks.

CRANBERRY NUT BREAD

½ cup butter, softened
1 cup granulated sugar
1 large egg
1 cup fresh orange juice
3 cups all-purpose flour

2 teaspoons baking powder
1 teaspoon fresh orange zest
1 cup fresh cranberries
1 cup chopped pecans

Makes 8 to 10 servings

For a special morning treat, use this bread to make French toast. Simply beat together an egg and ½ cup milk, then coat bread slices in the mixture and fry in a skillet on medium heat until lightly browned.

1. Preheat oven to 350°. Coat a 9" × 5" × 3" loaf pan with cooking spray or a light coating of cooking oil.
2. Mix together the flour and baking powder. Cream together the butter and sugar until light and fluffy. Add the egg, and beat for 2 minutes. Gradually stir in the juice, flour, baking powder, and orange zest; mix until just blended. Stir in the cranberries and pecans.
3. Pour the batter into the prepared baking pan. Bake for 50 to 60 minutes or until a toothpick inserted in the center comes out clean.
4. Let the bread stand in the baking pan for 8 to 10 minutes. Invert onto a wire cooling rack.

Hold the Yolk
Egg yolks contain all of the fat and cholesterol in an egg. Use egg whites instead of whole eggs when making pasta, cakes, and other dishes. Usually 2 egg whites can be substituted for 1 whole egg.

CRANBERRY-PECAN BARS

Makes 20 bars

Enjoy as an after-meal treat or with Irish Coffee (page 43).

1 cup unsalted butter, chilled
1½ cups roasted pecans
2 cups all-purpose flour
¾ packed cup brown sugar

1 (10-ounce) jar seedless raspberry preserves
¾ cup dried cranberries
⅓ cup flaked, dried coconut.

1. Preheat oven to 350°. Grease a 9" × 13" × 2" pan. Cut butter into bits.
2. In a food processor, coarsely chop ½ cup of the pecans and place in a bowl. Add the remaining 1 cup pecans to the processor along with the flour, brown sugar, and butter. Process until the dough clumps together, occasionally scraping down the sides of the processor bowl with a rubber spatula.
3. Remove the dough from the processor and measure out 1 cup. Add the reserved pecans to the 1 cup of dough and set aside. Pat the remaining dough onto the bottom of the prepared pan.
4. In a bowl, mix together the preserves and cranberries, then spread over the dough in the pan. Mix the coconut with the reserved nut mixture, pressing some together to form clumps. Sprinkle over the preserves layer in the pan.
5. Bake for 40 minutes or until the top browns. Let cool on a rack, then cut into 2-inch bars.

Sweet Vanilla Sauce

Mix ¼ cup nonfat buttermilk, 2 teaspoons sugar, and 1 cup vanilla yogurt in a small bowl. Use as a topping over fresh fruit or gingerbread.

PUMPKIN PIE

3 eggs
1 unbaked 9-inch pie pastry
   shell
1½ cups canned or mashed
   cooked pumpkin
¾ cup granulated sugar

½ teaspoon salt
1¼ teaspoons ground cinnamon
1 teaspoon ground ginger
½ teaspoon ground cloves
¼ cup milk
¾ cup evaporated milk

Serves 8

Serve as dessert for
a traditional
Thanksgiving meal
or for a fall dessert
at any meal.

1. Preheat oven to 400°. Lightly beat the eggs and set aside.
2. Line the pie pan with the pastry shell, forming a high edge by crimping the pastry in a tall, thick layer.
3. In a large bowl, combine the pumpkin, sugar, salt, and spices to taste. Stir in the eggs, milk, and evaporated milk until well blended. Pour into the pastry shell.
4. Bake for 50 minutes or until a knife inserted halfway between the edge and the center of the filling comes out clean. Let cool completely on a rack.

Problems with Cinnamon

While it tastes wonderful, cinnamon is a tricky spice. It can kill yeast, causing bread not to rise. It also does not permeate a soup or stew but tends to remain on top of the liquid.

PECAN PIE

Serves 8

Serve as a final course after Roast Turkey with Fruit Stuffing (page 3) and Oven-Roasted Asparagus (page 7).

1 unbaked 9-inch pie pastry shell
3 large eggs
1 cup dark corn syrup
½ cup granulated sugar
1 teaspoon vanilla extract
½ teaspoon salt
1 cup coarsely chopped toasted pecan pieces

1. Preheat oven to 350°.
2. Place the pie shell in a greased pie pan. Put in the oven and brown slightly, about 5 to 10 minutes. Remove.
3. In a large bowl, beat the eggs until foamy. Add the corn syrup, sugar, vanilla, salt, and pecans; mix well. Pour into the prepared crust.
4. Bake for 40 to 45 minutes or until the top is set. Transfer the pan to a wire rack to cool.

SPICED CRANBERRY GLOGG

Makes 6 servings

You can leave the raisins in for a special treat at the bottom of the glass. Or, remove the raisins and use them in spiced muffins.

1 orange
1 teaspoon whole cloves
1 cinnamon stick
½ cup raisins
1 (6-ounce) can apple juice concentrate
1 (6-ounce) can cranberry juice concentrate
4½ cups water

1. With a small knife, cut the orange peel into long strips, about ½-inch wide, so the peel begins to spiral. Poke the cloves into the orange peel. Break the cinnamon stick in half.
2. Squeeze the juice from the orange into a medium-sized saucepan. Add the studded orange peel, cinnamon stick, raisins, juice concentrates, and water; heat on medium until simmering.
3. Remove the orange peel and cinnamon stick. Serve promptly or refrigerate and reheat before serving.

APPLE BLOSSOM

2 ounces brandy

2 ounces apple juice

1 teaspoon lemon juice

Ice

Apple slice, for garnish

1. Pour the brandy, apple juice, and lemon juice into a mixing glass nearly filled with ice. Stir.
2. Strain into an old-fashioned glass over ice. Garnish with an apple slice.

Serves 1

This makes a perfect after-dinner drink to help settle stomachs that might have taken in just a little too much!

CRANBERRY CREAM COCKTAIL

3 ounces cranberry juice

2 ounces apple juice

1 ounce lime juice

1 ounce heavy cream

Dash grenadine

2 cups crushed ice or ice cubes

Combine all the ingredients in a blender; blend thoroughly. Pour into a large wineglass.

Serves 1

Kids and adults alike will enjoy this cool after-dinner drink. Make it extra-special by garnishing it with fresh apple slices or even some raspberries.

CRANBERRY GIN SOUR

Serves 1

Use this flavor-filled concoction as a before-dinner drink to get the taste buds in shape for all the flavors to come.

2 ounces gin
½ ounce Triple Sec
1 ounce lime juice
1 ounce lemon juice

2 ounces light cream
1 teaspoon granulated sugar
2 cups crushed ice or ice
   cubes

Combine all the ingredients in a blender; blend thoroughly. Pour into a large wineglass.

MAYFLOWER COCKTAIL

Serves 1

This is a wonderful after-dinner drink to soothe a too-full tummy.

1½ ounces sweet vermouth
½ ounce dry vermouth
½ ounce brandy

1 teaspoon Pernod
1 teaspoon orange bitters
Ice

Combine all the ingredients in a shaker half-filled with ice. Shake well. Strain into a cocktail glass.

TURKEY SHOOTER

¾ ounce Wild Turkey Bourbon   Ice
¼ ounce white crème de menthe

Pour all the ingredients into a mixing glass nearly filled with ice. Stir.
Strain into a cordial glass or a brandy snifter.

Serves 1

Serve as an after-dinner drink to calm the nerves during all those football games.

BRANDY COCOA

2 tablespoons unsweetened   1½ cups boiling water
  cocoa powder   4 cups whole milk
⅓ cup granulated sugar   3 teaspoons brandy

1. In a saucepan, scald milk.
2. In another saucepan, mix cocoa, sugar, and enough boiling water to make a smooth paste.
3. Add remaining water and boil 1 minute, then add to milk.
4. Mix well; add brandy, then beat mixture with egg beater for 2 minutes. Serve in large mugs.

Serves 2–3

This is a mellow and delicious drink for the holidays.

CHRISTMAS MEALS

PECAN-CRUSTED ROAST PORK LOIN

Serves 4

This meal is both festive and filling on a cold Christmas Eve. Serve it with Chocolate Mousse (page 139) for dessert.

1 garlic clove
1 teaspoon olive oil
1 teaspoon brown sugar
¼ teaspoon dried thyme
¼ teaspoon dried sage

¼ teaspoon freshly ground black pepper
½ pound boneless pork loin roast
¼ cup chopped or ground pecans

1. Crush the garlic with the side of a large knife. Remove the skin. Put the olive oil, garlic, brown sugar, and seasonings in a resealable plastic bag. Mix well. Add the roast and turn it in the bag to coat the meat. Marinate in the refrigerator for 6 to 12 hours.
2. Preheat oven to 400°.
3. Roll the pork loin in the chopped pecans and place it in a roasting pan. Make a tent of aluminum foil and arrange it over the pork loin, covering the nuts completely so that they won't burn. Roast for 10 minutes, then lower the heat to 350°. Continue to roast for an additional 8 to 15 minutes or until the meat thermometer reads 150° to 170°, depending on how well done you prefer it. Let sit for 10 minutes before serving.
4. Serve with Roasted Garlic Mashed Potatoes (page 2) and freshly steamed asparagus.

Create a Celery Roasting Rack

If you want to bake a roast in a casserole alongside potatoes and carrots, elevate the roast on 2 or 3 stalks of celery. The celery will absorb any fat that drains from the meat so that it's not absorbed by the other vegetables. Discard the celery.

CARAMELIZED PEARL ONIONS

2 cups pearl onions
2 teaspoons brown sugar
¼ teaspoon salt

1 tablespoon butter
1 cup cold water

Serves 8

Although you can use already-peeled onions or even frozen ones, you will get a far better taste from fresh pearl onions. It's worth the 15 to 20 minutes it will take to peel them!

1. Peel the pearl onions.
2. In a heavy-bottomed skillet over medium heat, combine the onions, sugar, salt, butter, and water. Bring to a simmer. Cook gently until all the water is absorbed and the onions are coated in a light glaze, about 5 minutes. Turn heat to low. Cook slowly until the glaze browns and the onions appear golden brown, about 5 minutes more.

HOLIDAY GOOSE WITH CRANBERRIES

1 wild goose, gutted and skinned
½ teaspoon table salt
½ teaspoon ground black pepper

1 (15-ounce) can whole-berry cranberry sauce
1 envelope dry onion soup mix
½ cup orange juice

Serves 4

Garnish with fresh orange slices, baked sweet potatoes, and parsley to create a festive-looking meal.

1. Wash the goose cavity with cold water and sprinkle with salt and pepper. Place the goose in a slow cooker.
2. Combine the cranberry sauce, dry onion soup mix, and orange juice. Pour the mixture over the goose.
3. Cook, covered, on low setting for 8 to 10 hours, depending on the size of the goose.

HERBED BEEF RIB-EYE ROAST WITH POTATOES

Serves 8

Serve with Oven-Roasted Asparagus (page 7) for a complete, festive meal.

2 large sweet potatoes
2 medium Yukon gold potatoes
4 small red potatoes
2 teaspoons dried rosemary
4 garlic cloves
1 teaspoon dry mustard
1 teaspoon salt
1 teaspoon cracked black pepper
4-pound boneless beef rib-eye
  roast
2 tablespoons vegetable oil

1. Preheat oven to 350°. Peel all the potatoes and cut them into pieces that are roughly 2 inches square.
2. Combine the rosemary, garlic, mustard, salt, and pepper, and divide in half. Rub or press ½ the mixture into the surface of the meat.
3. Place the meat on a rack in a shallow roasting pan and place a meat thermometer (if using) into the thickest part of the meat. Place the roast in the oven. The total roasting time will be 1½ to 2 hours for medium-rare (135°) or 2 to 3 hours for medium (150°).
4. Mix the remaining seasonings with the oil in a large bowl. Add the potatoes to the oil and herb mixture and toss well to coat.
5. About 1 hour before the meat will be done, place the potatoes in the roasting pan around the rack.

Meat Safety

Store meat unopened for up to 2 days in the refrigerator. Freeze it if it will not be used within 2 days. Meat wrapped in butcher paper should be unwrapped and rewrapped in foil, freezer bags, or freezer paper. Frozen meat is best used within 2 months. Meat in transparent film can be frozen in the package for up to 2 weeks.

SAUERKRAUT-STUFFED ROAST DUCK

1 domestic duck
1 cup distilled white vinegar
¼ teaspoon salt
¼ teaspoon ground black
   pepper

2 Granny Smith apples
1 medium-sized yellow onion
4 cups sauerkraut
1 pound pork spareribs

Serves 6

Serve with Garlic
Mashed Potatoes
(page 2) and
Caramelized Pearl
Onions (page 21).

1. Clean and wash the duck, then place it in a large kettle. Cover with water and add the vinegar. Soak for 3 hours. Remove the duck from the liquid, dry it off, and season with salt and pepper. Cover and place in the refrigerator overnight.
2. While the duck is being soaked, core and chop the apples. Peel and chop the onion into ½-inch chunks. Combine the apples, onion, sauerkraut, and spareribs in a slow cooker. Cook for 6 hours or until the meat from the ribs falls from the bones. Discard the bones and refrigerate the slow-cooker mixture.
3. The next day, stuff the spare-rib sauerkraut mixture into the duck. Place the stuffed duck into the slow cooker and cook on medium for 8 hours or until golden and tender.

High-Altitude Slow-Cooking

Since water boils at a lower temperature in high altitudes, you may want to cook most of your slow-cooker dishes on the high setting to ensure they're getting hot enough. You also can easily test the slow cooker by heating water in it and determining the temperature with a thermometer.

POACHED SALMON WITH BEARNAISE SAUCE

Serves 4

Serve with fresh green beans and carrots and a side of white rice for a light, festive meal.

½ cup water
¼ cup dry white wine
2 salmon steaks
¼ cup mayonnaise
2 tablespoons lemon juice
1 tablespoon Dijon mustard

1 teaspoon granulated sugar
1 teaspoon tarragon
½ teaspoon salt
1 teaspoon freshly ground
   black pepper

1. In a skillet, bring the water and wine to a gentle simmer. Add the salmon and cook without boiling for 8 to 10 minutes or until the fish flakes easily with a fork. Cut the steaks in half and arrange on warmed plates.
2. In a small saucepan, whisk together the mayonnaise, lemon juice, mustard, sugar, and tarragon. Cook over medium-low heat, whisking, for about 3 minutes or until warmed through but not boiling. Season with salt and pepper and spoon the sauce over the salmon.

HONEY-ORANGE BEETS

Serves 4

This is the perfect complement to turkey or beef. Pair with a green vegetable for the traditional holiday colors.

6 medium-sized fresh beets
1 teaspoon grated orange rind
2 tablespoons orange juice
2 teaspoons butter
1 teaspoon honey

¼ teaspoon ground ginger
½ teaspoon salt
¼ teaspoon ground black
   pepper

1. Remove and discard the green tops from the beets. In a pot of boiling water, cook the beets for 40 minutes or until tender.
2. Drain the beets and let cool slightly. Slip off the skins and cut the beets into ¼-inch-thick slices.
3. In a medium-sized saucepan, heat the orange zest, orange juice, butter, honey, and ginger over low heat until the butter melts. Add the beets and toss to coat. Season with salt and pepper.

TWICE-BAKED POTATOES WITH CHIVES

*4 medium-sized baking
  potatoes*
*¼ cup thinly sliced green
  onions*
¼ cup fresh chopped chives
¼ cup milk

*3 ounces cream cheese,
  softened*
¼ cup butter
½ teaspoon (or to taste) salt
*½ teaspoon (or to taste)
  ground black pepper*

> **Serves 4**
>
> Although they look complicated, twice-baked potatoes are an easy way to create an elegant side dish for holiday meals.

1. Bake the potatoes in a 350° oven. Remove from oven and let cool. Thinly slice the green onions. Chop chives.
2. Combine the milk and cream cheese. Cut the potatoes in half lengthwise and scoop out the flesh, being careful to leave a shell of at least ¼ inch.
3. In a medium-sized bowl, combine the potato, cream cheese, and butter. Mash them together thoroughly, then whip by hand or with an electric mixer. Stir in the chives, onions, salt, and pepper.
4. Mound the mixture in the potato shells and place them on an ungreased baking sheet. Bake at 350° for about 30 minutes, or microwave on high for about 10 minutes until well heated.

Potato Peelings

Whenever you cook potatoes, try not to peel them if there is a choice. Potato skins can add a nice crunch to the overall texture of a dish, plus they carry valuable dietary fiber and vitamins.

GINGERED MASHED SWEET POTATOES

Serves 6

Serve as a side dish to traditional holiday turkey or, for a unique taste, serve with Poached Salmon with Bearnaise Sauce (page 24).

4 medium-sized sweet potatoes or yams
¼ cup milk
2 tablespoons butter
1 tablespoon brown sugar
½ teaspoon ground ginger

1. Peel and quarter the sweet potatoes. Cook in boiling, salted water until tender, about 20 minutes. Drain and return to the pan.
2. In a small pan or in the microwave, heat the milk and butter. Add to the potatoes along with the brown sugar and ginger. Mash by hand or whip with an electric mixer. (The texture will be thicker than mashed white potatoes.)

BRUSSELS SPROUTS WITH MUSTARD CREAM

Serves 6

For more even cooking, crosshatch the bottom of the Brussels sprouts before placing them in the boiling water.

1½ pounds Brussels sprouts
2 tablespoons unsalted butter
1 large shallot
½ cup whipping cream
½ teaspoon dried tarragon
¾ teaspoon Dijon mustard
¼ teaspoon salt
¼ teaspoon freshly ground pepper

1. Trim the Brussels sprouts. Peel and mince the shallot.
2. Cook the Brussels sprouts in boiling water until tender, 5 to 6 minutes. Drain well.
3. Melt the butter in the same pan and add the shallot. Cook over medium-high heat until the shallot softens, about 2 minutes. Add the Brussels sprouts and toss gently.
4. Add all the remaining ingredients. Cook just until the cream thickens slightly, about 1 minute.

MEXICAN CHRISTMAS EVE SALAD

2 medium-sized sweet apples
1 medium-sized banana
2 cups pineapple chunks
1 (1-pound) can sliced beets
2 navel oranges

1 pomegranate
Several fresh lettuce leaves
Lemon juice
⅓ cup unsalted peanuts
Nondairy whipped topping

Serves 4

This salad is a Christmas Eve tradition in many Mexican homes but it's enjoyable in even the coldest climates.

1. Peel, core, and thinly slice the apples. Peel and slice the banana into ¼-inch rounds. Drain the pineapples and beets. Peel and section the oranges. Scoop out the pomegranate seeds.
2. Line a large serving platter with the lettuce leaves.
3. In a large bowl, mix together the sliced apples and bananas. Sprinkle with a little lemon juice to keep them from turning brown.
4. Arrange the apples, bananas, pineapple chunks, beets, and orange sections on the platter. Sprinkle peanuts and pomegranate seeds over the fruit.
5. Serve nondairy whipped topping on the side.

Fruit Compote
Nearly any combination of fresh fruits makes a wonderful fruit compote in a slow cooker. Add 1 cup of sugar for every 8 cups of fruit and cook on low until the sauce is thick.

OYSTERS ROCKEFELLER SOUP

Serves 12

This traditional soup frequently is served after Christmas Eve services.

5 celery stalks
2 large white onions
3 cups thinly sliced green onions
3 cups spinach
1¼ cups fresh flat-leaf parsley
1 garlic clove
½ teaspoon dried oregano
2 tablespoons butter
1 bay leaf
1 teaspoon dried thyme leaves
2 teaspoons salt

⅛ teaspoon freshly ground black pepper
⅛ teaspoon ground red pepper
⅛ teaspoon ground white pepper
1 tablespoon all-purpose flour
2 cups fresh oysters
Chicken stock, as needed
¾ cup Pernod (French anise-flavored cordial)
6 cups whipping cream

1. Peel the onions and finely chop the onions, celery, spinach, and parsley. Peel and mince the garlic. Crush the dried oregano.
2. Heat the butter in a Dutch oven over medium-high heat. When the butter starts to foam, add the celery, white onions, and bay leaf. Cook for 4 to 5 minutes or until the vegetables are tender. Reduce the heat to low. Add the spinach, green onions, and parsley. Cook, stirring constantly, for 3 to 4 minutes. Remove the bay leaf.
3. Add the garlic, thyme, oregano, salt, and peppers. Cook, stirring constantly, for 4 to 5 minutes. Add the flour and cook for 2 minutes, stirring constantly, and scraping the sides and bottom of the pan.
4. Drain the oysters, reserving the liquid. Add enough chicken stock to the oyster liquid, if necessary, to make 1 cup total. Set aside.
5. Increase the heat to medium-high and carefully add the Pernod to the vegetable mixture. Cook, stirring constantly, for 4 to 5 minutes. Add the oyster and stock liquid mixture, and cook for another 3 to 4 minutes. Let cool slightly. Transfer the vegetable mixture to a blender or food processor. Cover and blend or process to a smooth consistency.
6. Return the mixture to the Dutch oven. Stir in the whipping cream and cook over medium heat for 4 to 5 minutes or until heated through, whisking occasionally. Add the oysters and cook for about 5 minutes or until the oyster edges curl. Serve immediately.

OVEN-ROASTED WINTER VEGETABLES

½ pound rutabaga
½ pound carrots
½ pound parsnips
½ pound Brussels sprouts
1 tablespoon unsalted butter
1 tablespoon extra-virgin
   olive oil

2 teaspoons fresh thyme
2 teaspoons fresh sage
⅛ teaspoon freshly grated
   nutmeg
½ cup Marsala wine

Serves 6

This is the perfect complement to prime rib, turkey, or any winter holiday meal.

1. Preheat oven to 450°. Peel the rutabaga, carrots, and parsnips, and cut into 1-inch pieces.
2. Bring a large pot of salted water to a boil. Add the rutabagas, carrots, and parsnips, and simmer until they are somewhat tender when pierced with a fork, about 5 to 8 minutes. Drain well.
3. Place the rutabagas, carrots, parsnips, and Brussels sprouts in a large roasting pan. Melt the butter in a small saucepan and stir in the oil, thyme, sage, and nutmeg. Drizzle the butter mixture over the vegetables to coat them completely. Pour the Marsala into the bottom of the roasting pan.
4. Cover tightly with foil and bake in the oven for 40 minutes. Remove the foil, toss the vegetables, and continue to cook, uncovered, until the Marsala is evaporated and the vegetables can easily be pierced with a knife, about 20 to 30 minutes. Place on a platter and serve immediately.

Cleaning Roots

Clean root vegetables thoroughly by scrubbing them with a nail brush or scouring pad designated for that purpose. Because they grow in fertilized soil, they can harbor bacteria on their skins.

YORKSHIRE PUDDING

Serves 4

This traditional British dish is usually served as part of a main course.

1 cup milk
2 large eggs
1 cup all-purpose flour

¼ teaspoon salt
½ cup fresh beef fat from a roast

1. Preheat oven to 350°. Place a 9" × 9" pan in the oven.
2. Mix together the milk and eggs.
3. In a large mixing bowl, mix together the flour and salt. Stir the milk mixture into the flour mixture so that it forms a smooth paste.
4. Cover the bottom of the hot pan with the beef fat. Pour the batter over the beef fat.
5. Bake the pudding until golden, about 20 minutes.

CLASSIC BREAD PUDDING

Serves 8

There is nothing like hot bread pudding with vanilla ice cream and a mug of hot chocolate to make you feel all warm inside.

2 cups day-old bread
2 eggs
1¼ cups milk
½ packed cup brown sugar

1 teaspoon ground cinnamon
1 teaspoon vanilla extract
¼ teaspoon salt
½ cup raisins

1. Preheat oven to 350°. Grease an 8-inch square baking dish.
2. Tear the bread into 1-inch cubes. Place the bread cubes in a large bowl. Lightly beat the eggs in a small bowl. Stir in the milk.
3. Pour the milk mixture over the bread cubes. Add the brown sugar, cinnamon, vanilla, salt, and raisins. Toss lightly to blend.
4. Spread the mixture in the prepared baking dish. Place the dish in a baking pan and pour hot water into the pan to a depth of 1 inch.
5. Bake for 35 to 40 minutes or until a knife inserted halfway between the center and the outside edge comes out clean. Serve warm or cold.

CHAPTER 3

CHRISTMAS TREATS

ANISE OVAL COOKIES

Makes 3 dozen

For many people, especially those of Eastern European descent, the holidays aren't complete without these licorice-flavored cookies.

4 large eggs
1¾ cups confectioners' sugar
⅛ teaspoon salt

2 cups all-purpose flour
2 teaspoons anise seeds
¼ teaspoon baking powder

1. Separate the egg yolks from the whites.
2. Beat together the confectioners' sugar, egg yolks, and salt in a large bowl until creamy.
3. In a separate bowl, beat the egg whites until very stiff. Fold into the sugar mixture.
4. In another bowl, combine the flour, anise seed, and baking powder. Fold into the creamed mixture thoroughly.
5. Place the dough into a pastry bag fitted with a plain nozzle. Pipe small ovals onto ungreased baking sheets. Let stand overnight to dry.
6. Preheat oven to 325°. Bake the cookies for 18 to 20 minutes or until set. Let cool on a wire rack.

A Dessert Buffet

If you're looking for a fun way to celebrate a holiday, try having a dessert buffet. You can even turn it into a potluck event. Serve a nice mix of beverages to complement the buffet.

PFEFFERNUSSE

3 large eggs
½ packed cup dark brown sugar
3 cups all-purpose flour
½ teaspoon baking powder
½ teaspoon freshly ground
  black pepper
½ teaspoon ground cloves

½ teaspoon ground cardamom
  seeds
¼ cup finely ground almonds
¼ teaspoon salt
2 tablespoons lemon juice
Zest of 1 lemon
1 cup confectioners' sugar

Makes 3 to 4 dozen

These are traditional at holiday buffets and parties. However, they also are a popular gift. Place a few in a coffee mug, cover with plastic wrap, and add a red bow!

1. Preheat oven to 350°.
2. Break the eggs in a large bowl and beat with a fork until frothy. Add the sugar and beat until well mixed.
3. In a small bowl, mix the flour with the rest of the dry ingredients, except the confectioners' sugar. Slowly combine the dry mixture with the egg mixture. Blend in the lemon juice and zest. Cover the bowl with plastic wrap and place in the refrigerator for 1 hour.
4. With floured palms, roll the dough into 1-inch balls. Place on a greased or nonstick baking sheet and bake for 10 to 15 minutes or until the bottoms are just beginning to brown.
5. As each batch comes out of the oven, roll immediately in confectioners' sugar and let cool on a wire rack.
6. To keep the cookies soft, as soon as they are cool, place them in an airtight container with an apple slice. Replace the apple slice every 3 days. After 3 weeks, the flavors in the cookies will have blended and the cookies will be ready to eat.

CHRISTMAS THEME SUGAR COOKIES

Makes 1 to 3 dozen

These cookies are a traditional Christmas favorite.

---

1 cup granulated sugar
1 cup margarine
1 large egg
½ teaspoon almond or vanilla
  extract
1½ teaspoons baking powder

½ teaspoon salt
2½ cups all-purpose flour
Red and green sugar crystals
Colored jimmies
Small silver ball candies

1. Preheat oven to 350°. Grease a baking sheet.
2. In a large mixing bowl, beat together the sugar and margarine.
3. Beat in the egg, extract, baking powder, and salt. Gradually add in the flour. Mix well.
4. On a floured surface, knead the dough by hand and shape into a large ball. Wrap in plastic wrap and chill for up to 2 hours, until firm.
5. Roll out the dough on a floured surface to ¼-inch thick. Cut out shapes with Christmas theme cookie cutters. Decorate with trimmings.
6. Place on a baking sheet and bake for 10 to 12 minutes or until lightly browned on the edges.

Using Skim Milk

If a recipe calls for whole milk, half-and-half, or cream, you can easily substitute skim milk. You will get all the nutrition and most of the creamy taste with much less fat.

COCONUT WREATH COOKIES

½ cup butter or margarine,
  softened
½ cup granulated sugar
1 large egg

1 (3½-ounce) package
  shredded sweetened coconut
1¾ cups all-purpose flour
Red and green candied
  cherries, sliced

> **Makes 2 dozen**
>
> Another favorite at cookie swaps, buffets, and parties, this cookie also is perfect matched with Irish Coffee (page 43) during those long gift-opening sessions.

1. Preheat oven to 375°. Grease and flour a baking sheet.
2. In a large bowl, beat together the butter and sugar. Blend in the egg and coconut. On low speed, add the flour, ½ cup at a time, until blended.
3. Wrap the dough in plastic wrap and chill for several hours.
4. On a floured surface, roll out ⅓ of the dough at a time to ¼-inch thickness. Using a 2½-inch doughnut cutter, cut the dough into rings. Remove excess coconut from the edges of the cookies.
5. Place the cherry slices on the cookies to resemble flower petals. Press into the cookies. Place on a baking sheet and bake in batches for about 10 minutes, until brown.

Pretty Presentation

For a spectacular gift presentation, line the bottom of a container with gold foil gift wrap and place each cookie in gold foil candy cups (available at cooking specialty stores).

CRÈME BRÛLÉE

Serves 8

To make a meal even more special, make individual créme brûlées in large ramekin dishes. Decorate with your favorite fresh fruit or chocolate curls.

3 eggs
2 cups light cream
1 cup granulated sugar
¼ teaspoon salt

1 teaspoon vanilla extract
½ packed cup brown sugar
½ cup fresh raspberries

1. Lightly beat the eggs. Scald the cream by cooking it over medium heat in a medium-sized saucepan until a light blister forms on top. Do not let the cream boil.
2. In the top pan of a double boiler, combine the eggs, granulated sugar, and salt. Slowly stir in the hot cream and vanilla. Cook over hot (not boiling) water for about 8 minutes or until the custard coats a metal spoon. Continue cooking about 2 minutes longer, or until the custard thickens slightly. Pour into an 8-inch round baking dish with 3-inch-high sides. Cover and chill well.
3. Preheat broiler.
4. Sift the brown sugar evenly over the surface of the custard. Set in a shallow pan and surround the dish with ice cubes and a little cold water. Slip under the broiler about 8 inches from the heat and broil for about 5 minutes or until the custard has a bubbly brown crust.
5. Serve either hot or chilled. Decorate with fresh raspberries right before serving.

Chocolate Curls

Use a swivel vegetable peeler to make attractive shavings and curls from a block of chocolate. Just start with a large flat surface of chocolate, like the edge of a bar or the side of a hunk, and shave away, letting the curls fall onto whatever food you're garnishing. Don't pick them up with your fingers, though, because they melt very fast.

GINGERBREAD MEN

½ cup granulated sugar
½ cup solid vegetable shortening
1 large egg
½ teaspoon salt
1 teaspoon baking powder
½ teaspoon baking soda
1 teaspoon ground ginger

1½ teaspoons ground cinnamon
1 teaspoon ground cloves
½ cup light molasses
2¼ cups all-purpose flour
Prepared frostings
Candies for trimmings

Makes 1 to 3 dozen

If baking with toddlers in the house, be sure to make a big show of locking the door so the Gingerbread Man can't run away!

1. Preheat oven to 350°.
2. In a large mixing bowl, beat together the sugar and shortening. Add the egg, salt, baking powder, baking soda, ginger, cinnamon, cloves, and molasses. Add the flour ½ cup at a time, beating until dough forms.
3. Shape the dough into a ball, wrap in plastic wrap, and chill until firm, at least 1 hour.
4. On a floured surface, roll out the dough to ¼-inch thickness. Using a gingerbread man cookie cutter, cut out the cookies. Place on an ungreased cookie sheet at least 1 inch apart.
5. Bake the cookies in batches for 8 to 10 minutes for small cookies, 12 to 15 minutes for larger cookies. Transfer the baking sheet to a wire rack to cool.
6. Spread frosting over the cookies. Decorate with candies.

Easy Frosting

Put ½ cup confectioners' sugar into 3 different soup bowls. Add 2 drops of food coloring and 1 drop of vanilla flavoring to each bowl. Drizzle milk into the bowls while stirring with a spoon. It will take less than 1 tablespoon of milk to make a good, fairly stiff frosting.

PLUM PUDDING PIE

Makes 1 pie

This is a must if you have just attended The Nutcracker or if you have had a family reading of The Night Before Christmas.

1 cup pitted dates
1 cup crystallized plums
1 unbaked 9-inch pie pastry shell
2 large eggs
1 cup orange marmalade
1 cup shredded sweetened coconut

1 cup walnuts
¼ cup slivers of ginger-preserved watermelon rind (if available, or any dried fruit cut into slivers)
2 tablespoons milk
1 tablespoon butter

1. Preheat oven to 425°. Chop the dates and crystallized plums into ¼-inch pieces.
2. In a mixing bowl, beat the eggs. Add the dates, plums, marmalade, coconut, walnuts, watermelon rind, and milk, in that order. Blend well.
3. Place the pie crust in a greased pie pan. Pour the filling into the prepared crust. Dot the top with the butter. Bake for 25 minutes or until the crust is golden brown.

Prevent Overbrowning
Whether it's a turkey or a pie, you can prevent overbrowning on the top while baking by covering it with foil halfway through the cooking time.

PEPPERMINT-FLAVORED CANDY CANE COOKIES

1¼ cups margarine
1 cup confectioners' sugar
1 teaspoon vanilla extract
¼ teaspoon salt

1 large egg
3½ cups all-purpose flour
¼ teaspoon peppermint extract
3 drops red food coloring

Makes 2 to 3 dozen

Perfect with Minty Hot Chocolate (page 212) for the kids and with Irish Coffee (page 43) for the adults.

1. Preheat oven to 350°. Grease a baking sheet.
2. Beat together the margarine and sugar on medium speed until light and fluffy. Mix in the vanilla, salt, and egg. On low speed, beat in the flour ½ cup at a time until dough forms. Shape into a ball and divide in half.
3. In a small bowl, mix together the peppermint extract and red food coloring. Knead the food coloring mixture into 1 of the dough halves.
4. With lightly floured hands, roll 1 teaspoon of plain dough into a 4-inch rope. Repeat the process with 1 teaspoon of the red dough. Braid the ropes together and shape as a candy cane. Pinch together the ends to seal. Repeat with the remaining dough.
5. Place the cookies at least 1 inch apart on the prepared baking sheet. Bake in batches for 10 minutes or until golden brown. Transfer the baking sheet to a wire rack to cool.

Making Cookies Different Sizes?
Bake large cookies with large ones and small cookies with small ones for best results. Placing cookies of unlike sizes on the same sheet will result in uneven cooking.

MINCEMEAT PIE

2 eggs
1 (9-ounce) package mincemeat
1¼ cups water
1 cup granulated sugar

2 heaping tablespoons all-purpose
    flour
⅛ teaspoon salt
½ teaspoon vanilla extract
1 baked 9-inch pie pastry shell

1. Beat the eggs and set aside. Crumble the mincemeat into a bowl. Add the water and let soak for 30 minutes or until swollen.
2. Transfer the mincemeat to a medium-sized saucepan and add the sugar, flour, eggs, salt, and vanilla. Place over low heat and bring to a simmer. Stirring constantly, simmer for about 10 minutes or until thick.
3. Spread the mixture in the pastry shell. Let cool before serving.

CHRISTMAS TEACAKES

1 cup granulated sugar
1 cup margarine
3 large eggs
1 teaspoon nutmeg

3½ cups all-purpose flour
½ cup walnuts
1 cup confectioners' sugar

1. Preheat oven to 350°. Grease a baking sheet. Finely chop the walnuts.
2. In a large bowl, beat together the sugar and margarine until light and fluffy. Beat in the eggs and nutmeg. Beat in the flour ½ cup at a time.
3. Stir in the walnuts until well mixed.
4. Using 1 tablespoon of batter at a time, form cakes about ¼-inch thick. Place the cakes 1 inch apart on the prepared baking sheet. Bake the cakes in batches until golden and set, about 10 minutes.
5. When cool enough to handle but still warm, roll each cake in confectioners' sugar.

PEPPERMINT BAKED ALASKA

*1 sponge, angel food, or loaf
    pound cake*
4 egg whites
⅛ teaspoon cream of tartar
⅛ teaspoon salt

½ cup granulated sugar
½ teaspoon vanilla extract
1 quart peppermint ice cream

Serves 8

Baked Alaska may be prepared ahead and frozen, unwrapped, for up to 2 days. Brown just before serving.

1. Stack 2 pieces of corrugated 8" × 6" cardboard on top of each other and cover with aluminum foil. Cut the cake into ½-inch-thick slices and arrange the slices on the covered cardboard in a 7" × 5" rectangle. (You may not need all the cake.) Place in the freezer until frozen solid.

2. Let the egg whites stand at room temperature for 1 hour, then beat until frothy with a handheld electric mixer. Add the cream of tartar and salt, and continue beating until soft peaks form when the beaters are slowly raised.

3. Gradually beat in the sugar 2 tablespoons at a time, beating well after each addition. Continue beating for about 3 minutes until glossy. Mix in the vanilla.

4. Preheat oven to 500°.

5. Spoon the ice cream onto the frozen cake base. Quickly spread the ice cream evenly over the top and sides of the cake. Spoon the egg whites on top, spreading them over the top and down the sides onto the foil to seal completely. Make swirls in the egg whites on the top and sides.

6. Place on a baking sheet and bake for 3 minutes or until the meringue is light brown. Remove to a chilled platter and serve at once.

GINGERBREAD WITH LEMON TOPPING

Serves 9

Serve with Perfect Eggnog (page 45) or Hot Cinnamon Stocking (page 44).

½ cup water
½ firmly packed cup light brown sugar
⅓ cup butter
½ cup light molasses
1 teaspoon baking soda
1¼ cups all-purpose flour

1 teaspoon ground cinnamon
½ teaspoon ground ginger
1 large egg
2 tablespoons grated lemon rind
1 tablespoon lemon juice
1 cup confectioners' sugar

1. Preheat oven to 325°. Grease and flour an 8-inch square baking pan. Put the water in small saucepan on high heat and heat until boiling.
2. In a large bowl, mix together the brown sugar and butter. Mix in the molasses and baking soda. Add the flour, cinnamon, and ginger. Mix well.
3. Beat the egg, then add and mix. Add the boiling water and mix well.
4. Pour the batter into the prepared pan. Smooth the top.
5. Bake the gingerbread until a toothpick inserted into the center comes out clean, approximately 40 minutes.
6. While the gingerbread is cooling, mix together the lemon rind, lemon juice, and confectioners' sugar. Drizzle over the gingerbread pieces before serving.

Individual Portions
Foods bake faster in individual portions rather than in one large pan or dish. For example, use individual serving dishes for casseroles rather than one large casserole pan.

HOLIDAY PUNCH

½ medium-sized orange　　*1 cup brown sugar*
1 quart apple juice　　　*4 whole cinnamon sticks*
1 quart cranberry juice cocktail　　*4 whole cloves*

1. Peel and cut the orange into ¼-inch-thick slices.
2. Add the apple juice, cranberry juice, and brown sugar to a slow cooker. Cook on low setting, stirring occasionally, until the brown sugar is dissolved.
3. Add the cinnamon sticks and cloves. Cook, covered, for 1 hour on low setting.
4. Right before guests arrive, add the orange slices.

Serves 8

Keep this punch warm by keeping it in the slow cooker. Use a soup ladle to let guests serve themselves.

IRISH COFFEE

1½ ounces Irish whiskey　　*2 tablespoons whipped cream*
1 teaspoon granulated sugar　　*1 ounce Irish Cream or Kahlua*
1 cup very hot coffee　　　*liqueur*

1. Pour the whiskey into a glass or mug. Mix with the liqueur.
2. Stir in the sugar and add the hot coffee.
3. Top with whipped cream and serve immediately.

Serves 1

This mellow alcoholic drink is equally good alone or served as a dessert coffee. For a different twist, add a dollop of peppermint ice cream instead of whipped cream.

NONALCOHOLIC WASSAIL

Serves 8

For people who like their Wassail a little sweeter, add a teaspoon of honey to the pan and stir until the honey is dissolved.

2 quarts apple cider
2 cups orange juice
1 cup fresh lemon juice

1 teaspoon cloves
10 cinnamon sticks

1. Put the apple cider, orange juice, and lemon juice into a large saucepan. Add the cloves and 2 of the cinnamon sticks. Warm over medium heat for 20 minutes.
2. When ready to serve, strain off the cloves and cinnamon sticks and pour the liquid into mugs. Place a new cinnamon stick in each mug and serve.

HOT CINNAMON STOCKING

2 cups

Make a nonalcoholic version of this for children by adding cinnamon flavoring instead of liqueur.

2 cups prepared hot cocoa
2 tablespoons (or to taste)
*   cinnamon-flavor liqueur*
Whipped cream

2 red maraschino cherries,
*   halved*
2 green maraschino cherries,
*   halved*

Pour hot cocoa into 2 large mugs. Add 1 tablespoon of the cinnamon-flavored liqueur to each mug. Top each with whipped cream and red and green maraschino cherries.

PERFECT EGGNOG

6 large eggs
½ cup granulated sugar
1 pint heavy cream
1 pint milk

1 pint whiskey
2 ounces rum
1 tablespoon grated nutmeg

1. Separate the egg yolks and whites, and place the yolks in a large bowl.
2. Add the sugar to the yolks, beating at medium speed until the yolks are stiff.
3. Mix the egg whites into the yolk mixture. Stir in the cream and milk.
4. Add the whiskey and rum. Stir thoroughly.
5. Chill for 2 hours. Serve with grated nutmeg on top.

Makes 6 to 8 cups

Fresh eggnog is so much better than the store-bought varieties that you likely will never go back. Remember to keep some alcohol-free eggnog in the refrigerator for children and guests who don't imbibe.

TOM AND JERRY

1 egg
2 tablespoons granulated sugar
2 ounces light rum

1 ounce brandy
¾ cup hot milk
Nutmeg

1. Separate the egg white and yolk. Beat the egg white and yolk separately. Mix them together in a mug.
2. Add the sugar and mix vigorously. Pour in the rum and brandy. Fill with milk. Stir gently and sprinkle with nutmeg.

Serves 1

Here's something to lift your spirits on a cold holiday night!

CHAPTER 4
NEW YEAR'S

STUFFED MUSHROOMS

Serves 6

These make an excellent appetizer for any holiday meal.

1 pound fresh button
   mushrooms
1 small yellow onion
2 tablespoons fresh parsley
3 tablespoons butter
¾ cup bread crumbs

½ teaspoon salt
¼ teaspoon ground black pepper
1 teaspoon dried thyme
¼ cup half-and-half
¼ cup grated Parmesan cheese

1. Wash the mushrooms with a damp cloth and remove the stems. Set aside the caps. Chop the mushroom stems into ¼-inch pieces. Peel and finely chop the onion. Roughly chop the parsley.
2. Preheat oven broiler.
3. Heat the butter in a medium-sized skillet over medium heat. Add the onion and cook for 2 minutes, until translucent. Add the mushroom stems and cook for 2 to 3 minutes more. Stir in the bread crumbs, salt, pepper, and thyme. Cook for 1 minute more. Remove from heat and stir in the half-and-half and grated cheese.
4. Using a small spoon, fill each mushroom cap with the mushroom mixture. Place the filled mushrooms on a baking sheet and put under the preheated oven broiler for 5 to 7 minutes, until the tops are browned and the caps have softened and become juicy. Sprinkle the tops with chopped parsley and serve hot or warm.
5. Drizzle with garlic butter or top with an olive slice if desired to add a little extra flavor to these favorite hors d'ouvres.

Dried Mushrooms

Dried wild mushrooms are an excellent way to bring passionate flavors from forests to your dining table. Soak them for a few hours or overnight in room temperature water, then use them as you would fresh mushrooms. The soaking liquid acquires a wonderful flavor; use it in soups or stocks. Pour the water into a clear container and discard any sediment.

VEGETABLE GADO-GADO

*16–24 carrot sticks or baby
    carrots*
16–24 broccoli florets
16–24 trimmed green beans
16–24 yellow bell pepper strips
16–24 zucchini rounds
*Assorted other vegetables
    according to availability*

½ cup smooth peanut butter
¼ cup honey
¼ teaspoon salt
⅛ teaspoon cayenne pepper
1 tablespoon lime juice
¾ cup coconut milk

Serves 8

This appetizer has its origins in Indonesia. It can make a wonderful summer sampler when served with several dipping sauces.

1. Blanch all the vegetables quickly in lightly salted boiling water. Plunge immediately into ice-cold water to stop the cooking process. Drain and arrange in an attractive pattern on a serving platter.
2. Combine the peanut butter, honey, salt, cayenne pepper, and lime juice in a food processor or mixing bowl; Pulse or whisk together until smooth. Gradually work in the coconut milk until a saucy consistency is reached. Adjust consistency with hot water, if needed. Serve as a dipping sauce with the blanched vegetables.

Time-Saving Tip

You can purchase precleaned and precut vegetables in plastic bags or even prearranged on a platter. Just add a special dip for quick appetizers.

BROCCOLI DIP

1 small yellow onion
2 celery ribs
1 cup sliced fresh mushrooms
2 garlic cloves

2 cups chopped fresh broccoli
¼ cup butter
1 (10¾-ounce) can cream of
   mushroom condensed soup

1. Peel the onion and chop into ¼-inch pieces. Chop the celery into ¼-inch pieces. Clean the mushrooms by wiping with a damp cloth, then slice paper-thin. Peel the garlic and chop into ⅛-inch pieces. Chop the broccoli into ¼-inch pieces.
2. Combine all the ingredients in a slow cooker. Cover and cook on low setting for 3 to 4 hours.

CREAMY GARLIC AND RED PEPPER DIP

1 fresh red pepper
1 large garlic clove
1 teaspoon dried basil leaves

1 teaspoon hot pepper sauce
   of your choice
1 cup cottage cheese

1. Preheat oven to 350°. Cut the red pepper into ½-inch-wide strips. Place skin-side down on a baking sheet and spread cooking oil on top of the pepper strips. Bake for 1 hour or until well browned. Remove from the oven and cut into 1-inch pieces. Remove the peel from the garlic and crush the clove with the side of a large kitchen knife.
2. In a food processor, blend the red pepper strips, garlic, dried basil, and hot pepper sauce until chopped. Add the cottage cheese and blend well.
3. Chill for at least 1 hour before serving.

PARMESAN CRISPS

1 cup shredded (not grated)
  Parmesan cheese
1 teaspoon salt

1 teaspoon freshly ground
  white pepper

Serves 15

Use instead of traditional crackers or bread with Hot Artichoke Dip (page 56) or Eggplant Caviar (page 54).

1. Preheat oven to 325°. Line a baking sheet with parchment paper.
2. Place rounded teaspoons of the shredded cheese on the parchment, equally spaced with about 2 inches between each mound.
3. Lightly flatten each mound with your fingertips to a circle about 1½ inches across. Sprinkle with salt and pepper.
4. Place in the oven and remove when the cheese just starts to melt and very lightly begins to brown, about 3 to 5 minutes. Remove immediately.

ARTICHOKE BOTTOMS WITH HERBED CHEESE

1 can artichoke bottoms
2 tablespoons mix of fresh
  parsley, basil, and chives
6 fresh radishes

8 ounces cream cheese, softened
½ teaspoon salt
½ teaspoon freshly ground
  black pepper

Serves 15

Canned artichoke bottoms are a great item to have on hand when you need a quick appetizer with an elegant look.

1. Drain and rinse the artichoke bottoms, then slice into 30 neatly trimmed slices. Chop the herbs. Clean the radishes and slice into 30 rounds.
2. Mix together the cream cheese, herbs, salt, and pepper in a small bowl until smooth.
3. Use a pastry bag to pipe a small rosette of the cream cheese mixture (about 1 rounded tablespoon each) onto each artichoke slice.
4. Top with a radish slice and serve immediately.

HERBED CLAM DIP

Makes 1 cup

Use low-fat cottage cheese and low-fat yogurt for a low-fat, low-carb snack.

1 cup cottage cheese
1 (10-ounce) can minced
  clams, liquid reserved
⅓ cup chopped fresh parsley
3 tablespoons plain yogurt

1 tablespoon dried basil
1 tablespoon minced onion
1 tablespoon lemon juice
¼ teaspoon Tabasco sauce

1. Process the cottage cheese in a food processor until smooth. Transfer to a bowl.
2. Drain the clams, reserving 1 tablespoon of the liquid. Add the clams and 1 tablespoon of the liquid to the cottage cheese. Add the remaining ingredients and mix well.
3. Cover and chill well before serving.

LOUISIANA HOT WINGS

Serves 8

If you're going to an evening-long party, add a little water and stir the wings every hour or so; then they won't dry out.

1 small onion
1 jalapeño pepper
1 cup Louisiana red pepper
  sauce
2 tablespoons Worcestershire sauce

2 tablespoons powdered Cajun
  spice, divided
1 cup barbecue sauce
5 pounds thawed chicken wings,
  disjointed with tips removed

1. Preheat slow cooker on high setting. Peel the onion and chop it into ¼-inch pieces. Remove the stem and seeds from the jalapeño pepper and dice the pepper.
2. Add the onion, jalapeño pepper, red pepper sauce, Worcestershire sauce, Cajun spice, and barbecue sauce to the slow cooker and stir well.
3. Add the chicken wings and stir until all the wings are covered.
4. Cover and cook on high setting for 4 hours. Uncover and turn heat to low while serving.

PEARS WRAPPED IN PROSCIUTTO ON A BED OF MIXED GREENS

6 slices prosciutto

2 ripe pears

3 tablespoons extra-virgin olive oil

1/2 teaspoon salt

1/2 teaspoon ground black pepper

4 cups mixed salad greens

1/2 cup prepared vinaigrette salad dressing

1/2 cup fresh-grated Parmesan cheese

Serves 4

Use a good quality Parmesan cheese from the deli counter to enhance the flavor of this dish.

1. Cut each slice of prosciutto in half lengthwise. Cut each pear into 6 wedges and remove the core.
2. Toss the pear wedges in about 2 tablespoons of the olive oil until evenly coated, and season with the salt and pepper.
3. Heat a grill pan until very hot, almost smoking. Mark the pear slices with dark brown grill marks on each side, using tongs to turn the pears. This should take only a few minutes on each side.
4. Preheat broiler to low. Wrap a piece of prosciutto around the middle of each pear. Place all the wrapped pears on a lightly oiled baking sheet and cook for about 2 to 3 minutes on each side.
5. Toss the salad greens with the vinaigrette. Top with the Parmesan cheese and sprinkle with salt and pepper. Drizzle with the remaining olive oil and serve immediately.

Freezing Cheese

Placing a leftover hunk of cheese into the freezer not only conserves all those odd bits that are too small to use in another recipe, but also hardens up the soft cheeses enough for grating. Be sure to freeze soft cheeses when they have ripened. Semisoft and harder cheeses can be frozen as is, or sliced or grated beforehand.

EGGPLANT CAVIAR

Serves 4

Serve with crackers,
French bread, or
Parmesan Crisps
(page 51).

1 large white onion
3 garlic cloves
1 large eggplant
2 tablespoons olive oil

1 tablespoon tomato paste
1 teaspoon salt
½ teaspoon ground white pepper

1. Preheat oven to 400°. Peel and finely chop the onion and garlic.
2. Place the eggplant in a baking dish and roast on the middle rack of the oven until very well done, about 1 hour. Let cool. Cut the eggplant in half and scoop out the soft pulp with a serving spoon. Place on a cutting board and chop thoroughly, until it has the consistency of oatmeal.
3. Heat the olive oil in a large skillet over medium heat for 1 minute. Add the onions and cook until they are very soft but not brown, about 10 minutes. Add the garlic and cook 1 minute more. Stir in the tomato paste and cook for 1 minute.
4. Add the chopped eggplant and cook until the mixture is thickened. An indentation should remain when a spoon is depressed into the mixture. Season with salt and pepper.

About Eggplant

Eggplants vary widely in flavor and intensity, and some types' delicate bitter edge helps define this beautiful vegetable's character. Long, slender, violet-hued Japanese eggplants contain none of the bitterness of America's large black variety. Pear-sized Italian-style eggplants are similar to our regular ones, but white-skinned varieties are milder. When sliced eggplant is sprinkled with salt it sheds some of its bitterness along with the salty droplets that form along its surface.

FRIED GREEN TOMATO BRUSCHETTA

4 medium-sized green tomatoes
1/4 cup fresh basil leaves
12 pimiento-stuffed green olives
1 loaf crusty country bread
1 cup olive oil

2 eggs
1 cup all-purpose flour
1 cup bread crumbs
1 tablespoon balsamic vinegar
1/4 cup extra-virgin olive oil

Makes 12

This recipe combines the best of Italy with the best of the deep South. Serve it with champagne for a New Year's treat.

1. Cut the tomatoes into 1/2-inch-thick slices. Roughly chop the basil leaves. Cut the olives in half lengthwise. Cut the bread into slices about 1-inch thick. Pour the olive oil into a frying pan and preheat to about 325° (medium-low).
2. Lightly beat the eggs in a shallow bowl. Dredge the tomato slices in the flour, dip them in the eggs, and then in the bread crumbs, shaking off excess after each dip. Fry at low heat until golden and mostly tender. Place the still-hot tomatoes flat on a cutting board and dice them into 1/2-inch pieces.
3. In a large mixing bowl, gently toss the diced tomatoes with the vinegar, basil, and olives. Set aside.
4. Preheat oven to 400°.
5. Brush the bread slices with the extra-virgin oil and place on a baking sheet. Toast in the oven until lightly browned. Remove and top each of 6 slices with the tomato mixture. Cut each in half.

Tomato Types

All tomatoes are not alike. Substitute plum tomatoes for a more robust flavor. Choose golden tomatoes for a more mellow taste. Reserve pricier hot-house tomatoes for salads and recipes in which tomatoes are the main ingredient.

HOT ARTICHOKE DIP

Serves 10

This is excellent served with pita bread, Parmesan Crisps (page 51), or even crisp vegetables such as carrots and celery.

1 (10½-ounce) can artichoke
  hearts
2 garlic cloves
¼ cup mayonnaise
½ teaspoon Worcestershire sauce

½ cup grated Parmesan cheese
½ teaspoon salt
½ teaspoon ground white
  pepper

1. Preheat oven to 350°.
2. Drain and rinse the artichoke hearts. Chop into ¼-inch pieces. Peel and mince the garlic.
3. Combine all the ingredients in a 2-quart ovenproof glass dish. Mix well. Bake, uncovered, for 25 minutes.

SPINACH AND RICOTTA DIP

Serves 12

Serve with fresh trimmed vegetables, Parmesan Crisps (page 51), or toasted bread rounds. No one will guess how easy this was to make!

1 (10-ounce) package frozen,
  chopped spinach
4 green onions
1 small white onion
½ cup ricotta cheese
⅓ cup mayonnaise
¼ cup sour cream

3 tablespoons lemon juice
¼ teaspoon Worcestershire
  sauce
½ teaspoon salt
½ teaspoon ground black
  pepper

1. Thaw and drain the spinach. Peel and chop the green onions. Peel and grate the white onion, reserving the juice.
2. Combine all the ingredients in a food processor and pulse until smooth.
3. Transfer to a bowl and chill thoroughly.

HOT DUNGENESS CRAB APPETIZER

*1 (14-ounce) can artichoke
    hearts*
*½ pound fresh Dungeness
    crabmeat*
2 cups mayonnaise

1 small yellow onion
*1 cup shredded Parmesan
    cheese*
1 bunch fresh parsley

Makes 2 cups

When making this dish ahead of time, do not cover with aluminum foil, as the crab will discolor.

1. Preheat oven to 350°. Drain the artichoke hearts and chop into ¼-inch pieces. Drain the crabmeat and chop. Peel the onion and chop thinly. Chop the parsley.
2. Combine all the ingredients *except* the parsley and mix well. Place in a shallow baking dish and heat in the oven for 6 to 8 minutes or until the internal temperature is at least 140°.
3. Garnish with minced parsley. Serve with assorted breads.

PEANUT POPCORN FUDGE

2 cups granulated sugar
½ cup smooth peanut butter
½ cup milk
1 tablespoon margarine

*1 heaping cup of coarsely
    chopped popped popcorn*
1 teaspoon vanilla extract

Serves 12

This recipe calls for experimentation. Try adding peanuts, coconut, or crispy rice cereal until you find the perfect "fudge" for your family and friends.

1. Grease a medium-sized baking dish.
2. In a medium-sized saucepan, combine the sugar, peanut butter, and milk, and warm over low heat until smooth. Add the margarine, popcorn, and vanilla.
3. Beat until all the ingredients are well distributed and the mixture is of an even consistency.
4. Pour onto the prepared baking dish. Chill well.

IRISH CREAM

Makes about 4 drinks

To make an elegant-looking drink, top with whipped cream and drizzled chocolate syrup.

1 (12-ounce) can condensed milk
8 ounces Irish whiskey
4 large eggs

1 tablespoon chocolate syrup
1 teaspoon vanilla extract
1 teaspoon coconut extract

Mix together all the ingredients in a blender. Chill for 1 hour and serve.

CRUNCHY NUT TREATS

Makes about 3 dozen

These are a wonderful complement to those meat and cheese appetizers so prevalent at New Year's Eve parties.

1 cup solid vegetable shortening
¼ cup confectioners' sugar, plus extra for dusting
1 teaspoon vanilla extract

2 cups sifted all-purpose flour
½ cup chopped almonds
½ cup chopped walnuts

1. Preheat oven to 300°.
2. In a large bowl, beat together the shortening, confectioners' sugar, and vanilla extract. Beat in the flour at low speed. Stir in the nuts.
3. Shape the dough into round balls and place several inches apart on an ungreased baking sheet. Bake in batches for 15 to 18 minutes. Check frequently during the last 5 minutes to ensure they don't scorch.
4. Transfer cookies to a wire rack. Roll the warm cookies in confectioners' sugar. Let stand until cool.

PEANUTTY OATMEAL CANDY

1 cup granulated sugar
½ cup evaporated milk
¼ cup margarine
¼ cup crunchy peanut butter

½ teaspoon vanilla extract
1 cup old-fashioned dry oats
½ cup peanuts

1. In a saucepan, bring the sugar, evaporated milk, and margarine to a boil, stirring frequently.
2. When the sugar is dissolved, remove from heat and stir in the peanut butter and vanilla.
3. Mix in the oats and peanuts. Drop the mixture by rounded teaspoon onto wax paper so that each morsel has a peak. (If the mixture is too stiff, add a few drops of milk.) Chill until firm.

Makes 2 dozen

Try experimenting with this recipe by replacing the peanuts with coconut and the peanut butter with melted milk chocolate. Or use almonds instead of peanuts.

SCOTCH MILK PUNCH

2 ounces scotch
6 ounces milk

1 teaspoon sugar
⅛ teaspoon nutmeg

Pour the scotch into a highball glass. Add the milk and sugar. Stir well. Dust with nutmeg.

Serves 1

This is a traditional cure for New Year's Day hangovers, although it's pretty tasty during the party, too.

CHAMPAGNE COCKTAIL

Serves 1

A traditional treat to help ring in the New Year.

1 teaspoon fine sugar
3 dashes bitters

6 ounces chilled champagne
Lemon twist

Dissolve the sugar in the bitters in the bottom of a champagne flute. Add the champagne and stir. Top with a lemon twist.

CHAMPAGNE CHARISMA

Serves 1

It's just as good without the sherbet. Or try a different flavor of sherbet for a unique taste.

1 ounce vodka
½ ounce peach-flavored brandy
1 ounce cranberry juice

1–2 scoops raspberry sherbet
2 ounces chilled champagne

Combine all the ingredients *except* the champagne in a blender. Blend well. Pour into a large red wine goblet. Add the champagne and stir.

CHAMPAGNE MINT

½ ounce green crème de menthe   *Chilled champagne to fill glass*

Pour the crème de menthe into a champagne flute. Add the champagne and stir gently.

CHAMPAGNE FIZZ

2 ounces gin   *Ice*
1 ounce lemon juice   *4 ounces champagne*
1 teaspoon granulated sugar

1. Combine the gin, lemon juice, and sugar in a shaker half-filled with ice. Shake well.
2. Strain into a highball glass over ice. Add the champagne and stir gently.

NONALCOHOLIC CHAMPAGNE PUNCH

Serves 20

Even if everyone at your party is planning to drink, it's nice to have something nonalcoholic to wash down those appetizers.

1 cup fine sugar
1 cup water
2 cups grapefruit juice

Juice of 1 lemon
1½ quarts ginger ale

1. Dissolve the sugar in the water in a punch bowl.
2. Add the grapefruit and lemon juices to the sugar water and mix well.
3. Add the ginger ale to the punch bowl just before serving.

Serving Tips

Pouring a cold drink into a warm glass is not a crime, but it should be. It robs the drink of its chill and the pleasure of its proper temperature. Chilling glasses is not hard, of course—just difficult to remember. If refrigerator or freezer space allows, squeeze the glass in along with the ice cream. If not, fill a glass with ice just before serving, stir it a bit, and discard the ice.

CHAPTER 5

VALENTINE'S DAY

ARTICHOKES IN COURT BOUILLON WITH LEMON BUTTER

Serves 4

Serve as the first course to a romantic menu including Scallops and Shrimp with White Bean Sauce (page 65).

4 whole artichokes
4 lemons
2 tablespoons whole coriander
  seeds

2 tablespoons salt
1 cup butter

1. Trim the stems of the artichokes to about 2 inches. Bring 5 quarts water to a rapid boil. Halve 3 of the lemons, squeeze them into the boiling water, and toss the squeezed lemon fruits into the water along with the coriander seeds and salt. Boil for 5 minutes.
2. Place the artichokes in the cooking liquid and cover with a heavy plate or other object to keep them from floating. Boil until a paring knife inserted where the stem meets the bottom comes out easily, about 15 minutes. Meanwhile, melt the butter in the microwave for 30 seconds on high, then mix with the juice of the remaining lemon.
3. Serve each person a whole artichoke accompanied by a ramekin of butter sauce and a large bowl for discarded leaves.

How to Eat an Artichoke
Eat the artichoke leaf by leaf, dipping them in butter and nibbling at the tender bits at the bottoms of the outer leaves first and gradually reaching the fully edible inner leaves. When you reach the hairlike "choke," scoop it out with a spoon, discard it, and carve the prized "heart" at the bottom into pieces for easy consumption.

SCALLOPS AND SHRIMP WITH WHITE BEAN SAUCE

1 small white onion
2 garlic cloves
1⅓ cups canned white beans
½ pound medium-sized shrimp
2 teaspoons olive oil, divided
¼ cup dry white wine
¼ tightly packed cup fresh parsley leaves
¼ lightly packed cup fresh basil leaves
¼ cup chicken broth
½ pound scallops

> **Serves 4**
>
> Add 1 pound of crab-meat instead of the shrimp and scallops for a smoother texture. Mix with the bean purée and serve over egg noodles.

1. Remove the skins from the onion and garlic. Chop the onion into ¼-inch pieces. Mince the garlic. Drain and rinse the beans. Parboil the shrimp. Remove the shells and devein the shrimp.

2. In a medium-sized saucepan, sauté the onion and garlic in 1 teaspoon of the olive oil over moderately low heat until the onion is soft. Add the wine and simmer the mixture until the wine is reduced by half. Add the parsley, basil, ⅓ cup of the beans, and the chicken broth. Simmer the mixture for 1 minute, stirring constantly.

3. Transfer the bean mixture to a blender or food processor and purée it. Pour the purée back into the saucepan and add the remaining beans. Simmer for 2 minutes.

4. Heat the remaining 1 teaspoon of oil over moderately high heat in a medium-sized skillet until it is hot but not smoking. Sauté the shrimp for 2 minutes on each side, or until they are cooked through.

5. Using a slotted spoon, transfer the shrimp to a plate and cover to keep warm. Add the scallops to the skillet and sauté them for 1 minute on each side, or until they are cooked through. To serve, divide the bean sauce between 4 shallow bowls and arrange the shellfish over the top.

How to Parboil

The key to effective parboiling is not to let the shrimp cook for too long. Bring a large pot of water to boil (more than enough to cover the shrimp when added). Add the shrimp and boil for 2 to 3 minutes. Immediately drain and rinse in cold water.

CHEESE FONDUE

Serves 6

Turn down the lights, add a few candles, and let the conversation flow as people assemble their own meals.

1 garlic clove
¾ pound Swiss cheese
¾ pound Gruyère cheese
1 loaf French bread
Assorted bite-sized vegetables
   such as carrot sticks, broccoli,
   cauliflower, and green beans

2 cups dry white wine
1 tablespoon cornstarch
2 tablespoons kirsch

1. Cut the end off the garlic clove and remove the skin. Shred the cheeses. Cut the French bread into 1-inch cubes.
2. Put the vegetables in a vegetable steamer and cook until soft but not mushy.
3. Rub the inside of a medium-sized saucepot with the cut-side of the garlic. Leave the clove in the bottom of the pot. Add the wine and cook over medium heat until it simmers. Whisk in the cheese in small handfuls, making sure that the last addition has completely melted before adding the next.
4. Combine the cornstarch and kirsch to form a paste; whisk into the cheese mixture. Simmer the fondue gently for 5 to 7 minutes to allow the cornstarch to thicken.
5. Transfer the cheese mixture to a fondue pot and set a low flame under it, just hot enough to keep it at the border of simmering. Assemble a platter with the vegetables and bread cubes and set the table with either long fondue forks or long wooden skewers.

Making Your Own Pasta

Use semolina flour to make homemade noodles. It is made from high-gluten wheat and is more finely ground. The pasta is slightly stiffer than that made from regular flour so it also holds up better in slow-cooked casseroles.

SWEET FENNEL WITH LEMON AND SHAVED PARMIGIANO

2 bulbs fresh fennel

½ fresh lemon

1 wedge (at least 4 inches long) Parmigiano Reggiano cheese

1 tablespoon extra-virgin olive oil

Pinch of salt

> **Serves 4**
>
> This is the perfect hors d'oeuvres for an Italian meal, but it also makes an interesting treat for any dinner.

1. Trim the stems and hairlike fronds from the fennel tops. Break the bulbs apart, layer by layer, using your hands to make long, bite-sized pieces. Discard the core. Arrange the pieces in a pyramid-shape on a small, attractive serving plate.
2. Squeeze the lemon over the fennel. Using a peeler, shave curls of the cheese over the fennel, allowing them to fall where they may. Make about 10 curls. Drizzle the olive oil over the plate and sprinkle with salt.
3. Serve at room temperature.

Even-Seasoning Secret

To avoid salty patches in some parts of your food, and bland, unseasoned patches on other parts, take a cue from pro chefs: Season from a great height. Most chefs pinch salt between their thumb and forefinger and sprinkle it down onto food from about head height. It tends to shower broadly over the food this way, covering evenly.

PASTA WITH ARTICHOKES

1 (10-ounce) package frozen
    artichoke hearts
1¼ cups water
1 tablespoon lemon juice
¼ cup sun-dried tomatoes
    packed in oil
2 garlic cloves

1½ cups uncooked linguine
4 teaspoons olive oil
¼ teaspoon red pepper flakes
2 teaspoons dried parsley
¼ cup grated Parmesan cheese
½ teaspoon freshly grated
    black pepper

1. Cook the artichokes in the water and lemon juice according to package directions. Drain, reserving ¼ cup of the liquid. Let the artichokes cool, then cut into quarters. Drain the tomatoes and chop into ¼-inch pieces. Peel and finely mince the garlic. Cook the pasta according to package directions.
2. Heat the olive oil in a nonstick skillet over medium heat. Add the garlic and sauté for 1 minute. Reduce heat to low and stir in the artichokes and tomatoes. Simmer for 1 minute. Stir in the reserved artichoke liquid, the red pepper flakes, and parsley. Simmer for 5 minutes.
3. Pour the artichoke sauce over the pasta in a large bowl. Toss gently to coat. Sprinkle with cheese and top with pepper.

Low-Fat Garlic Toast

Instead of smearing the bread with butter before toasting, give it a light spritz of olive oil and bake in a 350° oven for 6 to 8 minutes. Rub a cut garlic clove across the top of each slice. The flavor is great and the fat is near zero.

SPINACH-WRAPPED ZUCCHINI FLAN

1 small zucchini (about 3/4 pound)
4–6 large leaves flat-leaf spinach
1/2 cup heavy cream
2 eggs
1 egg yolk
1 teaspoon fresh-grated nutmeg
1/8 teaspoon curry powder
1/8 teaspoon cayenne powder
1/2 teaspoon salt
1/2 teaspoon ground black pepper
1 teaspoon butter, softened

Serves 4

The flan can be made the day before and gently reheated just before serving.

1. Preheat oven to 300°. Trim the zucchini and cut into 2-inch pieces. Wash the spinach thoroughly and remove the stems.
2. Bring salted water to a boil in a medium-sized saucepan. Using a steamer insert, steam the zucchini, covered, until tender. Add the spinach leaves to the steamer when the zucchini is just about done. When the leaves just start to wilt, remove them from the water. Spread them out flat on paper towels and pat dray. Remove the zucchini and let cool.
3. Squeeze the zucchini with your hands to remove as much water as possible. Transfer the zucchini to a food processor and process for about 30 seconds. Add the cream, eggs, egg yolk, nutmeg, curry powder, cayenne, salt, and pepper; process until very smooth.
4. Lightly butter four 4-ounce ramekins. Use the spinach to line each ramekin, positioning the leaves with the ribbed side facing inward. Leave a little spinach overhanging the edges of the ramekins.
5. Pour the custard into the spinach-lined ramekins. Fold the overhanging spinach leaves over the custard.
6. Place the ramekins in a baking dish. Fill the pan with boiling water 2/3 of the way up the sides of the ramekins. Bake for about 45 minutes or until just set. Remove the ramekins from the water and let rest for at least 5 minutes before unmolding.

FRENCH ONION SOUP

4 large yellow onions
1 garlic clove
¼ cup butter, plus extra for buttering
3 cups rich beef stock
1 cup dry white wine

¼ cup medium-dry sherry
1 teaspoon Worcestershire sauce
1 loaf French bread
¼ cup fresh grated Romano cheese

1. Peel and thinly slice the onions. Peel and mince the garlic clove.
2. In a large frying pan, slowly sauté the onions in the butter until limp and glazed. Transfer to a slow cooker. Add the beef stock, white wine, sherry, Worcestershire, and garlic. Cover and cook on low for 6 to 8 hours.
3. Preheat broiler. Cut 6 slices of French bread about 1-inch thick, and butter the slices. (Reserve the remaining bread to serve with the meal.) Grate the cheese if necessary. Place the buttered French bread on a baking sheet. Sprinkle with the cheese. Place under the broiler until lightly toasted.
4. To serve, ladle the soup into 6 bowls. Float a slice of toasted French bread on top of each serving.

Cry for Onions?

If onions make you cry, try storing them in the refrigerator in a tightly sealed container. Peel them under cold, running water as needed and chop them in a food processor.

COQUILLES ST. JACQUES PROVENÇAL

2 pounds fresh scallops
½ teaspoon salt
½ teaspoon ground white pepper
1 small yellow onion
½ pound fresh mushrooms

2 large red tomatoes
1 tablespoon chives
1 garlic clove
6 tablespoons butter, divided
½ cup dry white wine

Serves 6

This also can be made with shrimp or crab-meat. It is best served with a dry white wine.

1. Pat the scallops dry. If they are large, cut them into smaller pieces about the size of a nickel. Sprinkle the scallops lightly with salt and pepper. Peel and mince the onion. Wash the mushrooms with a damp cloth and slice. Peel the tomatoes and chop into ¼-inch pieces. Mince the chives. Peel and mince the garlic clove.
2. Sauté the scallops along with the minced onion in 4 tablespoons of the butter until the onions look transparent, about 5 minutes, turning the scallops to brown all sides lightly. Remove the scallops and onions. Keep warm.
3. Add the remaining butter to the pan and sauté the mushrooms for 2 minutes. Add the tomatoes, wine, chives, and garlic. Simmer for 5 minutes. Pour over the scallops and serve.

Sautéing with Water

For a healthy alternative, sauté onions and garlic in a few table-spoons of water instead of oil or butter. They tend to get a little crisper this way, but this cooking method saves many grams of fat.

GRILLED LOBSTER WITH LEMON AND TARRAGON

Serves 2

Serve with Oven-Roasted Asparagus (page 7) and Champagne Charisma (page 60).

2 uncooked lobster tails
2 tablespoons fresh lemon juice
1½ teaspoons grated lemon zest
2 tablespoons chopped fresh chives

1 tablespoon chopped fresh tarragon
½ cup butter
½ teaspoon salt
½ teaspoon freshly ground black pepper

1. Thaw the lobster tails if necessary. Create lemon zest by grating the peel of a fresh lemon. Chop the chives and tarragon.
2. Preheat a charcoal or gas grill to high heat.
3. In a small saucepan over low heat, melt the butter and add the lemon zest, lemon juice, chives, tarragon, salt, and pepper. Set aside and keep warm.
4. Use heavy kitchen shears to split the lobster tails by cutting the length of the underside. Brush the cut-side of the tails with 1 tablespoon of the butter sauce.
5. Grill the lobsters cut-side down for about 4 minutes. Turn them and grill for another 4 minutes. Turn them again to the cut-side and grill until the lobster meat is just opaque but still juicy, about 2 minutes. Transfer to plates.
6. Brush the lobster with the butter sauce and serve the remaining sauce in a small ramekin on the side.

Serving Lobster Graciously

Provide your guests with a clean towel and small bowl of warm water with a floating lemon slice for use as a finger bowl. Another alternative is to remove the meat from the shell before serving. Use kitchen shears to split the shell. Brush the meat with the seasoned butter before serving.

GAME HENS IN RED WINE

2 game hens, fresh or thawed
1 cup all-purpose flour
½ teaspoon salt
¼ teaspoon ground black
   pepper

⅓ cup vegetable oil
1½ cups dry red wine
1 cup sour cream

1. Clean the game hens by running them under cold water. Combine the flour, salt, and ground black pepper. Roll the game hens in the mixture until lightly coated.
2. Heat the vegetable oil at medium temperature in a medium-sized frying pan. Place the game hens in the frying pan and brown on all sides.
3. Place the game hens in the slow cooker on low setting. Pour the red wine on top of the game hens. Cover and cook on low setting for 5 hours.
4. Add the sour cream and cook for another hour.

To Prevent Curdling

To prevent curdling of milk, yogurt, or sour cream in long-cooking dishes, mix it with an equal amount of cooking liquid from the dish being prepared. Add the milk products during the last hour of the cooking process and always cook them on low heat.

CARAMEL RUM FONDUE

Serves 2 to 8

Serve with apple wedges, fresh strawberries, marshmallows, or walnuts.

1 (14-ounce) package caramels
²⁄₃ cup cream
½ cup miniature marshmallows
1 tablespoon rum

1. Combine the caramels and cream in a slow cooker. Cover and cook on low setting for 2 to 3 hours or until the caramels are completely melted.
2. Stir in the marshmallows and rum. Continue cooking, covered, on low setting for 1 hour.
3. Transfer to a traditional fondue pot before serving.

SALMON IN WHITE WINE WITH DRIED PEACHES

Serves 4

Serve with fresh steamed broccoli drizzled with fresh-squeezed lime juice.

1½ pounds salmon fillets
¼ cup all-purpose flour
2 tablespoons extra-virgin olive oil
1 cup dry white wine
½ cup vegetable stock
1 cup dried peaches
½ teaspoon freshly ground black pepper

1. Preheat oven to 350°. Pat the salmon dry with the paper towels. Coat the salmon with a light layer of the flour.
2. Heat the olive oil in a frying pan at medium heat. Add the salmon and brown on all sides. Discard the oil and place the salmon fillets on paper towels to soak up additional oil.
3. Add the wine and vegetable stock to an oven-proof casserole. Place the salmon fillets in the bottom of the casserole. Quarter the dried peaches and place them on top of the salmon. Sprinkle with pepper. Cover and bake for 30 minutes.

HERB LINGUINE WITH SALMON, CREAM, AND PISTACHIOS

2 tablespoons chopped pistachio nuts
¼ red bell pepper
2 garlic cloves
¾ pound salmon fillet
2 teaspoons lemon zest
¼ cup freshly grated Parmesan
   cheese

¼ cup unsalted butter
1½ cups heavy cream
½ teaspoon, plus 1 tablespoon
   salt
½ teaspoon ground white
   pepper
12 ounces fresh herb linguine

Serves 4

Serve with a light,
sweet white or
blush wine.

1. Preheat oven to 300°. Chop the pistachio nuts, if necessary. Seed and dice the red bell pepper. Peel and mince the garlic. Dice the salmon fillet. Create the lemon zest by grating a fresh lemon peel. Grate the Parmesan cheese, if necessary.
2. Place the pistachios on a baking sheet and toast in the oven for about 5 minutes. Set aside to cool.
3. In a large, deep skillet, melt the butter over medium-low heat. Add the bell pepper and garlic. Raise the heat to medium and sauté for 1 minute. Add the salmon and sauté for 1 minute. Add the cream, lemon zest, the ½ teaspoon salt, and the pepper. Cook until reduced and thickened, stirring frequently.
4. Meanwhile, in a large pot, bring at least 4 quarts water to a rolling boil. Add the 1 tablespoon salt. Add the pasta, stir to separate, and cook until al dente. Drain.
5. Transfer the linguine to a large, warm bowl. Add the sauce and toss well. Sprinkle with the pistachios and Parmesan cheese.

Resist the Urge to Precook Pasta

Pasta that has been precooked will continue cooking from the heat it generates long after it's removed from the pan. The result will be a gooey, mushy, untasty mess. Even if it means keeping the sauce warm, make your pasta as fresh as possible.

PEARS POACHED IN WHITE WINE WITH STRAWBERRY SAUCE

Serves 8

This beautiful dessert is perfect in any season. It is light, contains no cholesterol, and makes the perfect finish for an elegant dinner or even an everyday lunch.

4 Bosc pears
1 pint strawberries
1 lemon
1 bottle white wine
    (Chardonnay or Riesling)
8 whole cloves

2 whole cinnamon sticks
1 cup granulated sugar,
    divided
1 teaspoon vanilla extract
8 sprigs fresh mint

1. Cut the pears in half lengthwise and scoop out the seeds. Hull the strawberries and cut in half. Create zest from the lemon peel by shaving off with a vegetable peeler in strips.
2. Combine the wine, lemon zest, cloves, cinnamon sticks, and ½ cup of the sugar in a large (4- to 5-quart) pot. Bring to a boil.
3. Reduce heat to a simmer and add the pears, arranging them so they are mostly submerged. Cover tightly and cook slowly for 5 minutes. Remove from heat and leave to steep for 20 minutes. Chill in the refrigerator.
4. In a blender or food processor, combine the strawberries, remaining ½ cup sugar, and vanilla. Purée until smooth, adding a few drops of water if necessary to get things started.
5. Spoon the sauce onto dessert plates to forms small pools midplate. Serve the pears cut-side down atop the sauce. Garnish with mint sprigs at the stem end.

Balancing Your Menu

If you're leafing through this book in order to design a balanced meal, keep in mind that opposites attract. In other words, if your entrée is rich, go for a light, fruit-based dessert. Or, if you are serving a light salad, choose a calorie-laden, chocolate dessert.

CHOCOLATE SOUFFLÉ

2 ounces unsweetened chocolate
8 eggs
¾ cup granulated sugar
4 drops vanilla extract

1 cup all-purpose flour
2 cups milk
Confectioners' sugar
Sweetened whipped cream

> **Serves 12**
>
> Soufflés can be easy to make as long as you follow directions carefully. The egg whites and yolks cannot meet until they are folded gently together. Note that a soufflé typically falls somewhat while cooling.

1. Melt the chocolate and let cool. Separate the egg yolks from the whites, placing 5 of the yolks in a medium-sized bowl and discarding the remaining 3 yolks. Divide the egg whites into 3 portions as designated in step 6, following. Make sure no yolk is in the whites. (Even a tiny amount will cause the soufflé not to rise.)

2. Beat the egg yolks with ½ cup of the granulated sugar and the vanilla until light and fluffy. Gradually beat in the flour until a paste forms.

3. Scald the milk in a saucepan by heating it until a thin film appears on top. Add the egg yolk mixture to the milk and bring to a boil. With a wire whisk, quickly and vigorously beat the mixture until the paste is well incorporated into the milk and the mixture is smooth. Continue to stir with a wooden spoon until the mixture is thick.

4. Add the melted chocolate, stirring to blend. Let cool.

5. Preheat oven to 350°. Grease 12 individual soufflé dishes or custard cups, each 2 inches in diameter.

6. Gradually add the remaining ¼ cup granulated sugar to the egg whites and beat in 3 stages as follows: Beat 3 egg whites, then add another 3 egg whites and beat them. Finally, add the remaining 2 egg whites and beat until stiff and shiny but not dry. (The egg whites should not slide when the bowl is tipped.)

7. Fold the egg whites into the soufflé batter just until no white streaks remain. Do not stir or mix well. Evenly divide the batter among the prepared dishes.

8. Bake for 30 minutes or until the tops are firm. Dust with confectioners' sugar and serve topped with whipped cream.

AMARETTO CAKE

Serves 10

This is the perfect romantic ending to a meal of Herb Linguine with Salmon, Cream, and Pistachios (page 75).

1 yellow sheet cake in 2 layers
2 eggs
½ cup cornstarch
½ cup granulated sugar
2 cups milk
1 teaspoon vanilla extract
1 teaspoon rum extract
1 cup amaretto liqueur, divided
1 (10-ounce) jar apricot pre-
   serves
2 cups whipping cream
Fresh strawberries

1. The cake should be cooled completely. It can be baked a day ahead of time, if necessary.
2. Beat the eggs well. Combine the eggs, cornstarch, sugar, milk, vanilla extract, rum extract, and ¾ cup of the amaretto liqueur in a saucepan over low heat. Cook, stirring constantly, for 15 minutes or until a skin begins to form. Remove from heat and let cool.
3. Using a serrated knife, cut each cake layer in half horizontally, to yield 4 layers. Place a layer on a serving plate. Spread with ⅓ of the preserves and top with ⅓ of the pudding. Repeat with the remaining layers.
4. Make the frosting by whipping together the cream and remaining ¼ cup amaretto until soft peaks form. Frost the top and sides of the cake with the cream. Arrange the strawberries on top.

Make Condensed Milk

To make your own sweetened condensed milk, use 1 cup powdered milk, ⅔ cup granulated sugar, ⅓ cup boiling water, and 3 table-spoons melted butter. Mix everything in the blender and you have the equivalent of a 14-ounce can of condensed milk.

APPLE-BUTTERED RUM PUDDING
WITH APPLE TOPPING

For the pudding:
2 cups light cream
1 cup cooked white rice
1/3 cup granulated sugar
1/2 teaspoon salt
1 tablespoon unflavored gelatin
1/4 cup water
2 tablespoons rum or
   1 teaspoon rum flavoring
1 cup sour cream

For the apple topping:
1/2 packed cup light brown
   sugar
2 tablespoons cornstarch
1/4 teaspoon salt
1/2 teaspoon ground cinnamon
1/2 cup water
1 (20-ounce) can pie-sliced
   apples
1 tablespoon butter
2 tablespoons rum or
   1 teaspoon rum flavoring

> **Serves 6 to 8**
>
> This is delicious hot or cold. Serve it as the finale to a meal of Cheese Fondue (page 66).

1. To make the pudding, combine the cream, rice, sugar, and salt in a saucepan and bring to a boil. Reduce heat to low and simmer for 20 minutes, stirring occasionally.

2. Meanwhile, in a bowl, soften the gelatin in the water for 5 minutes. Remove the rice mixture from the heat and stir in the gelatin mixture until the gelatin dissolves. Let cool until thickened but not set.

3. Fold in the rum and sour cream. Spoon into individual molds (about 1 cup in size) and chill until firm.

4. To make the topping, combine the brown sugar, cornstarch, salt, cinnamon, butter, rum flavoring, and water in a saucepan and stir well. Add the apples and bring to a boil. Reduce heat to low and simmer for 15 to 20 minutes, or until the apples are tender, stirring occasionally.

5. Release puddings from the molds and place on individual plates. Spoon warm topping over them right before serving.

BISHOP

Serves 1

This is the perfect accompaniment to any meal with red meat.

2 ounces orange juice
1 ounce lemon juice
1 teaspoon fine sugar

Ice
4 ounces red wine (such as
    Merlot)

1. Pour the juices and sugar into a mixing glass nearly filled with ice. Stir. Strain into a highball glass over ice.
2. Fill with red wine. Garnish with a fruit slice, if desired.

VALENTINE

Serves 1

This is the perfect drink with turkey, chicken, or pheasant.

4 ounces Beaujolais
1 teaspoon cranberry liqueur

2 ounces cranberry juice
Ice

Combine all the ingredients in a shaker half-filled with ice. Shake well. Strain into a wineglass.

SANGRIA

1 lemon
1 orange
1 bottle dry red wine
2 ounces Triple Sec
1 ounce brandy

2 ounces orange juice
1 ounce lemon juice
¼ cup fine sugar
10 ounces club soda
Ice

1. Cut the orange and lemon into slices. Do not peel.
2. Combine red wine, Triple Sec, brandy, orange juice, lemon juice, and sugar; mix well. Add the orange and lemon slices. Chill for at least 1 hour.
3. Add the club soda. Add ice and stir.

Serves 10

This traditional romantic drink is wonderful with pasta or heavier dishes.

MIDORI MIMOSA

2 ounces Midori
1 teaspoon lime juice

4 ounces chilled champagne

Combine all the ingredients in a champagne flute or white wine glass. Stir gently.

Serves 1

The Midori turns this from a brunch drink to a light evening drink perfect with salads or seafood.

BELLINI

Serves 1
This is a perfect after-dinner drink for any romantic meal. Add a slice of fresh peach to the glass for an elegant touch.

2 ounces peach nectar
½ ounce lemon juice

Chilled champagne to fill glass

Pour the juices into a champagne flute and stir to mix. Fill with champagne. Stir gently.

Fresh Lemon Juice

Fresher is always better. The acid zing of lemon juice is a catalyst for the successful mingling of flavors. A convenient way to use fresh juice is to use a small hand reamer or electric citrus reamer.

CHAPTER 6

EASTER

BAKED ORANGE ROUGHY WITH ORANGE-RICE DRESSING

Serves 4

Steamed carrots and zucchini rounds are the perfect color and nutritional complement to this meal.

2 celery ribs
1 medium-sized yellow onion
1 teaspoon orange zest
1⅓ cups cooked white rice
2 tablespoons ground cashews
½ cup fresh-squeezed orange juice
1 tablespoon lemon juice
1 pound orange roughy fillets
1 teaspoon sea salt
½ teaspoon ground white pepper
2 teaspoons butter

1. Preheat oven to 350°. Chop the celery into ¼-inch pieces. Peel the onion and chop into ¼-inch pieces. Grate orange peel to create zest. Cook the rice according to package directions. Grind the cashews.

2. In a microwave-safe bowl, mix the celery and onion with the citrus juices and orange zest. Microwave on high for 2 minutes or until the mixture comes to a boil. Add the rice and stir to moisten. Add water 1 tablespoon at a time if necessary so that the rice is thoroughly coated with liquid. Cover and let stand for 5 to 10 minutes.

3. Rinse the fillets and pat dry between paper towels. Prepare a baking dish with nonstick spray. Spread the rice mixture in the dish and arrange the fillets on top. Season the fillets with the salt and pepper.

4. Combine the butter and cashews in a microwave-safe bowl and microwave on high for 30 seconds, or until the butter is melted. Stir and spoon over the top of the fillets. Cover and bake for 10 minutes.

5. Remove the cover and bake for an additional 5 to 10 minutes or until the fish flakes easily when tested with a fork. The cashews should be lightly browned.

WHITE WINE AND LEMON PORK ROAST

1 garlic clove
3 shallots
½ cup dry white wine
1 tablespoon lemon juice
1 teaspoon olive oil

¼ teaspoon dried thyme
⅛ teaspoon ground black pepper
½ pound pork loin roast

Serves 4

Variation: Instead of white wine and lemon juice, use 1 teaspoon Dijon mustard and 1 tablespoon orange marmalade in the marinade.

1. Crush the garlic with the side of a large knife. Remove the skin and roughly chop the clove. Remove the skin from the shallots and roughly chop the shallots.
2. Combine the garlic, shallots, white wine, lemon juice, olive oil, thyme, and black pepper in a small mixing bowl. Mix well and transfer to a large sealable plastic bag. Add the pork loin and place in the refrigerator for 1 to 12 hours.
3. Preheat oven to 350°. Remove the meat from the marinade and place the roast on a rack in a roasting pan. Roast for 20 to 30 minutes or until the meat thermometer reads 150° to 170°, depending on how well done you like pork.

Flavorful Marinades

Prepare dishes that must marinate the night before. The extra hours marinating will impart even more flavor to the dish.

SCENTED ESCAROLE WITH FENNEL

2 garlic cloves
1 small yellow onion
12 cups escarole
1½ teaspoons fennel seeds
2 tablespoons extra-virgin olive oil

½ teaspoon salt
¼ teaspoon freshly ground black pepper
1 tablespoon freshly grated Parmesan cheese

1. Peel and mince the garlic cloves. Peel and finely chop the onion. Coarsely chop the escarole. Lightly toast the fennel seeds over medium heat in a dry skillet.
2. Heat the olive oil on medium in a medium-sized skillet. Add the garlic and cook for about 1 minute, until it starts to brown. Add the onion and cook until translucent, about 5 minutes.
3. Add the escarole and fennel seeds, season with salt and pepper, and cover. Cook until the escarole is wilted and simmering in its own juices.
4. Remove the cover and raise heat to medium-high; cook until most of the liquid has evaporated, about 5 minutes. Serve garnished with the grated cheese.

Bulgar Wheat

Bulgar is a crunchy, nutty wheat grain that can be substituted for rice or pasta in most dishes. To prepare, just pour boiling water over the bulgur and let it sit until the liquid is absorbed.

GLAZED CARROTS WITH BALSAMIC VINEGAR

3½ pounds baby carrots
¼ cup chopped chives
½ cup butter
6 tablespoons granulated sugar
⅓ cup balsamic vinegar
½ teaspoon salt
½ teaspoon freshly ground
   black pepper

> **Serves 10**
>
> This is a colorful and flavorful side for any holiday meal but complements Easter ham perhaps best of all.

1. Peel the carrots and cut into 2-inch pieces. Cut in half lengthwise. Chop the chives and set aside.
2. Melt the butter in a large sauté pan over medium heat. Add the carrots and cook for about 5 minutes. Cover and cook for another 7 minutes or until slightly tender.
3. Stir in the sugar and vinegar. Cook, uncovered, until the carrots are tender and glazed and the liquid has reduced. Season with the salt and pepper.
4. Serve in a warm bowl and garnish with fresh chives.

GLAZED BAKED HAM WITH ROSEMARY

4-pound boneless ham
30 whole cloves
3 tablespoons chutney of your
   choice
1 packed tablespoon dark brown
   sugar
2 tablespoons prepared horseradish mustard
2 teaspoons fresh rosemary leaves

> **Serves 12**
>
> This ham tastes great served either hot or cold. Serve it the next day as sandwiches.

1. Preheat oven to 325°. Place the ham in a roasting pan set on a rack. Insert the whole cloves all over the ham and bake for about 1½ hours or until the internal temperature reads 130°.
2. Meanwhile, in a small saucepan, combine the chutney, brown sugar, mustard, and rosemary. Cook over low heat until warm and liquefied.
3. Drizzle the glaze over the ham and bake for an additional 30 minutes or until the internal temperature reads 140°. The outside of the ham should be crusty and sugary brown.

APRICOT-STUFFED PORK TENDERLOIN

Serves 3–4

Serve with Glazed Carrots with Balsamic Vinegar (page 87).

6 dried apricots
1 cup red wine (such as Merlot)
1½-pound pork tenderloin
1 shallot
3 garlic cloves

½ cup pecans
3 fresh sage leaves
½ teaspoon salt
½ teaspoon fresh-cracked black pepper

1. Soak the dried apricots in the red wine for at least 1 hour to rehydrate. Preheat oven to 375°.
2. Butterfly the tenderloin by making a lengthwise slice down the middle, making certain not to cut completely through.
3. Mince the shallot and garlic. Chop the pecans and sage. Slice the apricots into quarters.
4. Lay out the tenderloin. Layer all the ingredients over the tenderloin and season with salt and pepper. Carefully roll up the loin and tie securely.
5. Place the tenderloin on a rack and roast for 1 to 1½ hours. Let cool slightly before slicing.

The Other White Meat

Although pork is not really "the other white meat," today's pigs are not fat. In fact, pork tends to be leaner than beef. Substitute pork for beef in any recipe but remember to remove the fat from around the edges.

CAULIFLOWER VICHYSSOISE

2 medium-sized leeks
1 medium-sized white onion
1 large head cauliflower
1 tablespoon vegetable oil

4 cups chicken stock
½ teaspoon salt
½ teaspoon freshly ground
  white pepper

Serves 4

Serve the soup in warm soup bowls and garnish with a drizzle of extra-virgin olive oil and a sprinkling of freshly minced chives.

1. Remove the green part of the leeks and discard. Peel and thinly slice the leeks. Peel and dice the onion. Cut the cauliflower into florets.
2. Heat the oil in a large soup pot over medium heat. Cook the leeks and onions for 3 to 4 minutes, stirring, until tender. Be careful not to overcook the leeks and onions; they should retain their original color.
3. Add the cauliflower and stock, and bring to a boil. Reduce the heat and simmer, covered, for about 20 minutes or until the cauliflower is tender.
4. Transfer the soup to a blender and purée until smooth. Return the soup to the pot to warm. Season with salt and pepper.

Food Processor Safety

When puréeing hot mixtures, leave the vent uncovered on your food processor. If using a blender, either remove the vent cover from the lid or leave the lid ajar so the steam can escape.

YOGURT AND CUCUMBER SOUP WITH MINT AND DILL

3 cups yogurt
1 large cucumber
2 garlic cloves
2½ tablespoons chopped fresh dill weed, divided
1 tablespoon finely chopped fresh mint

2 cups milk
2 tablespoons olive oil
2 tablespoons fresh lemon juice
½ teaspoon salt
½ teaspoon freshly ground white pepper
4 drops hot pepper sauce

1. Put the yogurt into a cheesecloth-lined strainer and let drip over a bowl for 2 hours at room temperature, or overnight in the refrigerator.
2. Peel the cucumber and cut 6 paper-thin slices. Set aside for garnish. Seed and coarsely grate the remaining cucumber. Peel the garlic cloves and put through a garlic press. Finely chop the dill weed. Finely chop the fresh mint.
3. Discard the water from the yogurt and place the yogurt in a medium-sized bowl. Whisk the milk into the yogurt until smooth. Stir in the cucumber, garlic, 2 tablespoons of the dill, the mint, olive oil, lemon juice, salt, pepper, and hot pepper sauce. Refrigerate for 1 to 2 hours, until ice cold.
4. Garnish each serving with a little of the remaining dill and a slice of cucumber.

Buying Garlic

When buying fresh garlic, look for heads that are plump, firm, and heavy for their size. Any green shoots or sprouts indicate that the garlic is old and will have an off flavor. Store whole bulbs in an open plastic bag in the vegetable drawer of your refrigerator.

BAKED PEAR CRISP

2 fresh pears
2 tablespoons frozen, unsweet-
    ened pineapple juice concen-
    trate
1 teaspoon vanilla extract
1 teaspoon rum (or ½ tea-
    spoon rum extract)

1 tablespoon butter
⅛ cup whole-wheat flour
⅓ firmly packed cup brown
    sugar
½ cup oat bran flakes

Serves 4

This dish has endless
varieties. Use
peaches, plums, or
apples. Mix your fruits
by adding a few
berries.

1. Preheat oven to 375°. Treat a 9" × 12" baking dish with nonstick cooking spray. Core and cut up the pears into the baking dish (leave the skins on).
2. In a glass measuring cup, microwave the frozen juice concentrate for 1 minute. Stir in the vanilla and rum, then pour over the pears.
3. Using the same measuring cup, microwave the butter for 30 to 40 seconds, until melted.
4. Toss together the remaining ingredients in a bowl, being careful not to crush the cereal. Spread uniformly over the pears and dribble the melted butter over the top of the cereal.
5. Bake for 35 minutes or until the mixture is bubbling and the top is just beginning to brown. Serve hot or cold.

Using Canned Fruit

If substituting canned fruit for fresh in a dessert recipe, choose fruit in a water base, not syrup. Syrup bases tend to draw the sugar out of the fruit while in the can.

NEW ORLEANS PRALINES

Makes 1 pound

Easter Bunny beware: When the kids start tasting these treats from the city that brought us Mardi Gras, you might be out of a job.

1½ packed cups light brown sugar
½ cup granulated sugar
½ cup evaporated milk
¼ cup light corn syrup
1 tablespoon margarine
1 teaspoon vanilla extract
1½ cups pecans

1. Line baking sheets with wax paper.
2. Stir together the sugars, evaporated milk, and corn syrup in a heavy 3-quart saucepan. Cook over very low heat, stirring frequently, for about 1 hour or until the mixture registers 236° on a candy thermometer. Test by dropping a nugget of the mixture into cold water; it should form a soft ball that flattens when removed from the water. Do not cook the mixture too fast, as it will curdle.
3. Remove from heat. Add the margarine and vanilla, and beat for about 1 minute or until well blended.
4. Add the nuts and stir until coated. Quickly drop by tablespoonfuls onto the prepared baking sheets. When cool and set, remove from the paper.

Fatty Oils
All oils are 100 percent fat, including butter and margarine. For a healthy diet, use them sparingly and substitute unsaturated vegetable oil or extra-virgin olive oil whenever possible.

LIGHT LEMON PUDDING

1 tablespoon unflavored gelatin
½ cup, plus 1 tablespoon cold
   water
1 cup boiling water
½ cup granulated sugar
¼ cup, plus ¼ teaspoon lemon
   juice

1 teaspoon lemon zest
½ cup regular nonfat dry milk
   powder
½ cup ice water

Serves 6

This makes a wonderful light dessert after a meal of Apricot-Stuffed Pork Tenderloin (page 88).

1. In a small bowl, soften the gelatin in the 1 tablespoon cold water. Add the boiling water to dissolve.
2. Add the sugar, the ½ cup cold water, the ¼ cup lemon juice, and the lemon zest. Chill until very thick, about 90 minutes.
3. Chill a deep mixing bowl and beaters. Add the dry milk, ice water, and the ¼ teaspoon lemon juice to the chilled bowl. Beat until fluffy, then cover and chill.
4. Break up the gelatin lemon mixture with a fork. Add to the whipped milk mixture. Using an electric mixer, beat until fluffy but not too soft. Cover and chill until firm before serving, about ½ hour.

Full-Flavor Herbs

Crushing dried herbs before you add them to a recipe will result in a stronger flavor. You can pinch them between your fingers or use a spoon to crush them on a plate before adding them to the dish.

EASTER COOKIES

Makes about 5 dozen

These traditional cookies are usually served as dessert with coffee.

½ pound butter, softened
1½ cups granulated sugar
3 eggs
½ cup orange juice
6 cups all-purpose flour
2 teaspoons baking powder
½ teaspoon baking soda
1½ teaspoons vanilla extract
1½ teaspoons anise flavoring
Sesame seeds
60 whole cloves

For the glaze:
1 egg
5 tablespoons milk

1. Preheat oven to 375°. Grease 2 baking sheets.
2. In a large bowl, cream the butter until soft. Add the sugar and mix thoroughly. Add the eggs 1 at a time, mixing well after each addition. Add the orange juice and mix well.
3. Add the flour, baking powder, and baking soda; beat to combine. Add the vanilla and anise flavorings; mix thoroughly. The mixture will be stiff and you will have to knead it by hand in order to mix thoroughly.
4. Shape it into desired forms—figure 8s are traditional—and place on the prepared baking sheets.
5. To create the glaze, beat the egg and milk together. Brush each cookie with the glaze, sprinkle with sesame seeds, and place a whole clove in the center of each cookie.

PINEAPPLE-PEAR MOLD

2 medium pears
2 tablespoons unflavored
*   gelatin*
2½ cups orange juice, divided

1 (20-ounce) can crushed
*   pineapple*

Serves 6

Gelatin molds are a traditional salad at many Easter dinners. Add your favorite fresh fruits or even some grated carrots to complement the meal.

1. Peel, core, and dice the pears.
2. In a small saucepan, soften the gelatin in ½ cup of the orange juice for 5 minutes. Place over low heat and stir until the gelatin dissolves.
3. Stir in the undrained crushed pineapple and the remaining 2 cups orange juice. Cover and chill until partially set, about 30 minutes.
4. Fold the pears into the pineapple mixture and transfer to a 6-cup mold.
5. Cover and chill until firm, about 30 minutes. To unmold, dip the bottom of the mold in hot water for 10 seconds, then invert onto a plate.

Broiled Grapefruit

Try this fun fruit as an elegant dessert. Cut a grapefruit in half and loosen the sections with a knife. Sprinkle a little brown sugar on the halves and top with a pat of butter. Broil a few minutes until heated through.

ALMOND COOKIES

Makes 2 dozen

Many families serve these with coffee and orange juice as a light breakfast before Easter morning church services.

½ cup butter or margarine
½ cup superfine sugar
½ teaspoon salt
¼ teaspoon almond extract

1 egg yolk
1 cup unsifted flour
Blanched almonds

1. Preheat oven to 350°. In a large bowl, cream together the butter, sugar, salt, and almond flavoring until light and fluffy. Thoroughly beat in the egg yolk. Stir in the flour. Cover and chill for 1 hour before shaping.
2. Using a level tablespoon for each, shape the dough into small balls and place them 1 inch apart on an ungreased baking sheet. Press an almond onto the center of each cookie. The sides will crack slightly.
3. Bake for 15 to 18 minutes or until the bottoms of the cookies are browned but the tops are still light. The edges will turn tan. Carefully remove to a rack to cool.

MINT MERINGUE COOKIES

Makes about 1 dozen

These are the perfect Easter morning surprise. Perhaps the Easter Bunny left them there for the adults to find?

2 egg whites
½ teaspoon cream of tartar
¾ cup granulated sugar
¼ teaspoon peppermint flavoring

3 drops green food coloring
1 cup semisweet chocolate morsels

1. Preheat oven to 350°. In a medium-sized bowl, beat together the egg whites and cream of tartar until fluffy.
2. Add the sugar and beat until very stiff. Add the flavoring and the food coloring.
3. Fold in the chocolate morsels.
4. Drop by teaspoonfuls onto an ungreased baking sheet. The cookies will not spread during cooking, so they can be placed close together.
5. Turn off the oven and place the cookies inside. Leave the cookies in the oven overnight or until the oven cools.

CREAMY PEACH DRINK

2 ounces frozen peaches　　*1 ounce light cream*
1 teaspoon granulated sugar　*Lemonade to fill glass*

1. Put the peaches and sugar in blender and blend well.
2. Pour into a tumbler. Add the cream and lemonade. Stir well. Garnish with a peach slice, if desired.

Serves 1

Serve with Yogurt and Cucumber Soup with Mint and Dill (page 90) for a true spring treat.

LEMONY APPLE DRINK

3 ounces apple juice　　*8 ounces ginger ale*
1 ounce lemon juice　　*1 ounce grenadine*

Pour the apple and lemon juice into a tumbler. Stir. Add the ginger ale. Drizzle in the grenadine.

Serves 1

This is a wonderful complement to Baked Orange Roughy with Orange-Rice Dressing (page 84).

APRICOT SPARKLER

Serves 1

Serve this to comple-
ment Apricot-Stuffed
Pork Tenderloin
(page 88).

2 ounces apricot nectar
1 ounce lemon juice
Ice

Club soda to fill glass
Lemon twist

1. Combine the apricot nectar and lemon juice in a shaker half-filled with ice. Shake well.
2. Strain into an old-fashioned glass with a few ice cubes. Add the club soda and stir gently. Add a lemon twist.

PEACH BUNNY

Serves 1

This is a good after-
dinner drink or end-
of-day tummy settler.
It also complements
desserts such as
Amaretto Cake
(page 78).

1 ounce peach-flavored brandy
¾ ounce white crème de cacao

¾ ounce light cream
Ice

1. Combine all the ingredients in a shaker half-filled with ice. Shake well.
2. Strain into a cordial glass.

CHAPTER 7
PASSOVER FOODS

ZUCCHINI-STUFFED CHICKEN

Serves 8

Serve with Chocolate Raspberry Torte (page 109) for dessert.

8 bone-in, skin-on chicken breasts
2 medium zucchini
1 small yellow onion
2 eggs
3 cups matzo farfel
2 tablespoons chicken bouillon powder
¼ teaspoon garlic powder
¼ teaspoon onion powder
½ teaspoon salt
½ teaspoon ground black pepper

1. Preheat oven to 375°. Grease a 9" × 13" baking pan.
2. Rinse the chicken breasts under cold, running water. Pat dry. Shred the zucchini using a vegetable grater. Peel and chop the onion. Beat the eggs and set aside.
3. Place the farfel in a bowl and cover with hot water for 5 minutes. Drain and squeeze out water.
4. In a medium-sized mixing bowl, combine the zucchini, farfel, eggs, chicken bouillon, onion, garlic powder, onion powder, salt, and pepper.
5. Place 2 to 3 tablespoons of the stuffing under the skin of each chicken breast and arrange them in the baking pan.
6. Bake for 40 to 50 minutes. Drain off excess fat and serve.

Onion Varieties

Onions vary in sweetness. Vidalia tend to be the sweetest, followed by red, then yellow. White onions are the least sweet and are better in meat dishes than in soups.

BRAISED LAMB WITH A SOUR ORANGE MARINADE

4 sour oranges
4 garlic cloves
1 large white onion
1 tablespoon dried oregano
2 bay leaves

1 cup dry white wine
6 pounds deboned leg of lamb
1 teaspoon salt
1 teaspoon ground black pepper
2 tablespoons vegetable oil

16 servings

If you are unable to find sour oranges, substitute a combination of orange and lemon juice.

1. Juice the sour oranges. Peel and mince the garlic. Peel the onion and slice thinly. Combine the orange juice with the garlic, onion, oregano, bay leaves, and white wine in a large bowl.
2. Place the meat in the marinade. Make sure all the meat is covered. Cover the bowl and refrigerate for 2 to 4 hours.
3. Remove the meat from the marinade, reserving the marinade. Sprinkle the meat with the salt and pepper. In a large pot, heat the oil on medium-high. Place the meat in the pan and sear on all sides.
4. Decrease heat to low. Pour the reserved marinade over the meat in the pan and cover. Cook until the meat is fork-tender, about 3 hours. Add water to the pot if necessary to keep the meat from scorching.

Cooking with Lamb
Lamb is underused in North America, yet it has a wonderful flavor. Substitute it for pork in your next slow-cooker recipe for an unexpected treat.

FISH IN RED SAUCE

¼ cup minced fresh parsley
8 ounces pimientos
3 red tomatoes
2 carrots
2 celery ribs
2 garlic cloves
½ teaspoon salt
½ teaspoon ground black pepper

1 (28-ounce) can tomato purée
¼ cup water
3 tablespoons fresh lemon juice
6 (3-ounce) cod fillets
1 teaspoon white granulated sugar

1. Mince the parsley. Chop the pimientos into ¼-inch pieces. Chop the tomatoes into ¼-inch pieces. Peel and slice the carrots. Slice the celery. Peel and mince the garlic.
2. In a large saucepan, combine the parsley, pimientos, tomatoes, salt, pepper, and tomato purée. Bring to a boil. Add the carrots, celery, and garlic. Cook until the carrots can easily be pierced with a fork but are still firm.
3. Stir in the water and lemon juice. Place the fish into the pan without stirring. Baste the fish with the liquid. Sprinkle the sugar on top of the fish but do not stir. Continue basting periodically.
4. When the fish is opaque and warmed through, remove from heat. Let cool and serve cold.

Grilling Fish

When grilling fish, place the fish steaks or fillets on a hot, well-oiled grill. Grill for about 10 minutes per inch of thickness of the fillet, measured at its thickest part. Turn once during grilling. Thoroughly brush the fish with vegetable oil or basting sauce several times during grilling. Grill until the fish flakes when tested with a fork at its thickest part.

LEEK AND MEAT FRITTERS

1 garlic clove
4 leeks
1 pound ground lamb
2 eggs

1 teaspoon salt
½ teaspoon white pepper
1 cup matzo meal
½ cup vegetable oil

Makes 30 fritters

These are a fun treat
served with fresh fruit
and vegetables.

1. Peel and crush the garlic. Cut the white part of the leek stalks into 4 or 5 pieces each and cook uncovered in boiling water until tender. Drain and grind in a meat grinder.
2. In a large bowl, mix together the ground leeks, lamb, and eggs. Add the salt, pepper, and garlic; mix well. Add the matzo meal until the mixture is stable but not too hard. (If the mixture is too firm, add another egg.)
3. Form small, bite-sized patties. Heat the oil in a frying pan to medium temperature. Fry the patties until golden.

Skillet Sense

When using a greased griddle or skillet, it is hot enough for cooking when a drop of water "skitters" across it. Do not allow oil or butter to brown. The griddle or skillet is ready just before the oil or butter begins to sizzle.

GEFILTE FISH

1½ pounds salmon fillets
1½ pounds red snapper fillets
1 pound black cod fillets
1 pound ling cod fillets
4 large onions
6 carrots
5 eggs
½ cup white granulated sugar, divided

4 teaspoons salt, divided into 3 teaspoons and 1 teaspoon
4 teaspoons ground white pepper
3–4 cups ice water
¾ cup matzo meal
½ teaspoon paprika
½ teaspoon ground black pepper

1. Clean the fish fillets, reserving the skins. Peel the onions and carrots. Slice 2 of the onions and 2 of the carrots, and set aside.
2. In a meat grinder, grind together the fish, the 2 whole onions, and the 4 whole carrots. Place the fish mixture in a wooden bowl. Using a hand-held chopper (a mallet with several dull knives on the end), add the eggs 1 at a time. Add ¼ cup of the sugar, 3 teaspoons of the salt, and white pepper. Continue to chop until very well blended.
3. Stir in the ice water a little at a time throughout this process. Add the matzo meal and chop again. If the mixture is not thick enough to bind together to make an oval gefilte fish ball, add more matzo meal.
4. Fill 2 large, heavy stockpots halfway with water. Add the sliced onions, sliced carrots, fish skins (if desired), paprika, the remaining salt, the black pepper, and the remaining sugar, dividing each ingredient evenly between the 2 pots. Bring to a boil over medium heat and let boil for 10 minutes.
5. With wet hands, shape the fish balls and carefully drop into the boiling stock. Cover slightly and cook over medium-low heat for 2 hours.
6. When done, let the fish sit in the pot for 10 minutes, then carefully transfer the pieces to containers. Strain the remaining stock over the fish balls until covered. Chill and serve.

WHITE BEAN AND ARTICHOKE SALAD

3 cups cooked white beans
1 cup canned artichoke hearts
⅔ cup diced green bell pepper
⅓ cup black olives
¼ cup chopped red onion
¼ cup fresh chopped parsley

¼ ounce chopped fresh mint leaves
¾ teaspoon dried basil
⅓ cup olive oil
¼ cup red wine vinegar

> **8 servings**
>
> This dish is so flavorful it can be served simply with matzo crackers.

1. Drain the white beans. Drain the artichoke hearts and quarter. Dice the green bell pepper. Chop the black olives, red onion, parsley, and mint leaves.
2. In a large bowl, combine the beans, artichoke hearts, bell peppers, olives, onion, parsley, mint, and basil; mix well.
3. In a small container with a lid, combine the oil and vinegar. Cover and shake well.
4. Pour the oil and vinegar over the salad and toss to coat.
5. Cover and chill in the refrigerator for several hours or overnight, stirring occasionally, to let the flavors blend.

Fresh Versus Dry

If you don't have fresh herbs, you can always use dry ones. Just make sure to experiment with the proper amount. Some dry herbs have a more concentrated flavor while others have a weaker one.

MATZO BREI

1 matzo cracker
1 egg
¼ teaspoon salt
¼ teaspoon ground black pepper
2 tablespoons vegetable oil

1. Break the matzo cracker into small pieces in a medium-sized bowl. Cover with hot water for 1 minute , then squeeze out the water.
2. In a small bowl, beat the egg with the s alt and pepper. Add to the matzo and mix well.
3. Heat the oil to medium in a medium frying pan. Pour the mixture into the pan. Brown 1 side and turn over.

APPLE HAROSET

2 large Red Delicious or other sweet apples
1 cup walnuts
1 teaspoon granulated sugar
1 teaspoon ground cinnamon
2 tablespoons kosher red wine

1. Peel, core, and finely chop the apples. Finely chop the walnuts.
2. Mix together the apples, nuts, sugar, and cinnamon in a bowl. Add the wine and thoroughly blend. Refrigerate.

Hold the Salt

Resist the urge to salt. Salt draws flavors and juices out of meat and vegetables. Let the flavors release on their own time for the best result. Guests can salt their own dishes if they prefer. They'll also use less than if you add it while cooking.

PASSOVER BROWNIES

5 eggs
2½ cups granulated sugar
1¼ cups vegetable oil
1¼ cups matzo cake meal

1½ cups unsweetened cocoa
  powder
1¼ cups chopped walnuts

1. Preheat oven to 325°. Grease a 9" × 13" pan.
2. Beat together the eggs and sugar. Add the oil. Mix in the cake meal and cocoa. Add 1 cup of the nuts, and mix. Pour into the prepared baking pan. Top with the remaining nuts.
3. Bake for 30 to 35 minutes. If doing the toothpick test, the toothpick will not come out completely clean even though the brownies are done.

Makes 2 dozen

The secret to moist brownies is to under-bake them. Check these after 25 minutes and every couple minutes afterward.

APPLE-CINNAMON FARFEL KUGEL

Nonstick cooking spray
2 large Red Delicious or other
  sweet apples
3 egg whites

1 cup hot water
1 cup matzo farfel
½ cup granulated sugar
2 teaspoons ground cinnamon

1. Preheat oven to 375°. Spray an 8" × 8" baking dish with nonstick cooking spray.
2. Peel, core, and shred the apples. Stiffly beat the egg whites and set aside.
3. In a large bowl, combine the water and farfel. Add the sugar, apple, and 1 to 1½ teaspoons of the cinnamon. Fold in the egg whites. Pour the mixture into the prepared baking dish and dust the top with the remaining cinnamon.
4. Bake for 45 minutes.

Serves 6

Serve this kugel as a dessert with Gefilte Fish (page 104).

SPINACH FRITATTA

3 servings

Serve with Apple-Cinnamon Farfel Kugel (page 107).

2 (10-ounce) packages frozen chopped spinach
½ cup water
4 eggs
3 matzo crackers
½ teaspoon salt
½ teaspoon ground black pepper
¼ teaspoon ground nutmeg
2 tablespoons grated Parmesan cheese, plus extra for garnish
3 tablespoons butter

1. Heat the spinach in a saucepan with the water until completely thawed. Strain the spinach, reserving ½ the liquid.
2. Beat the eggs and set aside. Crumble the matzo into a medium-sized mixing bowl and pour the spinach and the remaining liquid over them. Mix thoroughly until the matzo are softened. Add the eggs, salt, pepper, nutmeg, and cheese.
3. Heat the butter in a medium-sized skillet to medium temperature. Add the spinach mixture. Cook, uncovered, for 5 minutes on each side. Garnish with a sprinkling of grated Parmesan and serve immediately.

Frozen Vegetables

Frozen vegetables will quickly separate if you place them in a colander and run hot water over them.

CHOCOLATE RASPBERRY TORTE

16 ounces semisweet chocolate
2 cups unsalted butter
1 cup cola-flavored carbonated
  beverage
⅓ cup raspberry jam
1 teaspoon lemon juice
8 eggs, at room temperature
1 cup granulated sugar
2 tablespoons vanilla sugar

For the glaze:
1 cup semisweet chocolate
  chips
2 tablespoons unsalted butter

Serves 16

Dress up this cake by trimming it with fresh whole raspberries, chocolate leaves, or cocoa powder.

---

1. Preheat oven to 350°. Line the bottom of a 10-inch springform pan with parchment paper. Chop the semisweet chocolate.
2. In a heavy saucepan over low heat, mix together butter and cola, and heat through. Remove the pan from the stove and add the chocolate, stirring to melt the chocolate. When melted, set aside and let the mixture cool completely.
3. In a small mixing bowl, blend the raspberry preserves and lemon juice together. Set aside.
4. In another bowl, whip the eggs with the sugar and vanilla sugar for 10 minutes on high speed. Whisk the cooled, melted chocolate into the egg mixture until thoroughly incorporated. (The mixture will deflate.) Stir in the raspberry preserve mixture. Pour into the prepared springform pan.
5. Place the springform pan on a baking sheet in the oven and reduce the oven's heat to 325°. Bake for 55 to 60 minutes, until the cake is done. (The top will have a slight crust and the middle will seem set.) The cake may rise and fall, but that is fine. Remove the cake and refrigerate for several hours.
6. To make the glaze, melt the chocolate chips with the butter. Stir to melt evenly. Pour over the chilled cake before serving.

CHAPTER 8
CINCO DE MAYO

CARNE ASADA

4 garlic cloves
1 medium-sized white onion
½ cup tequila
¼ cup lime juice
¼ cup lemon juice
¼ cup orange juice

1 teaspoon Tabasco sauce
1 teaspoon ground black pepper
2 pounds flank steak
1 dozen corn tortillas
1 cup tomato salsa
1 cup guacamole

1. Peel and crush the garlic. Peel the onion and chop into ¼-inch pieces.
2. Mix together the garlic, onion, tequila, juices, Tabasco sauce, and pepper in a bowl. Add the meat, turning to coat. Cover and marinate in the refrigerator for 4 to 12 hours, turning occasionally.
3. Preheat grill to medium heat. Wrap the tortillas in aluminum foil and place on the grill.
4. Remove the meat from the marinade, reserving the marinade. Grill the steak for 12 to 18 minutes, turning and basting halfway through with the reserved marinade. Turn the tortillas occasionally.
5. Remove the meat from the grill and cut into thin slices. Serve the steak slices on the tortillas. Garnish with salsa and guacamole.

What Is a Tomatillo?

Tomatillo is a fruit and is also known as a Mexican green tomato. Tomatillos should be used while they are green and still quite firm. They come with a parchmentlike covering. To use tomatillos, remove the covering and wash. Tomatillos have a flavor with hints of lemon, apples, and herbs. Cooking enhances the tomatillo's flavor and softens its thick skin.

TOTOPOS

1 small yellow onion
2 avocados
¼ head lettuce, shredded
3 dill pickles
1 fresh red tomato
2 cups Carne Asada meat
 (page 112)
1 tablespoon butter
2 cups canned kidney beans,
 undrained

1 teaspoon salt
½ teaspoon ground black
 pepper
1⅓ cups vegetable oil, divided
12 corn tortillas
2 tablespoons white wine
 vinegar
1½ teaspoons granulated sugar
¼ teaspoon garlic salt
¾ cup crumbled goat cheese

> **Serves 6**
>
> Change the ingredi-ents to suit your whims. Hot peppers, spicy chicken, and guacamole also make good toppings.

1. Peel the onion and chop finely. Peel and pit the avocados and slice into crescents ⅓-inch thick. Shred the lettuce. Slice the pickles into ¼-inch rounds. Remove the stem from the tomato and cut into ¼-inch slices. Cut the beef into ½-inch pieces and warm in a small pan on low heat.
2. Melt the butter in a medium-sized frying pan on medium heat. Add the onion and sauté until limp but not brown. Add the kidney beans, with their liquid, and the salt and pepper. Cook until the liquid is reduced by half.
3. In a large skillet, heat 1 cup of the vegetable oil to medium-high. Fry the tortillas 1 at a time, turning when first side is lightly browned. Transfer to paper towels to drain and cool.
4. Mix together the vinegar, sugar, garlic salt, and the ⅓ cup remaining vegetable oil in a small container with a cover. Cover and shake until well mixed.
5. Combine the lettuce, avocado, pickles, and meat in a medium-sized bowl. Mix with the vinegar and oil dressing.
6. Spread the beans about ½-inch thick on the tortillas. Pile the salad mixture on top. Add the tomato slices and sprinkle with the cheese.

MEXICAN CHICKEN ROLL-UPS

Serves 4

This recipe also is perfect for Totopos (page 113). Make beef and chicken with all the trimmings for a wonderful Cinco de Mayo buffet.

1 green bell pepper
1 red bell pepper
1 medium-sized yellow onion
3 cups chopped red tomatoes
4 cups shredded lettuce
2 garlic cloves
4 scallions

1 skinless, boneless whole
    chicken breast
1 tablespoon olive oil
4 large flour tortillas
¼ cup shredded Cheddar
    cheese
¼ cup salsa of your choice

1. Chop the green and red peppers, onion, and tomatoes into ¼-inch pieces. Shred the lettuce. Peel the garlic and scallions, and chop into ⅛-inch pieces. Dice the chicken breast. Set oven to 250°. Wrap the tortillas in aluminum foil, and place in the oven to warm.
2. In a large skillet, heat the oil on high. Add the bell peppers, onion, and garlic; sauté until soft, about 7 minutes. Add the chicken, cover, and reduce heat to low; cook until the chicken is tender, about 8 minutes.
3. Transfer the chicken mixture to a serving bowl. Set out the warmed tortillas. Place the lettuce, scallions, cheese, and salsa in separate small bowls. Let diners make their own roll-ups.

Anaheim Peppers

The Anaheim, also known as the New Mexico chili pepper, can range from 3 to 6 inches long. Its shade of green is a little lighter than either the jalapeño or poblano, and it is also the chili with the least bite.

BAJA LOBSTER TAILS

6 shallots
2 garlic cloves
3 fresh jalapeño peppers
3 fresh limes
4 medium-sized lobster tails
3 tablespoons olive oil
2 teaspoons ground cumin

2 teaspoons paprika
½ teaspoon cayenne pepper
2 tablespoons unsalted butter
1 teaspoon sea salt
1 teaspoon freshly ground
    black pepper

Serves 4

Serve with Gazpacho
(page 117) and
Margarita Pie
(page 120).

1. Peel the shallots and chop into ¼-inch pieces. Peel and mince the garlic. Seed the jalapeño peppers and chop into ¼-inch pieces. Juice 2 of the limes and cut the third lime into wedges.
2. Preheat grill to medium.
3. Cut the lobster tails in half lengthwise. Sprinkle lightly with salt and black pepper.
4. Heat the olive oil in a medium-sized skillet to medium temperature. Add the shallot and sauté until golden, about 4 minutes. Add the garlic and jalapeños; sauté for another 1 to 2 minutes. Add the cumin, paprika, and cayenne pepper; cook, stirring, for another 1 to 2 minutes.
5. Remove from the heat. Stir in the lime juice, butter, the 1 teaspoon salt, and 1 teaspoon black pepper.
6. Place the lobsters on the grill, shell-side down, approximately 4 inches from the heat source. Grill for 8 to 9 minutes, occasionally turning the tails onto their sides to cook through. Spoon the butter mixture over the lobsters during cooking. Garnish with fresh lime wedges.

MEXICALI SHRIMP ON THE GRILL

Serves 4

This recipe also can be used with baby shrimp, cooked in the oven for ½ hour, then put into Enchiladas (page 121) or served as Totopos (page 113).

2 pounds large shrimp
½ cup fresh cilantro
2 jalapeño peppers
2 garlic cloves
¼ cup white wine vinegar
3 tablespoons lemon juice
¾ cup olive oil

½ teaspoon ground cayenne pepper
½ teaspoon red pepper flakes
½ teaspoon salt
½ teaspoon ground black pepper

1. Peel and devein the shrimp but leave on the tails. Finely chop the cilantro. Remove the stems and seeds from the jalapeño peppers and mince the peppers. Peel and mince the garlic.
2. Combine all the ingredients except the shrimp in a large bowl. Whisk together. Add the shrimp and toss lightly, coating on all sides.
3. Lay the shrimp flat in a large glass or ceramic pan. Pour the remaining sauce over the shrimp and cover with plastic wrap. Refrigerate for 3 to 12 hours, stirring occasionally.
4. Preheat grill to medium. Place the shrimp in a vegetable basket and place on the grill. Turn frequently to cook thoroughly, about 5 minutes.

Poblano Peppers
Like the jalapeño, the poblano is dark green, but shaped like a cone and has a milder flavor. The flavor comes out when roasted.

GAZPACHO

4 large red tomatoes
1 small yellow onion
1 green bell pepper
2 medium carrots
2 celery stalks
4 cups canned condensed
   tomato soup

2 tablespoons olive oil
2 tablespoons white wine vinegar
2 teaspoons salt
1 teaspoon ground black
   pepper
1 medium cucumber

Serves 8

Gazpacho makes an excellent first course to a heavier beef or chicken meal. It also makes a good lunch served with white bread and cheese.

1. Peel the tomatoes and cut into quarters. Remove the skin from the onion and cut into quarters. Remove the stem and seeds from the green pepper and cut into quarters. Peel the carrots and cut into quarters. Remove the leaves from the celery and cut the stalks into quarters.
2. Combine 2 cups of the tomato soup, the olive oil, wine vinegar, salt, pepper, and ½ of the vegetables in a blender. Blend until liquefied, about 1 minute. Pour into a bowl. Repeat with the remaining tomato soup and vegetables. Combine with the previous mixture.
3. Cover and chill in the refrigerator for at least 2 hours before serving.
4. Cut the cucumbers into thin slices and place on top right before serving.

Bell Peppers

Bell peppers have different flavors depending on their color. Green is the most acidic and sour tasting. Red has the most peppery flavor. Yellow and orange have a gentle flavor. Combine them to create unique flavors and a beautiful dish.

GUACAMOLE

Serves 8

Serve with tortilla chips or as an accompaniment to spicy food.

2 garlic cloves
1 small red onion
1 small jalapeño pepper
4 ripe Hass avocados
1 plum tomato

¼ cup fresh cilantro
2 tablespoons lime juice
½ teaspoon salt
½ teaspoon freshly ground
    black pepper

1. Peel the garlic and chop into ⅛-inch pieces. Peel the onion and chop into ¼-inch pieces. Remove the stem and seeds from the jalapeño pepper and chop into ⅛-inch pieces. Halve, pit, and scoop the meat from the avocados. Seed and chop the tomato into ¼-inch pieces. Chop the cilantro.
2. In a medium-sized mixing bowl, mash together the garlic, onion, and jalapeño with a fork.
3. Add the avocado and mix until it forms a chunky paste.
4. Add the lime juice, salt, pepper, tomato, and cilantro. Stir to combine.

Pitting an Avocado
To remove the pit of an avocado, start by cutting through the skin, down to the pit, and scoring the fruit lengthwise. Gripping both halves, give a quick twist to separate 1 half from the pit, leaving the other half holding that large nut. If you plan to use only ½ of the avocado, it's best to leave the pit in the unused portion, since it prevents the fruit from turning brown overnight. To remove the pit, hack into the middle of it with the blade of your knife, gripping the fruit in the palm of your other hand. Twist the knife clockwise to loosen the pit. It should fall right out of a ripe avocado.

CHURROS

3 cups vegetable oil
1 cup water
½ cup butter
1 cup all-purpose flour

¼ teaspoon salt
3 eggs
1 cup confectioners' sugar
¼ cup ground cinnamon

1. Pour the oil into a medium-sized frying pan. The oil should be 1 to 2 inches deep. Heat to 375°.
2. Heat the water to a rolling boil in a medium-sized saucepan. Add the butter and continue to boil.
3. Quickly stir in the flour and salt. Reduce heat to low and stir vigorously until the mixture forms a ball.
4. Remove from heat and beat in the eggs 1 at a time, until the mixture is smooth and glossy.
5. Form the dough into round sticks about 10 inches long and 1-inch thick.
6. Fry the sticks 2 or 3 at a time until light brown. Place the sticks on paper towels and let cool.
7. Mix together the confectioners' sugar and cinnamon on a large plate. As soon as the churros are cool, roll them in the mixture. Set aside until completely cool.

Frying Food

Although it seems easy, frying food is a great art. The oil must be hot enough to cook the food without soaking into the food. At the same time, if the oil is too hot, it will cook the outside of the food before the inside is completely cooked.

ORANGE LIQUEUR MOUSSE

Serves 4

If serving a light meal, try using this as a dessert for Gazpacho (page 117).

1 (3-ounce) package orange-
  flavored gelatin
1 cup boiling water
¼ cup cold water

¼ cup orange liqueur
1 cup whipping cream
½ teaspoon ground cinnamon
½ cup shredded coconut

1. Dissolve the gelatin in the boiling water. Add the cold water and cool the mixture to room temperature. Stir in the orange liqueur. Chill in the refrigerator until the mixture starts to thicken, about 30 minutes.
2. Whip the cream until it piles softly. Gradually add the gelatin mixture and cinnamon, stirring gently until evenly blended. Pour into a mold. Chill until set, about 1 hour.
3. Turn the mold onto a serving plate and top with the shredded coconut.

MARGARITA PIE

Serves 8

For a low-fat version of this recipe, use egg substitute and nonfat whipped topping. It tastes the same and has very few calories.

1 tablespoon unflavored gelatin
⅔ cup granulated sugar
¼ teaspoon salt
2 eggs
½ cup lime juice

1 teaspoon fresh lime zest
¼ cup tequila
1½ cups whipped cream
1 prebaked 9-inch pie shell

1. In a small saucepan, combine the gelatin, sugar, and salt. In a bowl, beat together the eggs and lime juice until blended.
2. Add the gelatin mixture to the egg mixture. Cook in a medium-sized saucepan over medium heat, stirring until the gelatin dissolves, about 5 minutes.
3. Stir in the lime zest and tequila. Cover and chill until the mixture thickens to a pudding consistency.
4. Fold the whipped cream into the tequila mixture. Spoon into the pie shell and chill well.

PEPITA BALLS

*1 pound unsalted, hulled
    pepitas (pumpkin seeds).*

*1 cup sweetened condensed
    milk*
3½ cups confectioners' sugar

1. Grind the pepitas finely.
2. Mix the pepitas with the condensed milk and 3 cups of the confectioners' sugar.
3. Shape into 1-inch balls and roll in the remaining sugar. Place on wax paper on a baking sheet.
4. Refrigerate for 2 to 3 hours or until set.

Makes 6 dozen

This is the perfect treat to accompany Classic Margaritas (page 123).

ENCHILADAS

3 cups refried beans
12 corn tortillas
*2 cups shredded Monterey jack
    cheese*

*2 cups canned red or green
    chili sauce*

1. Preheat oven to 375°. Shred the cheese.
2. Ladle ½ cup of the chili sauce into a 9" × 12" baking pan.
3. Put ¼ cup of the beans in the center of each tortilla. Add 2 tablespoons shredded cheese to each tortilla. Roll up and place in a baking pan.
4. When all the enchiladas are in the baking pan, cover with the remaining sauce and cheese. Bake for 15 to 20 minutes.

Serves 4

Try mixing beans and meat or adding spicy chicken. Or for a cheesy enchilada, mix 3 different cheeses and don't include meat or beans.

MOLASSES CANDY

Makes 1 pound

Mexican cooks love their sweets and will serve these equally as appetizers or dessert.

1 cup light molasses
1 firmly packed cup brown
    sugar
2 tablespoons butter
1 teaspoon cider vinegar

¼ teaspoon almond extract
1½ cups toasted, slivered
    almonds

1. Combine the molasses, brown sugar, butter, and vinegar into a heavy saucepan. Bring to a boil. Boil hard for 7 to 12 minutes or until the mixture reaches 260° on a candy thermometer. The mixture should form a firm ball when a small amount is dropped in cold water.
2. Remove from heat. Add the almond extract and almonds. Stir well.
3. Pour onto a greased baking sheet. Spread out in as thin a layer as possible. Let cool. Break into 2-inch pieces.

MEXICAN COFFEE

Serves 6

Too many margaritas? Use this as a nightcap or with a dessert of Pepita Balls (page 121) and Molasses Candy (page 122).

6 cups water
¼ packed cup brown sugar
3-inch stick cinnamon

6 whole cloves
¾ cup regular grind, roasted
    coffee

1. In a medium-sized saucepan, combine the water, brown sugar, cinnamon, and cloves. Heat at medium temperature, stirring periodically, until the sugar is dissolved.
2. Add the coffee and bring to a boil. Reduce heat and simmer, uncovered, for 1 to 2 minutes. Remove from the heat.
3. Cover and let stand for 15 minutes. Strain before serving.

SPARKLING FRUIT DRINK

4 cups watermelon meat
1 mango
1 papaya
1 pineapple
1 guava

2 cups fresh strawberries
1 cup white granulated sugar
2 gallons sparkling water
2 pounds ice cubes

1. Remove the rind, stems, seeds, and cores from the fruits. Cut the fruit into ½-inch pieces. Reserve all the juices.
2. Stir the sugar into the water until it dissolves.
3. Add the fruit and juices to the water. Stir well.
4. Add the ice cubes and serve immediately.

Serves 12 to 24

This festive drink is often served at parties where children are present. Everyone loves snacking on the fruit once the water is gone.

CLASSIC MARGARITA

1½ ounces tequila
1 ounce lime juice
½ ounce Triple Sec

Ice
Salt and lime wedge to rim glass

1. Combine the tequila, lime juice, and Triple Sec in a shaker half-filled with ice. Shake well.
2. Rim a cocktail glass by running the lime wedge along the top, then dipping the rim in salt.
3. Strain the drink into the glass. Garnish with the lime wedge.

Serves 1

Nothing says Cinco de Mayo like fresh margaritas. Involve your guests in making their own drinks for a truly festive atmosphere.

FRUITY MARGARITA

Serves 1

This drink is especially fun when you're having an open-air party. Serve mounds of fresh fruit as hors d'oeuvres with it.

1½ ounces tequila
1 ounce fruit-flavored liqueur
1 ounce Triple Sec

Ice
Lime wedge and sugar
   to rim glass

1. Combine tequila, liqueur, and Triple Sec in a shaker half-filled with ice. Shake well.
2. Rim a glass by running the lime wedge over the top and dipping the rim into the sugar.
3. Strain the drink into the glass. Garnish with fresh fruit, if desired.

Making It Nonalcoholic

If you want to make uncooked foods calling for liqueur nonalcoholic, simply substitute 1 tablespoon of the flavored extract mixed with half water and half corn syrup. You will get a very similar flavor without the alcohol.

Chapter 9

MOTHER'S DAY AND FATHER'S DAY

SMOKED MUSSELS IN CREAM SAUCE WITH PASTA

Serves 4

Serve with fresh fruit and steamed broccoli for a festive, healthy meal.

2 garlic cloves
1 large leek
4 cups fresh mushrooms
4 ounces smoked mussels
1 bunch fresh parsley
1⅓ cups uncooked linguine
3 teaspoons extra-virgin olive oil, divided

2 teaspoons butter
½ cup dry white wine
2 cups cottage cheese
1 teaspoon all-purpose flour
½ teaspoon cracked black pepper

1. Crush the garlic with the back of a large knife. Remove the skins. Remove the skin from the leek and chop into ½-inch pieces to yield ½ cup. Thinly slice the mushrooms. Drain any oil from the mussels. Roughly chop the parsley.

2. Place the mushrooms in a vegetable steamer; steam for 5 minutes on medium-high heat. Boil the pasta in 2 quarts water and 1 teaspoon of the olive oil until tender but not mushy.

3. Melt the butter in a deep nonstick skillet. Add the garlic and leeks, and sauté just until transparent. Add the wine and bring to a boil. Cook until reduced by half. Add the mushrooms and toss in the wine mixture.

4. In a blender or food processor, purée the cottage cheese. Add it to the wine-mushroom mixture and bring to serving temperature over low heat. Make sure the mixture does not boil. If the mixture seems too thin, sprinkle flour over the mixture, stir until blended, and cook until thickened.

5. Add the mussels to the cottage cheese mixture just prior to serving. Stir well to bring the mussels to serving temperature. Toss the pasta with the remaining 2 teaspoons olive oil. Divide onto 4 plates. Ladle the mixture over the noodles right before serving. Top with cracked pepper and parsley.

BROCCOLI FLORETS WITH LEMON BUTTER SAUCE

2 small shallots
1 lemon
8 ounces cold unsalted butter
¼ cup white cooking wine

½ teaspoon salt
¼ teaspoon white pepper
1 large head broccoli

Serves 4

This sauce can be used with any vegetable. It is especially good over carrots and zucchini rounds.

1. Remove the skins from the shallots and mince. Juice the lemon. Cut the butter into small pieces. Break the broccoli into bite-sized florets.
2. Place the shallots, ½ of the lemon juice, and the wine in a small saucepan over medium heat. Simmer until almost dry.
3. Reduce heat to very low and stir in a few small pieces of the butter, swirling it in with a wire whisk until it is mostly melted. Gradually add the remaining butter, whisking constantly until all the butter is added and the sauce is smooth. Take care that the sauce does not boil.
4. Season the sauce with the salt, white pepper, and remaining lemon juice. Keep in a warm place but not over a flame.
5. Wash the broccoli and boil in 4 quarts of rapidly boiling, salted water. Drain and serve with the lemon-butter sauce.

Reducing Saltiness

If a dish tastes too salty, add 1 teaspoon each of cider vinegar and sugar to help cut down on the salty flavor in the recipe.

HOT DILL PASTA WITH SCALLOPS

Serves 4

This meal is best accompanied by a slightly sweet white wine.

1 pound sea scallops
2 large carrots
3 garlic cloves
3 green onions
6 ounces fresh snap peas
8 ounces fettuccine
2 tablespoons olive oil, divided
1 tablespoon butter
½ cup dry white wine
⅓ cup water

1 tablespoon fresh dill
1 teaspoon instant chicken
    bouillon granules
¼ teaspoon crushed red
    pepper
2 tablespoons cornstarch
2 tablespoons cold water
¼ cup grated Parmesan cheese
½ teaspoon freshly cracked
    black pepper

1. Thaw the scallops if frozen. Cut any large scallops in half and set aside. Peel and thinly slice the carrots. Peel and mince the garlic cloves. Peel and thinly slice the green onions. Remove the stems from the snap peas.

2. Cook the fettuccine in boiling water with 1 tablespoon of the olive oil until al dente. Drain, toss with the butter, and set aside.

3. Pour the remaining oil into a wok or large skillet. Preheat over medium-high heat. Add the carrots and garlic; stir-fry for 4 minutes. Add the green onions and snap peas; stir-fry for 2 to 3 minutes or until crisp. Remove the vegetables and set aside.

4. Reduce heat to low and let the wok cool for 1 minute. Carefully add the wine, the ⅓ cup water, the dill, bouillon granules, and crushed red pepper to the wok. Add the scallops. Simmer, uncovered, for 1 to 2 minutes or until the scallops are opaque, stirring often.

5. Stir together the cornstarch and 2 tablespoons cold water. Add to the wok. Cook and stir until the mixture is thickened and bubbly. Return the vegetables to the work. Add the pasta and toss to mix. Heat through.

6. Transfer to dinner plates. Sprinkle with Parmesan cheese and cracked black pepper.

FIGS WITH BRIE AND PORT WINE REDUCTION

2 cups port wine
1 tablespoon cold, unsalted
   butter

12 ounces Brie cheese
6 fresh figs
¼ cup confectioners' sugar

Serves 6

A tiny piece of dark chocolate is the perfect addition to this appetizer.

1. Heat the wine on medium in a medium-sized saucepan, and let reduce by half. Remove from heat and add the cold butter.
2. Cut the Brie into 6 equal portions. Cut the figs in half.
3. To serve, drizzle the wine reduction on plates, sprinkle with confectioners' sugar, and arrange figs and Brie on top.

BEER SOUP

1 cup all-purpose flour
1½ tablespoons butter
1 (12-ounce) bottle of your
   favorite beer

1½-inch piece cinnamon
1 teaspoon granulated sugar
2 egg yolks
½ cup milk

Serves 4

Sometimes all Dad, or Mom, wants to do is laze around and watch a game. This is the perfect treat for helping him, or her, do just that.

1. In a large stockpot, brown the flour in the butter, then add the beer.
2. Add the cinnamon and sugar and bring to a boil.
3. Whisk together the egg yolks and milk, then stir into the hot (but not boiling) beer.
4. Strain and serve with croutons, fresh popcorn, or toasted slices of French bread on top.

VENISON MEDALLIONS WITH CRANBERRY DIJON CHUTNEY

> **Serves 4**
>
> Venison should never be cooked past medium or it will become very dry and tough.

2 small shallots
2 cups mushrooms
1 cup fresh cranberries
1 teaspoon honey
1 tablespoon Dijon mustard
2 teaspoons butter, divided
1 teaspoon salt

1 teaspoon ground black pepper
8 (2½-ounce) venison medallions
1 cup dry red wine
¼ cup cider vinegar
½ cup chicken stock
1 tablespoon red currant jelly

1. Peel and mince the shallots. Clean and quarter the mushrooms.
2. In a small sauté pan, combine the cranberries, honey, mustard, and 1 teaspoon of the butter. Season with salt and pepper. Cook over low heat for about 4 minutes until the cranberries just start to pop. Remove from heat and set aside.
3. Season the venison with salt and pepper. Melt the remaining butter in a large sauté pan over high heat until very hot. Add the venison and sear for about 2 minutes or until golden brown. Turn over and sear for another 2 minutes. The meat should be medium-rare at this point. Transfer to a warm platter and keep warm.
4. Return the sauté pan to medium heat. Add the shallots and cook for about 2 minutes or until tender. Stir in the mushrooms and cook until softened. Add the wine, vinegar, and stock, and scrape the bottom of the pan with a wooden spoon to loosen any browned bits. Raise the heat to high and cook for about 10 minutes or until the liquid is reduced to about ½ cup. Stir in the jelly and adjust seasoning to taste.
5. Spoon a small amount of the cranberry sauce on top of each venison medallion. Ladle the sauce on top and around the venison.

Venison Definition

Venison isn't necessarily deer meat. It also is the term used for elk or caribou meat. These meats can vary widely in taste depending on what the animal has eaten. As a result, they are best served in stews or other dishes that blend many flavors.

SHRIMP SCAMPI

16 jumbo shrimp
16 clams
3 garlic cloves
1 pound fettuccine
1 tablespoon olive oil
¼ cup butter

1 cup dry white wine
1 teaspoon dried oregano,
   crumbled
1 teaspoon dried basil,
   crumbled

Serves 6
Serve with a dry white wine or champagne.

1. Peel and devein the shrimp. Split each shrimp along the back from the tail to the head, but not all the way through. Scrub the clams well. Peel and mince the garlic.
2. Cook the fettuccine in boiling salted water until al dente. Drain the fettuccine, place in a warmed bowl, and toss with the olive oil.
3. Meanwhile, melt the butter in a large skillet over medium heat. Add the garlic and sauté until soft and translucent, about 10 minutes.
4. Add the shrimp, clams, wine, oregano, and basil. Cook until the shrimp are pink and the clams have opened, 5 to 10 minutes. Discard any clams that did not open.
5. Toss the shrimp and clams with the pasta and serve.

Preparing Fresh Shrimp

When using fresh shrimp, boil them for 3 minutes. Run under cold water. Remove all of the shell, although you can keep the tail on if you like. Take a small fork and run it along the back of the shrimp to remove the black vein.

FILET SOUTHWESTERN

Serves 4

Chipotle peppers canned in adobo sauce are available at most large grocery stores. Purée the entire contents of the can and store what you don't need for this dish in a covered bowl in the refrigerator.

6 shallots
1 tablespoon cilantro
2 teaspoons chipotle peppers
  in adobo sauce

¼ cup butter, softened
1 tablespoon lime juice
4 (1-inch-thick) filets mignons
1 tablespoon vegetable oil

1. Peel and mince the shallots. Mince the cilantro. Purée the chipotle peppers in adobo sauce in a blender or food processor.
2. Adjust oven rack so the filets will be 4 inches from the heating element, and preheat broiler.
3. Beat the butter and lime juice with an electric mixer until light and fluffy. Mix in the shallots, cilantro, and peppers.
4. Remove the filets from the refrigerator about 15 minutes before you are ready to begin cooking them. Flatten them slightly by pressing with a plate. Oil 1 side of the filets lightly and place on the broiler pan, oiled-side down. Spread about 1 teaspoon of the butter mixture on each fillet. Broil for 4 minutes for rare or 6 minutes for medium.
5. Turn the filets. Top each with another teaspoon of the butter mixture and broil an additional 4 to 6 minutes. To serve, top each filet with a quarter of the remaining butter mixture.

What Fish Tastes Best?

If adding sauces and spices to fish, look for a firm, mild-flavored white-fleshed fish that holds up well to cooking. Bass, flounder, shark, swordfish, and red snapper all work well. Some fish can have surprisingly strong flavors, so if you want to try a new fish, take a small piece home and steam it to see if you like the flavor before putting it in your recipe.

CLASSIC WALDORF SALAD

2 large Red Delicious apples
2 celery stalks
½ cup walnuts
½ cup mayonnaise

1 tablespoon granulated sugar
1 teaspoon lemon juice
½ teaspoon salt

Serves 6

Serve as a salad before Filet Southwestern (page 132).

1. Dice the apples into ½-inch pieces. Finely slice the celery. Coarsely chop the walnuts.
2. Blend the mayonnaise with the sugar, lemon juice, and salt.
3. Combine the apples, celery, and nuts, and fold in the dressing mixture.
4. Chill for at least 1 hour before serving.

CHEESY GOLDEN APPLE OMELET

1 Golden Delicious apple
2 tablespoons butter, divided
4 eggs
1 tablespoon water
¼ teaspoon salt

¼ teaspoon ground black pepper
2 tablespoons crumbled blue cheese
2 tablespoons grated Parmesan cheese

Serves 2

This is the perfect way to greet your Mom or Dad in the morning. Serve with a Mimosa (page 141).

1. Pare, core, and slice the apple. Sauté in 1 tablespoon of the butter in a medium-sized pan on medium heat until barely tender. Set aside.
2. Combine the eggs, water, salt, and pepper until blended. Heat the remaining butter in a skillet. Add the egg mixture. Cook slowly, lifting the edges to allow the uncooked portion to flow under.
3. When the eggs are cooked, arrange the apple slices on half of the omelet. Sprinkle with cheeses. Fold in half.

BEEF AND HORSERADISH SALAD

Serves 4

This salad is a meal in itself. Serve with Cherries Jubilee (page 140) for dessert.

1 cup fresh green beans
1½ cups fresh baby carrots
¾-pound beef sirloin steak, 1-inch thick
4 cups torn Boston or Bibb lettuce
1 (16-ounce) can julienne-cut beets

For the dressing:
1½ ounces softened cream cheese
2 tablespoons prepared horse-radish sauce
3–4 tablespoons milk

1. Wash the green beans. Remove the ends and strings and cut in half lengthwise. Cook the beans, covered, in boiling water in a medium-sized saucepan for 5 minutes.
2. Add the carrots and cook for 10 to 15 more minutes or until the vegetables are tender. Drain. Cover and chill the vegetables for 4 to 24 hours.
3. Remove broiler pan from the oven. Preheat broiler.
4. Place the steak on unheated rack of broiler pan. Broil 3 inches from the heat for 13 to 15 minutes for medium, turning once.
5. In the meantime, combine the cream cheese, horseradish sauce, and milk in a small container with a cover. Cover and shake until well mixed.
6. Arrange the torn lettuce on plates. Top with steak. Drizzle with dressing.

BAR HARBOR FISH CHOWDER

¼ pound salt pork
4 cups cubed small red
   potatoes
3 medium-sized onions
2 teaspoons salt, divided
3 pounds flounder, haddock,
   or cod

2 cups milk
1 tablespoon butter
¼ teaspoon freshly ground
   black pepper

Serves 6

Although the recipe calls for discarding the salt pork, many people like to add it to the soup at the end to create an interesting array of flavors.

1. Dice the salt pork into ½-inch pieces. Cut the red potatoes into ½-inch pieces. Peel and thinly slice the onions. Scald the milk by heating it in a saucepan on medium heat until a thin film appears on top.
2. Fry the salt pork in a large skillet. Set aside, leaving the drippings in the pan. Add the potatoes, onions, and ½ teaspoon of the salt. Cover with hot water and cook over medium heat, covered, for 15 minutes or until the potatoes are just tender.
3. Meanwhile, cut the fish into large chunks and place in another saucepan. Add boiling water to cover and the remaining 1½ teaspoons salt. Cook slowly, covered, until the fish is fork-tender, about 15 minutes. Remove from heat. Strain and reserve liquid.
4. Remove any bones from the fish. Add the fish and strained liquid to the potato-onion mixture. Pour in the milk and heat through, about 5 minutes. Mix in the butter and pepper. Serve at once.

Selecting Fish

When purchasing fresh fish, check for clear and bright eyes, firm skin that bounces back when touched, and a fresh, clean smell. Try not to keep fresh fish more than a day in your refrigerator before cooking.

EASY CHICKEN CORDON BLEU

Serves 2

Serve with fresh peas and carrots for a well-balanced meal.

2 whole chicken breasts
4 small ham slices
4 small Swiss cheese slices
¼ cup all-purpose flour
¼ cup grated Swiss cheese

½ teaspoon fresh or ¼ teaspoon dried sage
¼ teaspoon ground black pepper
1 (10¾-ounce) can condensed cream of chicken soup

1. Remove the skin and bones from the chicken breasts. Cut each breast in half and pound with a kitchen mallet until about ¼-inch thick.
2. Place a ham slice, then a Swiss cheese slice on each piece of chicken. Roll up and secure with toothpicks.
3. Combine the flour, cheese, sage, and black pepper in a small bowl. Dip the chicken rolls into the mixture. Place in the bottom of a slow cooker. Pour the condensed soup over the chicken rolls. Cook, covered, on low heat for 4 to 6 hours.

Grate Your Own Cheese

As a time and money saver, buy blocks of cheese and grate them yourself. To keep the cheese from sticking together, add a little cornstarch and toss the cheese until mixed through.

QUAIL BAKED IN WHITE WINE

*2 quail or game hens (fresh
     or frozen)
2 garlic cloves
1 small yellow onion
1 tablespoon shortening
2 whole cloves
1 teaspoon black peppercorns
1 bay leaf*

*1 teaspoon fresh-chopped
     chives
1 cup dry white wine
½ teaspoon salt
⅛ teaspoon ground black
     pepper
⅛ teaspoon cayenne pepper
1 cup heavy cream*

Serves 2

If you don't have wine handy for your recipe, substitute 1 tablespoon of red or cider vinegar mixed with 1 cup of water.

1. Thaw the quail, if necessary, and clean by running under cold water. Peel and chop the garlic and onion into ¼-inch pieces.

2. Melt the shortening in a medium-sized frying pan on medium heat. Add the garlic, onions, cloves, peppercorns, and bay leaf. Cook for several minutes. Add the quail and brown on all sides.

3. Place the quail and the mixture from the frying pan into a slow cooker. Chop the chives into ¼-inch pieces. Add the chives, wine, salt, pepper, and cayenne pepper to the slow cooker. Cook, covered, on low setting for about 6 hours.

4. Remove the quail and set aside. Remove the bay leaf and discard. Strain the liquid, then add the cream to the liquid. Stir well for 5 minutes. Pour over the quail to serve.

Game Hens

Rock Cornish game hens weigh only 1 to 1½ pounds and are all white meat. They are a separate bread of poultry, unlike capons, which are small male chickens that have been neutered.

CHOCOLATE FONDUE

1 quart water
½ cup granulated sugar
Angel food cake
Canned pineapple chunks
Canned mandarin oranges
Fresh bananas
Fresh strawberries

12 ounces milk chocolate
½ cup whipping cream
3 tablespoons orange-flavored
 liqueur
½ cup chopped toasted
 almonds
1 tablespoon honey

1. Mix the sugar into the water and place in a large bowl. Cut the angel food cake into 1-inch squares. Drain the pineapple and mandarin oranges. Slice the bananas and dip them in sugar water to prevent browning. Chill the fruit in the refrigerator. Chop the toasted almonds.
2. Combine the almonds, chocolate, cream, liqueur, and honey in a saucepan. Heat slowly until the chocolate is melted, stirring well. Pour the chocolate into a fondue pot placed over a low flame.
3. Arrange the cake and fruit on a platter.

Melting Chocolate

The easiest way to melt chocolate morsels is to use the microwave. Place the chocolate in an uncovered, microwave-safe container. A cover could cause moisture condensation to build up, ruining the chocolate. Stop the microwave and stir the chocolate every few seconds, because chocolate will be melted without looking melted.

CHOCOLATE MOUSSE

6 eggs
1½ tablespoons kirsch or
 cherry brandy
1½ tablespoons dark rum
1 tablespoon, plus a few
 drops vanilla extract

6 ounces bittersweet chocolate
1½ cups heavy cream
2½ tablespoons confectioners'
 sugar
Whipped cream and chocolate
 shavings, for garnish

> **Serves 8**
>
> This is actually a lighter version of traditional French chocolate mousse, which contains egg yolks. However, it is just as tasty and equally glamorous.

1. Chill eight 8-ounce wineglasses. Separate the egg yolks from the whites. Discard the yolks. Whip the egg whites to medium-soft peaks and refrigerate.
2. Combine the kirsch, dark rum, 1 tablespoon vanilla extract, and the chocolate in a double boiler. Warm, stirring occasionally, until melted and smooth.
3. Whip together the cream, confectioners' sugar, and a few drops of vanilla until it forms soft peaks when the whisk is lifted from it.
4. Gently fold ⅓ of the whipped cream into the chocolate mixture. Fold the chocolate mixture back into the rest of the whipped cream, mixing only as much as is necessary to incorporate it most of the way. (A few streaks of chocolate are okay.) Fold the whipped egg whites very gently into the chocolate cream mixture, just barely enough to incorporate.
5. Put the mousse into a pastry bag with a star tip (or a plastic bag with a corner cut out), and pipe into the prepared wineglasses. Cover the glasses individually with plastic wrap and chill for at least 6 hours until set. Garnish with a spoonful of whipped cream and chocolate shavings.

Don't Have a Double Boiler?

Find a steel mixing bowl that will fit securely into a pot. It shouldn't fit too low but shouldn't be so high that it is not sturdy. Simply fill the pot halfway with water and you have your double boiler.

ROAST DUCKLING WITH ORANGE GLAZE

2 cups prepared poultry stuffing
1 duckling, fresh or thawed
½ cup granulated sugar
½ teaspoon salt
1 teaspoon cornstarch
1 (6-ounce) can frozen orange juice concentrate, thawed.

1. Prepare the stuffing according to the package directions and stuff into the duckling cavity. Place the duckling, breast-side up, in a slow cooker. Cover and cook on low setting for 6 hours.
2. One hour before serving, combine the sugar, salt, and cornstarch in a medium-sized saucepan. Add the thawed orange juice concentrate. Stir over moderate heat until slightly thickened. Brush the entire surface of the duckling with the glaze. Repeat every 15 minutes for the remaining 1 hour.

CHERRIES JUBILEE

1 (16-ounce) can pitted sweet cherries
⅓ cup granulated sugar
2 tablespoons cornstarch
1 tablespoon lemon juice
⅓ cup brandy
Vanilla ice cream

1. Drain the cherries, reserving the juice in a measuring cup. Add enough water to the juice to make 1 cup liquid.
2. In a small saucepan, mix together the sugar and cornstarch. Gradually stir in the diluted cherry juice until smooth. Bring to a boil over medium heat, stirring constantly. Boil for 1 minute.
3. Add the cherries and lemon juice. Remove from the heat and keep warm.
4. Just before serving, add the brandy. Ignite while still in the saucepan. After the flame dies down, spoon the cherries over the ice cream.

MIMOSA

3 ounces chilled champagne   *3 ounces orange juice*

Combine in a champagne flute or white wine glass. Stir gently.

Serves 1
Serve this with Cheesy Golden Apple Omelet (page 133) to wake up your Mom or Dad.

WHITE WINE COOLER

4 ounces white wine (such as   Sparkling water to fill glass
   Chablis)   *Ice*
2 ounces pineapple juice   1 fresh lime wedge

1. Pour the wine, juice, and sparkling water over ice into a large wine-glass. Stir gently.
2. Garnish with the lime wedge.

Serves 1
This is the perfect complement to any fish or poultry dish.

MEMORIAL DAY

TEXAS CAVIAR

Serves 12

Serve with taco chips or crackers.

2 ripe, firm avocados
1 bulb fresh garlic
1 small red onion
2 medium-sized red tomatoes
1 bunch fresh cilantro
1 (15-ounce) can whole-kernel corn
1 (15-ounce) can black-eyed peas

1 (15-ounce) can black beans
2 tablespoons vegetable oil
3 tablespoons Tabasco sauce
2 tablespoons red wine vinegar
1 teaspoon coarse ground black pepper

1. Remove the pit and skin from the avocados. Cut the flesh into ½-inch cubes. Peel and mince the garlic cloves. Peel and chop the onion. Remove the stems from the tomatoes and chop the tomatoes into ½-inch pieces. Chop the cilantro. Drain and rinse the corn, black-eyed peas, and black beans.
2. In a small bowl, mix together the vegetable oil, Tabasco sauce, vinegar, pepper, and garlic.
3. Place the avocados in a medium-sized mixing bowl. Pour the vegetable oil mixture over the avocados and stir gently to coat.
4. In a large mixing bowl, mix together the onion, tomatoes, cilantro, corn, peas, and beans. Add the avocado mixture to the large bowl and gently mix with the other ingredients.

Garlic in Jars?

Beware of prepared garlic. While preminced garlic looks like a good buy and certainly sounds easier, chopped garlic releases an oil while stored. This affects both the taste and consistency in your recipes. Fresh garlic is always best.

GREEN BEANS IN LEMON HONEY

½ lemon
2 tablespoons butter
3 tablespoons honey
1 teaspoon cider vinegar
½ teaspoon salt

1 tart apple
1 teaspoon cornstarch
1 tablespoon water
3 cups fresh green beans
1 medium-sized yellow onion

1. Slice the lemon into wedges no thicker than ⅛ inch. In a small saucepan, combine the lemon slices with the butter, honey, vinegar, and salt. Bring to a boil, stirring constantly, for 5 minutes.
2. Core and dice the apple into pieces about ¼-inch square. Do not remove the peel. Add to the lemon mixture and cook on medium heat for about 5 minutes.
3. Stir together the cornstarch and water until you have a light paste. Stir this into the apple-lemon mixture. Bring to a boil, then cook on low heat for about 3 minutes.
4. Snap off the ends of the green beans and discard. Wash the green beans thoroughly in cold water. Peel and slice the onion into ¼-inch rings. Place the green beans and onions in a large saucepan and pour the apple-lemon mixture over them. Cook, covered, for 15 minutes or until the beans are cooked through but not soggy.

Add Some Tartness

Use lemon juice when cooking casseroles or other slow-cooked dishes. Sprinkle a little juice on top and the vegetables will retain their color better. The lemon juice also adds a tang that is a nice substitute for fatty butter.

CHICKEN SKEWERS WITH
SPICY ISLAND MARINADE

Serves 4

The marinade may be made up to 3 days in advance and refrigerated until ready to use.

For the marinade:

4 scallions

2 garlic cloves

¼ cup fresh lime juice

2 tablespoons chopped parsley

½ teaspoon dried thyme

½ teaspoon dried rosemary

1 fresh jalapeño pepper

⅛ teaspoon hot sauce

½ teaspoon salt

½ teaspoon ground black pepper

For the skewers:

1 pound boneless, skinless
  chicken breast

8 white mushrooms

4 metal or bamboo skewers

2 tablespoons vegetable oil

1. Peel the scallions and garlic. Remove the seeds and stem from the jalapeño pepper. Trim the stems from the mushrooms and clean the mushrooms with a damp cloth.
2. Combine all the marinade ingredients in a food processor and mix until finely chopped.
3. Slice the chicken into 8 equal pieces. Place the chicken in a plastic storage bag with a leak-proof seal. Pour the marinade over the chicken. Refrigerate for at least 3 hours.
4. Remove the chicken from the marinade. Discard the marinade. Thread a rolled-up strip of chicken on a skewer. Add a mushroom and another strip of chicken. Repeat with the remaining skewers.
5. Prepare a charcoal grill or preheat a gas grill to high heat. Lightly oil the grill rack. Grill the skewers on each side for about 5 minutes or until done. Turn the skewers several times to ensure all sides cook evenly.

Boneless Chicken

Buying chicken breasts that are already deboned and skinned is a great time-saver. They cost more, but one way to save money is to buy larger quantities when they are on sale and freeze them.

LONDON BROIL WITH MUSHROOMS

5 garlic cloves
1 green onion
½ cup dry red wine
¼ cup olive oil
2 tablespoons red wine vinegar
1¼ teaspoon Worcestershire
   sauce

2-pound London broil
1 teaspoon salt
1 teaspoon ground black pepper
1 pound fresh mushrooms
1 tablespoon butter

Serves 4

To serve, slice the
meat against the grain.
Top with mushrooms.

1. Peel and mince 2 of the garlic cloves. Peel and sliver the remaining 3 garlic cloves. Keep separate. Finely chop the green onion, including the green top.
2. In a small mixing bowl, combine the minced garlic, green onion, red wine, oil, vinegar, and Worcestershire sauce.
3. Poke several small holes in the London Broil and place the garlic slivers in the holes. Place the meat in a shallow baking pan and pour the wine mixture over the meat. Cover and refrigerate, turning once, for several hours.
4. Preheat grill to medium-high. Grill the London broil for 3 minutes. Turn and sprinkle the cooked side with salt and pepper. Cook for another 3 minutes or until cooked to your liking.
5. During the last few minutes of cooking the meat, sauté the sliced mushrooms in butter.

STRAWBERRY CHICKEN SALAD

Serves 4

This is a wonderful luncheon meal. Finish the theme by ending with Strawberry Sorbet (page 153).

2 cups diced cooked chicken
1 cup sliced celery
¼ cup chopped red onion
1½ pints fresh strawberries
½ cup mayonnaise
2 tablespoons chutney of your choice

1 tablespoon lemon juice
1 teaspoon grated lemon zest
1 teaspoon salt
1 teaspoon curry powder
4 lettuce leaves
Fresh mint sprigs

1. If necessary, cook the chicken and cut into ½-inch pieces. Slice the celery into ½-inch pieces. Peel the onion and chop into ¼-inch pieces. Remove the stems from the strawberries.
2. In a large bowl, stir together the mayonnaise, chutney, lemon juice, zest, salt, and curry powder, mixing well.
3. Add the chicken, celery, and onion. Toss well, cover, and chill.
4. Just before serving, slice 1 pint of strawberries. Add to the chicken mixture and toss gently.
5. Line a platter of individual serving plates with the lettuce leaves. Mound the chicken mixture on the lettuce. Garnish with the whole strawberries and mint. Serve at once.

Strawberry Garnish

Using a strawberry with the green cap and stem still on, make thin slices nearly up to the cap, being careful not to cut all the way through. Press gently to create a strawberry fan. The color and flavor complement poultry dishes but it looks beautiful with any meal.

SMOKED SALMON SALAD WITH CILANTRO DRESSING

For the dressing:

2 tablespoons plain yogurt

1 tablespoon fresh lemon juice

1 tablespoon white wine vinegar

1 tablespoon minced fresh
   cilantro

¼ teaspoon salt

⅛ teaspoon freshly ground
   black pepper

⅛ teaspoon ground red pepper

½ cup olive oil

For the salad:

1 head romaine lettuce

½ pound smoked salmon

1 cup pitted ripe olives

1 (15-ounce) can chickpeas
   (garbanzo beans)

½ medium-sized red onion

Serves 4
This is excellent served with crusty French bread and a Lemon-Spiked Pineapple Smoothie (page 154).

1. Combine all the dressing ingredients *except* the olive oil in a small bowl. Set aside.
2. Trim the romaine and discard the stem ends. Slice the remaining inner leaves into 1½-inch pieces. Wash and dry the lettuce pieces. Flake the fish into bite-sized pieces. Cut the olives in half. Drain the chickpeas. Cut the onion into thin slices.
3. In a large bowl, combine lettuce, salmon, olives, chickpeas, and onion. Whisk the olive oil into the dressing and pour over the salad. Toss gently.

Olives

Avoid buying canned supermarket-grade factory-pitted olives. They have usually been overprocessed and retain little or no true olive flavor. It is best to select olives from the delicatessen department, or buy good imported olives in a glass jar and pit them by hand.

BURGERS WITH LEMON PEPPER

2 pounds lean hamburger
3 tablespoons lemon pepper
1 tablespoon dried thyme
1 tablespoon paprika
1 teaspoon garlic powder

½ teaspoon granulated sugar
½ teaspoon salt
¼ teaspoon ground coriander
⅛ teaspoon ground cumin
⅛ teaspoon cayenne pepper

1. Form the hamburger into 8 equal-sized patties.
2. Stir together all the ingredients *except* the hamburger in a small mixing bowl. Generously sprinkle the mixture on the raw burgers and let stand for 1 hour in the refrigerator.
3. Cook the burgers on broiler or grill until desired doneness.

MARINATED GINGER CHICKEN

1 (2–3 pound) frying chicken
½ cup lemon juice
½ cup vegetable oil
¼ cup soy sauce

1 teaspoon fresh grated ginger-root (or 1 tablespoon ground ginger)
1 teaspoon onion salt
¼ teaspoon garlic powder

1. Cut the chicken into serving pieces. Place in a shallow baking dish.
2. In a small bowl, combine the lemon juice, oil, soy sauce, ginger, onion salt, and garlic powder. Pour over the chicken. Cover and refrigerate at least 4 hours or overnight, turning occasionally.
3. Grill or broil for about 20 minutes, basting frequently with the marinade, and turning after 10 minutes. Cook until the meat is no longer pink and the juices run clear.

CALIFORNIA TRI-TIP

1 tablespoon freshly cracked
   peppercorns
2 teaspoons garlic salt
1 teaspoon dry mustard

¼ teaspoon cayenne pepper
2–3 pound tri-tip roast
Oak, mesquite, or hickory
   chips for grilling

Serves 6

This works equally well hot as a main dish, room temperature over lettuce as a salad, or cold in sandwiches.

1. Mix together the pepper, garlic salt, mustard, and cayenne. Rub into the surface of the tri-tip. Cover with plastic wrap and refrigerate overnight.
2. Soak the wood chips in water for at least 30 minutes. Preheat grill to medium. Add the soaked woods chips to the coals.
3. Sear the tri-tip directly over medium heat, turning once, to seal in juices, about 2 minutes on each side. Then grill the tri-tip indirectly over medium heat, turning once, until the internal temperature is about 140°. Grill an additional 30 minutes.
4. Remove from heat and let stand for 5 minutes. Slice diagonally against the grain.

Meat Grades

The higher the grade of meat, the more marbling (fat) contained in the cut. For a healthy alternative, use a lower grade of meat and cook it slowly to tenderize. "Select" is the least fatty grade.

BRUSSELS SPROUTS A L'ORANGE

Serves 4

Serve with Marinated Ginger Chicken (page 150).

4 cups fresh Brussels sprouts
1¼ cups fresh-squeezed orange juice
½ teaspoon cornstarch
¼ teaspoon ground cinnamon

1. In a slow cooker, combine all the ingredients. Stir until well mixed. Cover and cook on low for 1 hour.
2. Uncover and cook on low for 1 additional hour until the sauce has thickened and the Brussels sprouts are tender.

GRILLED RIB-EYE STEAKS WITH ONIONS

Serves 4

Serve with Brussels Sprouts a l'Orange (page 152).

4 large white onions
4 garlic cloves
2 tablespoons olive oil
4 boneless ribeye steaks, 1-inch thick
½ teaspoon salt
½ teaspoon ground black pepper
4 teaspoons dry vermouth

1. Peel and slice the onions. Peel the garlic cloves and split in half.
2. In a large skillet, heat the olive oil on medium; cook the onions in the oil until golden brown, about 10 to 15 minutes. Cover and keep warm.
3. Rub both sides of the steaks with the cut-side of the garlic and season with salt and pepper. Grill the steaks for 3 to 4 minutes on each side, or to the desired degree of doneness.
4. Pour 1 teaspoon vermouth over each steak immediately before removing from the grill. Serve with grilled onions.

STRAWBERRY SORBET

2 cups fresh strawberries
¾ cup orange juice
½ cup 1% milk

¼ cup, plus 1 tablespoon honey
2 egg whites

Serves 8

This is a perfect
dessert for Burgers
with Lemon Pepper
(page 150).

1. Remove the stems from the strawberries.
2. In a blender, combine the berries, orange juice, milk, and the ¼ cup honey. Blend until smooth, about 1 minute. Pour into a 9-inch square baking pan. Cover and freeze until almost firm, about 3 hours.
3. Beat the egg whites with an electric mixer at medium speed until soft peaks form. Increase the speed to high and gradually add the 1 tablespoon honey, beating until stiff peaks form.
4. Break the frozen mixture into chunks. Transfer the pieces to a chilled large bowl. Beat with an electric mixer until smooth. Fold in the egg whites with a rubber spatula.
5. Return the mixture to the baking pan. Cover and freeze until firm, 6 to 8 hours. To serve, scrape across the surface of the frozen mixture with a spoon and mound in dessert dishes.

Making Nonstick Pans

There is no need to buy special nonstick pots and pans. Just use a bit of vinegar before you cook in a new pan the first time. Pour enough vinegar into the pan to cover the bottom of the pan, and then bring it to a boil. Wipe out the pan. Let cool and wash the pan.

MINT JULEP

Serves 1

The first Saturday in May is the Kentucky Derby and always the day to toast your sweetheart with a Mint Julep. This drink even has its own silver "julep cup," but a highball or Collins glass will do.

4 sprigs fresh mint
1 teaspoon fine sugar
1 teaspoon water

Crushed ice
2½ ounces bourbon

1. In a Collins glass, muddle the mint leaves, sugar, and water.
2. Fill the glass with crushed ice and add the bourbon.
3. Garnish with mint and serve with straws.

LEMON-SPIKED PINEAPPLE SMOOTHIE

Serves 6

If you like a sweeter drink, add ½ cup honey to the drink. Stir well before serving.

1 fresh lemon
1 medium-sized ripe pineapple
6 tablespoons freshly squeezed
  lemon juice

4 cups cold water
Ice

1. Cut the lemon into thin slices and set aside.
2. Peel the pineapple and cut out the core. Cut the fruit into pieces about 1-inch square. Place in a food processor and process to a somewhat smooth, pulpy consistency. Transfer to a large pitcher.
3. Add the lemon juice and cold water. Stir until mixed. Serve in glasses over ice with a thin slice of lemon for garnish.

CHAPTER 11
SUMMER PICNICS

ZESTY FETA AND OLIVE SALAD

1 small red onion
1 celery rib
1 small cucumber
1 garlic clove
1 fresh lemon
1 fresh orange
12 small cherry tomatoes
½ cup kalamata olives
2 tablespoons fresh Italian
  parsley
2 teaspoons fresh oregano
1 teaspoon fresh mint
1 tablespoon fresh cilantro
2 ounces crumbled feta
1 tablespoon olive oil
12 large romaine or butter
  lettuce leaves
½ teaspoon freshly ground
  black pepper

1. Remove the skin from the onion and dice into ⅛-inch pieces. Chop the celery into ⅛-inch pieces. Dice ½ of the cucumber into ⅛-inch pieces and cut the other ½ into slices. Remove the peel from the garlic and mince finely. Use the lemon and orange to create 1 teaspoon each of zest. Peel the lemon and orange and cut into thin slices. Cut the cherry tomatoes in half (or quarters if they are large). Pit the olives and cut each into 8 slices. Mince the parsley, oregano, mint, and cilantro.
2. Place the feta in a large bowl and add the onion, celery, diced cucumber, garlic, lemon and orange zest, cherry tomatoes, and olives; mix gently. Add the fresh herbs and olive oil, and toss.
3. Arrange the lettuce leaves on 4 salad plates. Arrange the cucumber, lemon, and orange slices around the sides. Spoon the feta salad on top. Top with freshly ground pepper.

Cracked Black Pepper

Like many seeds, black pepper's best flavor remains locked inside until it's smashed. Place 10 peppercorns at a time on a flat, hard surface. Using a small saucepot or skillet, apply pressure with the heel of your hand to break the seeds a few at a time.

AVOCADO AND PEACH SALAD

1 garlic clove

1 avocado

1 peach

1 small Vidalia onion

⅛ cup water

⅛ cup frozen orange juice concentrate

1 teaspoon rice wine vinegar

1 tablespoon olive oil

½ teaspoon vanilla

1½ tightly packed cups baby arugula

2 tablespoons fresh tarragon leaves

½ teaspoon sea salt

¼ teaspoon freshly ground black pepper

> **Serves 4**
>
> This is a perfect first course for any summer meal. Use it to complement a heavier dish such as a roast or ribs.

1. Crush the garlic with the side of a large knife. Remove the skin. Peel the avocado and dice into ¼-inch pieces. Peel the peach and dice into ¼-inch pieces. Remove the skin from the onion and slice thinly.
2. In a large measuring cup, whisk together the garlic, water, orange juice concentrate, vinegar, oil, and vanilla until well mixed.
3. Prepare the salad by arranging layers of the arugula and tarragon, then the avocado, peach, and onions. Drizzle the salad with the orange juice vinaigrette. Season with salt and pepper.

Salad Dressing

Greens should be thoroughly dry before adding dressing, to enable it to stick to the leaves. Don't dress a salad until you are ready to serve it. Use only enough to coat the greens lightly. If desired, you can serve additional dressing at the table.

SPINACH SALAD WITH APPLE-AVOCADO DRESSING

Serves 4

This is a wonderful first course for virtually any meal. It complements any meat or pasta meal.

1 ripe avocado
1 garlic clove
1 small red onion
6 radishes
¼ cup unsweetened apple juice
1 teaspoon cider vinegar

1 teaspoon soy sauce
½ teaspoon Worcestershire sauce
2 teaspoons olive oil
2½ tightly packed cups spinach greens
½ cup bean sprouts

1. Remove the skin and pit from the avocado. Peel and mince the garlic. Peel the onion and slice thinly. Clean the radishes and slice thinly.
2. Place the avocado, garlic, apple juice, cider vinegar, soy sauce, Worcestershire sauce, and oil in a food processor or blender; process until smooth.
3. In a large bowl, combine the onion, radishes, spinach greens, and bean sprouts; mix well. Pour the dressing over the salad and toss.

HONEY DIJON TUNA SALAD

Serves 2

Variation: To make a complete meal, add 1 cup cooked pasta to the salad before placing on the greens. Serve with fresh melon cubes.

½ cup water-packed tuna
2 celery ribs
1 small yellow onion
1 small red pepper
8 ounces nonfat plain yogurt

2 teaspoons Dijon mustard
2 teaspoons lemon juice
½ teaspoon honey
2 tablespoons raisins
2 cups iceberg lettuce

1. Drain the tuna and flake with a fork. Cut the celery into ¼-inch pieces. Remove the skin from the onion and cut into ¼-inch pieces. Remove the stem and core from the red pepper. Chop ½ of the red pepper into ¼-inch pieces. Slice the other ½ into ¼-inch strips.
2. Add the tuna, celery, onion, chopped red pepper, yogurt, mustard, lemon juice, honey, and raisins to a medium-sized bowl; mix well.
3. Arrange lettuce leaves on plates and top with the tuna salad. Use the red pepper strips for garnish.

POLYNESIAN BANANA SALAD

4 bananas
1 cup coconut cream
2 tablespoons curry powder

1 cup soft raisins
4 teaspoons shredded coconut

Serves 4

Excellent with spicy food and rice, this rich, sweet salad can be part of a meal, snack, or dessert.

1. Slice the bananas about ½-inch thick on a slight diagonal.
2. Whisk together the coconut cream and curry powder. Add the bananas and raisins. Toss gently to coat.
3. Transfer to a serving dish and sprinkle with the shredded coconut.

Plump Raisins
If you find your raisins are a bit too dry, soak them in a light white wine for an hour or so. They will plump up nicely while the wine will add extra flavor to your dish.

RISOTTO WITH FRESH SUMMER VEGETABLES

1 tablespoon butter
1 large white onion
1 cup chopped fresh zucchini
1 cup uncooked white rice
4 cups chicken broth

1 cup fresh green beans
½ teaspoon salt
½ teaspoon ground black pepper
1 cup fresh snow peas
⅓ cup chopped fresh parsley

Serves 8

While it is excellent served warm, this is a great dish to make 1 or 2 days ahead of time and serve cold at your picnic. Bring assorted gourmet crackers and cheeses as well as a light white wine.

1. Melt the butter in a small skillet on medium-high heat. Peel and chop the onion into ¼-inch pieces. Sauté the onions in the butter for 3 to 5 minutes, until translucent. Drain.
2. Chop the zucchini into 1-inch pieces. Place the onions, zucchini, uncooked white rice, chicken broth, green beans, salt, and pepper in a slow cooker. Mix well. Cover and cook on low setting for 7 to 8 hours or until the rice is soft. Add the peas and cook for 1 to 2 hours more.
3. Chop the parsley into ¼-inch lengths, add it to the slow cooker, and stir well. Cook, uncovered, for 15 to 30 minutes.

SUNSHINE BEAN SALAD
WITH GOLDEN GATE DRESSING

Serves 8

Perfect as a first course
with fried chicken
or hamburgers.

For the dressing:
⅓ cup granulated sugar
½ teaspoon dry mustard
1 teaspoon salt
2 tablespoons all-purpose flour
1 egg
½ cup white wine vinegar
1½ cups water
1 tablespoon butter

For the salad:
1 (16-ounce) can chickpeas
   (garbanzo beans)
1 (8-ounce) can corn kernels
1 cup diced celery
½ cup chopped red onion
2 tablespoons diced pimientos
¼ cup diced green bell peppers

1. To make the dressing, stir together the sugar, mustard, salt, and flour in a small bowl. In another small bowl, beat the egg with a fork, then beat into the dry mixture.
2. In a small saucepan, combine the vinegar, water, and butter; cook over low heat until the mixture simmers. Remove from the heat and gradually add the egg mixture, stirring vigorously.
3. Return to heat and cook, stirring constantly, until smooth and thick, 2 or 3 minutes.
4. Drain the chickpeas and corn kernels. Dice the celery. Peel and chop the onion into ¼-inch pieces. Dice the pimientos into ⅛-inch pieces. Remove the seeds and stem from the green pepper and chop into ¼-inch pieces.
5. Combine the chickpeas, corn, celery, onion, pimiento, and green pepper in a large glass bowl. Moisten to taste with the dressing. Chill before serving.

TRICOLOR PEPPER SALAD

2 red bell peppers
2 green bell peppers
2 yellow bell peppers
2 celery stalks
2 large cucumbers
1 large red onion
2 cups cherry tomatoes
4 garlic cloves

¼ cup chopped fresh parsley
3 tablespoons lime juice
1 tablespoon lemon juice
2 tablespoons white wine
    vinegar
1 tablespoon olive oil
½ teaspoon salt
¼ teaspoon cayenne pepper

> **Serves 8**
>
> Serve with hot dogs,
> hamburgers,
> or grilled chicken.

1. Remove the stems and seeds from the bell peppers and chop into ½-inch pieces. Chop the celery into ¼-inch pieces. Peel the cucumbers and dice into ¼-inch pieces. Peel the onion and chop into ½-inch pieces. Halve the cherry tomatoes. Peel and mince the garlic cloves. Roughly chop the parsley.
2. In a large salad bowl, combine the bell peppers, celery, cucumbers, onion, and tomatoes; mix well.
3. In a small bowl, stir together the garlic, parsley, lime and lemon juices, vinegar, oil, salt, and cayenne pepper. Add the dressing to the salad and toss well to combine.
4. Cover and chill for 1 hour, tossing occasionally before serving.

Seedless Cucumbers

If slippery cucumber seeds bother you, look for specifically grown seedless cucumbers in the grocery store. These longer, thin cucumbers taste just as good.

CALIFORNIA GARDEN SALAD WITH AVOCADO AND SPROUTS

Serves 4

The fruity taste of large, green Florida avocados gives this salad a lighter, more summer flavor, although the smaller Haas avocadoes are more authentic for this California salad.

For the dressing:
1 tablespoon fresh-squeezed
    lemon juice
3 tablespoons extra-virgin
    olive oil
1 tablespoon chopped shallots
½ teaspoon salt
¼ teaspoon freshly ground
    black pepper

For the salad:
2 heads Boston or
    Bibb lettuce
2 large red tomatoes
1 ripe avocado
1 cup alfalfa sprouts

1. Peel and mince the shallots. Combine all the dressing ingredients in a small bowl, mixing well.
2. Wash the lettuce and trim away outside leaves. Core the tomatoes and cut into 8 wedges each. Remove the skin and pit from the avocado. Cut the avocado into 8 wedges.
3. Arrange the lettuce leaves, stem-end in, on 4 plates, making a flower-petal pattern. You don't need to use the smallest inner leaves.
4. Toss the tomatoes in 1 tablespoon of the dressing. Place 4 onto each salad. Toss the avocado pieces with 1 tablespoon dressing and place 2 wedges on each salad. Divide the sprouts into 4 bunches and place a bunch in the center of each salad. Drizzle the salads with the remaining dressing.

Avocados

Avocados are one of the few vegetables high in fat. Substitute cucumber for avocado for a fresh flavor with none of the fat grams. Choose a seedless cucumber and remove the skin before dicing it.

SUMMER VEGETABLE SLAW

1 small head green cabbage
2 medium carrots
1 red bell pepper
1 green bell pepper
1 yellow bell pepper
1 small red onion
2 ears fresh sweet corn
¼ pound snow peas

12 fresh green beans
½ teaspoon granulated sugar
¼ cup cider vinegar
1 tablespoon peanut oil
½ teaspoon celery seeds
½ teaspoon salt
½ teaspoon ground black
  pepper

Serves 8

This is an excellent accompaniment to crispy fried foods like chicken and onion rings.

1. Quarter and core the cabbage. Slice as thinly as possible. Peel the carrots, then shave as thinly as possible. (Discard the small amount that can't be shaved.) Remove the stems and seeds from the bell peppers and cut into fine julienne strips. Peel the onion and cut into julienne strips. Cut the corn kernels from the cob.
2. Combine all the vegetables in a large mixing bowl. Mix together the sugar, vinegar, oil, celery seeds, salt, and pepper. Toss the vegetables with the dressing. Allow to sit for at least 10 minutes before serving.

Wilted Spinach Salad

Stir-fry fresh spinach in a little butter or olive oil until wilted. Sprinkle with allspice, onion powder, or a splash of lemon juice. Add a little crumbled bacon and chopped, hard-boiled egg. Serve with simple oil and vinegar for dressing.

WILD BLACKBERRY PIE

Serves 12

This recipe also can be used to create a mixed berry pie. Use a combination of black raspberries, blueberries, and blackberries.

Uncooked pastry for a double-crust, 9-inch pie
½ cup black walnuts
4 cups blackberries
1 tablespoon lemon juice
½ cup granulated sugar
½ packed cup brown sugar
½ teaspoon ground cinnamon
3 tablespoons all-purpose flour
5 tablespoons butter

1. Preheat oven to 350°. Line a deep-dish 9-inch pie plate with ½ of the pastry, leaving 1 inch of the pastry hanging over the edge of the plate. Chop the nuts.
2. In a large bowl, combine the nuts, blackberries, lemon juice, sugars, cinnamon, and flour; mix lightly. Spoon into the prepared shell. Dot with 3 tablespoons of the butter cut into small pieces.
3. On a lightly floured work surface, roll out the remaining pastry into a thin round and cut into ½-inch-wide strips. Moisten the edge of the bottom pastry with water. Arrange the pastry strips on top of the pie, forming a lattice top. Trim the ends of the strips as necessary and press the ends together with the bottom crust.
4. Turn the edge of the bottom crust and strips under and flute to make an attractive rim. Melt the 2 remaining tablespoons of butter over a low heat in a small saucepan. Brush the lattice and edges with the melted butter. Sprinkle lightly with cinnamon and sugar, if desired.
5. Bake for 45 minutes or until the top crust is golden.

Freeze Nuts

Squirrels know to freeze their nuts under the cold ground in winter. The reason is that nuts go rancid within a couple of months at room temperature. Store them in the freezer in airtight containers.

FISH HOUSE PUNCH

½ cup fine sugar
1½ cups lemon juice
1 pint peach brandy
1 pint light rum

2 bottles dry white wine
1 quart sparkling water
Ice

1. Dissolve the sugar in the lemon juice and brandy. Add the rum and wine. Stir well. Refrigerate.
2. Pour into a punch bowl over ice. Add the club soda just before serving.

CAPE COD PUNCH

½ cup fine sugar
2 quarts cranberry juice
1 quart orange juice
½ cup lemon juice

3 cups vodka
Ice
1 quart sparkling water

1. Dissolve the sugar in the juices in a large bowl. Add the vodka and stir well.
2. Pour over ice in a punch bowl. Add the water just before serving.

Chilled Cups

For a delightful drink presentation for a summer party, chill the drink glasses and keep them in a cooler outside. As you fill drinks, grab an ice-cold glass and give people a frosty treat on a steamy day.

CHAPTER 12
FOURTH OF JULY

GRILLED CINNAMON PORK TENDERLOINS

Serves 4

Serving tip: Slice thinly and drape over garlic mashed potatoes. Drizzle with thinned horseradish mustard.

4 teaspoons soy sauce
4 teaspoons burgundy wine
2 teaspoons brown sugar
1/4 teaspoon honey

1/4 teaspoon garlic powder
1/4 teaspoon ground cinnamon
4 (8-ounce) pork tenderloins

1. Combine the soy sauce, burgundy wine, brown sugar, honey, garlic powder, and ground cinnamon in a sealable plastic bag; shake well. Add the tenderloins and shake gently until the meat is well coated. Place in the refrigerator for at least 1 hour.
2. Heat coals or gas grill until moderately hot. Grill the tenderloins on both sides until meat thermometer hits 160°. Allow the meat to rest for 10 minutes in its juices.

ORANGE-AVOCADO SLAW

Serves 10

Use as a unique complement to backyard barbecues or as the perfect potluck surprise.

1 avocado
1/4 cup orange juice
1/2 teaspoon curry powder
1/8 teaspoon ground cumin
1/4 teaspoon granulated sugar
1 teaspoon white wine vinegar

1 tablespoon olive oil
5 cups broccoli slaw mix
1/2 teaspoon sea salt
1/4 teaspoon freshly ground
   black pepper

1. Peel the avocado, remove the pit, and chop the meat into 1/4-inch pieces.
2. In a medium-sized bowl, whisk together the orange juice, curry powder, cumin, sugar, and vinegar. Add the oil in a stream, whisking until emulsified.
3. In a large bowl, toss the avocado with the slaw mix. Drizzle with the vinaigrette. Chill until ready to serve, and season with the salt and pepper.

CLASSIC AMERICAN POTATO SALAD

2 pounds potatoes (any variety)
1 small carrot
¾ cup mayonnaise
2 teaspoons Dijon mustard
1 teaspoon granulated sugar
½ teaspoon salt
¼ teaspoon ground black
  pepper
1 tablespoon Italian parsley

Serves 8

For a fun treat, try making this potato salad with one of the specialty potatoes such as the purple or Yukon gold varieties.

1. Peel and cut the potatoes into ½-inch cubes. Boil in salted water until soft. Drain. Peel and grate the carrot. Roughly chop the parsley.
2. Whisk together the mayonnaise, mustard, sugar, salt, and pepper. Add the potatoes and carrot. Toss gently until the potatoes are all coated. Garnish with chopped parsley.

JUMBO BEER-BATTERED ONION RINGS

Peanut oil, for frying
2 extra-large eggs
1 (12-ounce) bottle pilsner or
  lager beer
½ cup peanut oil
3 cups cornstarch
½ teaspoon salt
2 extra-large Spanish or
  Bermuda onions

Serves 4

Who can resist this all-American treat? They are a must-have for any kid's party or backyard barbecue.

1. Heat oil to 360° in a medium-sized deep fryer or deep skillet.
2. Beat the eggs. Whisk together the eggs, beer, ½ cup oil, 2 cups of the cornstarch, and the salt until it makes a thick batter.
3. Remove the skin from the onions. Cut them into 1-inch-thick slices. Separate into rings. Dredge the onion rings in the remaining 1 cup cornstarch, dip into the batter, and add to the pot 1 at a time, making sure the first has started to sizzle before adding the next. Flip each ring so it cooks evenly on both sides. Drain on paper towels.

THREE-BEAN SALAD

Serves 6

This classic is the perfect complement to hamburgers, hot dogs, or any summertime treat.

1 (16-ounce) can green beans
1 (16-ounce) can yellow wax beans
1 (16-ounce) can red kidney beans
1 medium-sized red onion
½ cup granulated sugar
⅔ cup vinegar
⅓ cup vegetable oil
½ teaspoon salt
⅛ teaspoon ground black pepper

1. Drain the beans. Peel the onion and slice thinly, then cut the slices into quarters.
2. Whisk together the sugar, vinegar, oil, salt, and pepper.
3. In a large bowl, combine the beans, onion, and dressing; mix well. Chill for at least 4 hours, mixing occasionally. Drain before serving.

FRIED GREEN TOMATOES

Serves 4

This Southern dish was made popular when a movie by the same name became a hit. Now it's served at barbecues across the country.

2 large green tomatoes
1 teaspoon salt
1 teaspoon freshly ground black pepper
1 cup yellow cornmeal
1 cup extra-virgin olive oil

1. Slice the tomatoes about ¼-inch thick. Season both sides with salt and pepper. Dredge the tomato slices in the cornmeal, coating well on both sides.
2. Heat the oil in a medium-sized skillet over medium heat. Fry the tomatoes in the oil until golden brown, turning them only once. Drain excess oil on paper towels. Serve immediately.

DEVILED EGGS

4 large eggs
2½ tablespoons mayonnaise
1½ teaspoons Dijon mustard
½ teaspoon hot red pepper
    sauce
½ teaspoon salt

½ teaspoon ground white
    pepper
2 tablespoons minced fresh
    chives
1 teaspoon paprika

Makes 8

This update of a summer tradition is sure to appeal to traditionalists as well as newcomers to the deviled egg scene.

1. Place the eggs in a medium-sized saucepan and cover with water. Bring to boil, reduce to a simmer, and cook for 9 minutes. Plunge the eggs into a bowl filled with ice water. Allow the eggs to cool completely.
2. Carefully peel the shells from the eggs. Cut the eggs in half and remove the yolks from the whites. Place the yolks in a bowl and add the mayonnaise, mustard, hot pepper sauce, salt, pepper, and chives. With the back of a fork, mash all of the ingredients until blended.
3. Fill the egg whites with the yolk mixture using a teaspoon or a pastry bag fitted with a star tip. Dust with paprika. Chill until served.

Raw Eggs

Raw eggs can be harmful to some people, especially pregnant women, infants, and people with immune disorders. Although foods such as eggnog and mayonnaise contain raw eggs, these foods are pasteurized so they pose no risk. You can find pasteurized eggs at most large grocery stores.

FRIED CHICKEN

Serves 4

Serve with Three-Bean Salad (page 170) and Strawberry Pie (page 178).

3-pound fryer chicken
1½ cups buttermilk
½ cup all-purpose flour
1½ teaspoons salt
½ teaspoon black pepper

1 teaspoon paprika
½ teaspoon garlic powder
½ teaspoon grated nutmeg
3 cups vegetable oil

1. Wash the chicken and cut into 8 serving pieces.
2. Pour the buttermilk into a large nonmetallic bowl. Add the chicken pieces and turn to coat. Cover and refrigerate, turning occasionally, for 2 to 3 hours.
3. In a large bowl, combine the flour with the salt, pepper, paprika, garlic powder, and nutmeg. Remove the chicken pieces from the buttermilk and shake off any excess liquid. Allow to drain. Toss the chicken pieces in a plastic food storage bag with the flour mixture to ensure the pieces are evenly coated.
4. Pour ¾ inch of oil into a deep skillet and heat to 350°.
5. Fry the chicken in batches to avoid overcrowding the pan. Cook for about 10 to 15 minutes, turning occasionally so the pieces cook to an even crispy golden brown. Drain the chicken on paper towels.

Roasting Chickens
Roasting chickens are older and larger than broiler-fryers, usually weighing from 4 to 6 pounds. They are not as tender as broiler-fryers but when cooked by a slow method, like roasting, they become tender and flavorful.

GRILLED ZUCCHINI WITH BALSAMIC VINEGAR

3 garlic cloves
4 medium zucchini
¼ cup extra-virgin olive oil
½ teaspoon salt
¼ teaspoon ground black pepper

2 tablespoons balsamic vinegar
¼ cup coarsely chopped fresh
herbs (mint, basil, chives,
parsley, etc.)

Serves 6

Serve with Fried
Chicken (page 172)
or Grilled Cinnamon
Pork Tenderloins
(page 168).

1. Peel the garlic and chop finely. Scrub the zucchini and cut in half lengthwise.
2. Heat the oil in a small saucepan over low heat. Add the garlic and cook until just fragrant. Remove from the heat.
3. Preheat the grill to high temperature. Brush the zucchini with the garlic oil and season with salt and pepper. Grill the zucchini, skin-side down, until it begins to soften, about 3 minutes. Turn, and cook the other side until tender.
4. Cut each piece of zucchini in half at an angle into 2 or 3 pieces and place in a bowl. Drizzle the vinegar over the zucchini and add the chopped herbs and the remaining garlic oil. Toss well and season with salt and pepper.

Chopping Fresh Herbs
Although recipes might call for chopping leafy herbs, it's best to bunch gentle leaves like basil, oregano, or mint into small stacks, then slice them against the cutting board with the sharpest knife you can find. Chopping can result in unattractive black edges, clumps, and rapid spoilage.

ALL-AMERICAN BARBECUED CHICKEN

Serves 8

This sauce is equally good used for ribs or pork chops.

2 (3-pound) roasting chickens
1 medium-sized yellow onion
2 tablespoons vegetable oil
2 (15-ounce) cans tomato sauce
1 cup red wine vinegar

1 teaspoon prepared mustard
½ cup dark molasses
¼ cup Worcestershire sauce
⅓ packed cup brown sugar
¾ teaspoon cayenne pepper

1. Split the chickens in half. Peel the onion and chop into ¼-inch pieces. Preheat grill to medium temperature.
2. Heat the oil in a skillet over medium heat. Add the onion and sauté until tender, about 10 minutes.
3. Mix in the tomato sauce, vinegar, mustard, molasses, Worcestershire sauce, brown sugar, and cayenne. Heat to boiling over high heat, stirring frequently. Reduce heat and simmer, uncovered, for 30 to 45 minutes or until the sauce thickens slightly. Reserve 1½ cups of the mixture to serve as a sauce.
4. Place the chicken on the grill over medium heat. Cook for 25 to 30 minutes. Turn and baste generously with sauce. Cook for 25 minutes more, turning the pieces often and basting frequently. To test for doneness, pierce the chicken with a fork. The juices will run clear when the chicken is fully cooked.

Adding Smoky Flavor to Vegetarian Dishes

For a smoky flavor, most nonvegetarian recipes call for smoked pork bones or bacon. Vegetarians can achieve a similar result by adding smoked chilies, such as chipotles (smoked jalapeños) to those dishes.

BARBECUED PORK AND BEANS

*2 tablespoons chopped yellow
  onion
1 pound canned or fresh
  baked beans
½ cup prepared mustard*

*½ cup prepared ketchup
4 lean pork chops
¼ cup lemon juice
¼ cup granulated sugar*

Serves 4

Serve with Classic
Apple Pie (page 179)
for dessert.

1. Chop the onion into ¼-inch pieces. Mix with the beans and place in
   the bottom of a slow cooker.
2. Spread the mustard and ketchup over both sides of the pork chops.
   Sprinkle both sides with the lemon juice and sugar.
3. Lay the pork chops on top of the beans. If possible, do not layer
   them. Cook on low heat for 4 to 6 hours.

HAM BARBECUE

*2 pounds chopped ham
1 bottle chili sauce
½ cup ketchup*

*½ cup water
¼ cup corn syrup
8 whole-wheat bulky rolls*

Serves 8

This is the perfect
meal for those not-
quite-perfect summer
days. Cold tempera-
tures and rain won't
take the fun out of
this summer meal.

1. Mix together all the ingredients in a slow cooker. Cover and cook on
   low setting for 1 to 2 hours, stirring occasionally.
2. Serve on the whole-wheat rolls.

Make-Ahead Meals
*Cooked meats can be refrigerated for up to 3 months. Freeze in
1- or 2-cup measures. Thaw in the refrigerator or microwave.
Do not refreeze thawed meats that have not been cooked.*

SUMMERTIME STRAWBERRY SOUP

Serves 6

Serve as a dessert
for Fried Chicken
(page 172).

3 cups strawberries
½ teaspoon ground cinnamon
4 ounces frozen orange juice
    concentrate
½ cup water
¼ cup dry red wine

¼ teaspoon ground cloves
2 tablespoons cornstarch
2 tablespoons water
1 pint vanilla frozen yogurt
1 pint plain yogurt

1. Clean the strawberries and remove the stems. Mix the strawberries, cinnamon, orange juice concentrate, water, wine, and cloves in a large saucepan. Bring to a boil, reduce heat to medium-low, and simmer for 10 minutes.

2. Mix together the cornstarch and water in a small bowl. Stir ⅓ cup of the strawberry mixture into the cornstarch mixture until smooth and then add to the saucepan. Bring to a boil, stirring until thick, about 5 minutes.

3. Remove from the heat, let cool for 1 hour or longer, and then add both yogurts. Stir until the frozen yogurt melts. Cover and refrigerate for 1 hour before serving.

Freezing Soups and Stews

Label all items and use within 3 months. When freezing stews, leave the potatoes out. Undercook the vegetables so they don't become mushy when reheated.

BUBBLY BERRY BLAST

1 cup fresh strawberries
1 cup fresh blueberries
2 tablespoons unflavored
*   gelatin*

½ cup frozen, unsweetened
*   apple juice concentrate*
3 cups unsweetened sparkling
*   water*

Serves 6

A delicious treat on a
hot summer day.

1. Wash the blueberries and strawberries. Slice the strawberries into eighths.
2. Mix the gelatin and apple juice in a small saucepan. Stir and let stand for 1 minute. Place the mixture over low heat and stir until completely dissolved, about 3 minutes.
3. Stir in the sparkling water. Refrigerate until the mixture begins to gel or is the consistency of unbeaten egg whites.
4. Fold the fruit into the partially thickened gelatin mixture. Pour into a 6-cup mold. Refrigerate for 4 hours or until firm.

Microwave It

Try this in the microwave: Blend the gelatin and apple juice. Let stand for 1 minute, then heat in a microwave-safe bowl on high setting for 45 seconds. Stir the mixture until the gelatin is completely dissolved. Continue with steps 3 and 4.

STRAWBERRY PIE

Serves 8

Serve with Fried
Chicken (page 172).

2 pints fresh strawberries
1 prebaked 9-inch pie shell
1 pound cream cheese, softened
¼ cup granulated sugar
2 teaspoons grated lemon rind
4 tablespoons lemon juice,
  divided

2 tablespoons cornstarch
¼ cup water
1 (12-ounce) jar strawberry
  preserves
1 container whipped cream

1. Clean the strawberries, remove the hulls, and slice. Put the pie shell into a 9-inch pie pan.
2. In a medium-sized bowl, combine the cream cheese, sugar, lemon rind, and 2 tablespoons of the lemon juice; mix well. Spread in the bottom of the prebaked pie shell. Top with the fresh strawberries.
3. In a small saucepan, combine the cornstarch and water. Stir well to dissolve the cornstarch, then stir in the preserves. Bring to a boil, stirring constantly. Cook and stir for about 5 minutes, or until thick and clear.
4. Remove from heat and stir in the remaining 2 tablespoons lemon juice. Let cool to room temperature. Pour the cooled preserves over the berries. Chill well.
5. Garnish with whipped cream right before serving.

Fat Facts

Unsaturated fats are better for your body than saturated fats. Animal fats are saturated fats and most vegetable fats are unsaturated fats. But remember, coconut and palm oil are saturated vegetable fats and are used in most bakery and processed snack foods.

CLASSIC APPLE PIE

*1 prepared 9-inch graham
    cracker pie crust*
*6 medium-sized tart apples
    such as Granny Smith*
½ cup granulated sugar
1 teaspoon ground cinnamon

¼ teaspoon ground nutmeg
¼ teaspoon salt
¾ cup water
1 tablespoon lemon juice
2 tablespoons cornstarch
1 tablespoon butter

Serves 8

Tradition says this must be served with a huge scoop of vanilla ice cream, preferably 1 or 2 hours before the Fourth of July fireworks begin.

1. Put the pie crust in the pie pan. Peel the apples and slice thinly. Preheat oven to 350°.
2. Combine the sugar, cinnamon, nutmeg, and salt in a large saucepan. Stir in ½ cup of the water, the lemon juice, and apples. Place over medium heat and stir gently until the mixture comes to a boil. Cover and simmer for 13 to 20 minutes or until the apples are almost tender, stirring occasionally.
3. Meanwhile, in a small bowl, dissolve the cornstarch in the remaining ¼ cup water. When the apples are done cooking, stir in the cornstarch until thickened and clear. Stir in the butter.
4. Pour the apple filling into the pie crust. Bake for 30 minutes or until bubbling hot and the apples are tender.

Blender or Food Processor

They seem interchangeable sometimes, but they're not. Blenders and food processors are different tools with different strengths. For ultra-smooth purées, a blender is the first choice. For rougher purées or chopping jobs with drier ingredients, use a processor.

KEY LIME PIE

Serves 8

Don't try to use regular limes for this recipe. Key limes are much sweeter and have a very distinctive taste. They are readily available at most large grocery stores.

½ cup key lime juice
1 teaspoon key lime zest
4 eggs
1 tablespoon unflavored gelatin
1 cup granulated sugar, divided
¼ teaspoon salt
¼ cup water
3 drops green food coloring
1 cup whipped cream
1 prebaked 9-inch pastry shell
1 tablespoon pistachio nuts
1 key lime

1. Juice key limes to yield ½ cup of juice. Grate the rind of a key lime to yield 1 teaspoon zest. Separate the egg yolks from the egg whites.
2. In a saucepan, combine the gelatin, ½ cup of the sugar, and the salt; mix well.
3. In a bowl, beat together the lime juice, egg yolks, and water until well blended; stir into the gelatin mixture. Place over medium heat and cook, stirring, just until the mixture comes to a boil.
4. Remove from the heat. Stir in the 1 teaspoon grated rind. Add the food coloring. Chill, stirring occasionally, until the mixture mounds slightly when dropped from a spoon.
5. Whip the cream until stiff.
6. In a large bowl, beat the egg whites until soft peaks form. Gradually add the remaining ½ cup sugar, beating until stiff peaks form. Fold the gelatin mixture into the egg whites. Fold in ½ of the whipped cream. Pile into the pastry shell and chill until firm.
7. Grate the pistachio nuts and thinly slice the remaining key lime. Use the remaining whipped cream, the nuts, and lime slices for garnish.

CHAPTER 13
LABOR DAY

SWEET CORN PUDDING

Serves 8

Serve to complement
Baby Back Ribs with
Sauerkraut
(page 186).

2 (10-ounce) cans whole-kernel
  corn with juice
3 (10-ounce) cans creamed corn

2 cups corn muffin mix
½ pound margarine, softened
1 cup sour cream

Mix together all the ingredients in a medium-sized mixing bowl. Pour
into a slow cooker. Cover and heat on low setting for 2 to 3 hours.

ITALIAN BEETS

Serves 8

Serve this to comple-
ment Grilled Beef and
Onion Kebabs
(page 185).

4 medium beets
3 cups water

1 cup Italian salad dressing
¼ cup balsamic vinegar

Remove the tops and stems from the beets. Peel the beets and slice
into ¼-inch-thick rounds. Mix together with the water, dressing, and
vinegar in a slow cooker. Add the beets to the mixture. Cover and
cook on low setting for 9 to 10 hours.

SPICY CHILLED SHRIMP

3 pounds fresh shrimp
3 fresh jalapeño chilies
3 garlic cloves
½ cup chopped fresh cilantro
3 fresh lemons
1 large red onion
¾ cup olive oil

¼ cup white wine vinegar
3 tablespoons fresh lemon juice
¼ teaspoon cayenne pepper
1 teaspoon salt
½ teaspoon ground white
   pepper

Serves 12

Keep the shrimp chilled and put the serving bowl on ice while serving.

1. Peel and devein the shrimp, leaving the tails on. Remove the stem and seeds from the jalapeño peppers and mince the peppers. Peel and mince the garlic cloves. Chop the cilantro. Slice the lemons. Peel and slice the onion.
2. Boil the shrimp in fresh water in a large pot until pink and opaque, about 3 minutes. When done, chill the shrimp in ice water. Drain and place in the refrigerator.
3. Whisk together the chilies, garlic, cilantro, olive oil, vinegar, lemon juice, cayenne pepper, salt, and white pepper until well blended. Pour over the shrimp. Toss to coat.
4. Layer the shrimp, lemon slices, and onion in a large glass bowl. Cover and refrigerate for 4 hours.

Flavor Your Oil

To infuse oil with flavor and complexity, stuff herbs, spices, and garlic cloves into a bottle of it, and steep for at least 3 days. Fine olive oil becomes a transcendent condiment when perfumed by rosemary, thyme, savory, garlic, peppercorns, dried mushrooms, or truffles.

FENNEL- AND GARLIC-CRUSTED PORK ROAST

Serves 6

Serve with Italian
Beets (page 182).

1 small head fennel
½ cup coarsely chopped onion
6 garlic cloves
¼ cup chopped assorted fresh
  herbs (thyme, sage, rosemary, parsley, oregano, etc.)

4½-pound pork rib roast, tied
2 tablespoons olive oil
2 teaspoons fennel seeds
1 teaspoon freshly ground
  black pepper
Salt to cover meat

1. Coarsely chop the fennel. Peel the onion and garlic, and chop roughly. Roughly chop the herbs.
2. In a blender or food processor, combine the fennel, onion, garlic, and olive oil; purée into a paste. Add the herbs, fennel seeds, and pepper; pulse to combine.
3. With a small, sharp knife, make shallow diamond cuts in the skin of the pork roast. Season the meat all over with salt, rubbing it in well. Rub the garlic-fennel paste over the roast to cover it with a layer about ¼-inch thick. Cover and refrigerate for up to 8 hours. Remove from the refrigerator and let stand at room temperature for about 20 minutes.
4. Preheat oven to 375°.
5. Transfer the roast to a roasting pan with a rack. Roast for about 1 hour and 15 minutes or until the internal temperature reads 150° on a meat thermometer. Remove the roast from the oven and allow to rest for at least 20 minutes. Slice the roast into thick chops.

What Is Fennel?

Fennel is a broad bulblike vegetable cultivated in the Mediterranean and the United States. In many cultures, it has long been believed to have medicinal qualities. Both the base and stems can be eaten raw as a flavorful addition to salads. Fennel can be cooked in a variety of ways, including braising, grilling, roasting, and sautéing. Fennel is often mislabeled as "sweet anise." The flavor of fennel is much lighter and sweeter than licorice-tasting anise.

GRILLED BEEF AND ONION KEBABS

1½ pounds boneless sirloin
    steak
12 pearl onions
1 tablespoon minced garlic
4 teaspoons finely ground
    whole coriander seeds
4 teaspoons finely ground
    anise seeds

1 tablespoon ground paprika
¼ teaspoon cayenne pepper
1 teaspoon salt, divided
½ teaspoon ground black
    pepper, divided
½ cup olive oil, divided

Serves 4

Serve with Strawberry
Sorbet (page 153)
for dessert.

1. Trim excess fat from the steak and cut the meat into 1-inch cubes. Peel and mince the garlic. Peel the pearl onions. Preheat grill to medium heat.

2. Place the ground coriander and anise seeds in a medium-sized bowl. Add the garlic, paprika, cayenne pepper, ½ of the salt, ½ of the black pepper, and ¼ cup of the olive oil; stir until combined. Add the sirloin cubes and stir to coat. Set aside.

3. In a medium-sized bowl, combine the onions, the rest of the salt and pepper, and the remaining olive oil. Toss to coat.

4. Divide the steaks cubes and onions among 8 skewers. Thread the meat and onions on the skewers, alternating a steak cube with an onion.

5. Grill the kebabs until well browned and medium-rare, 5 to 7 minutes.

Preparing Pearl Onions

When using pearl onions, cook them first in boiling water for 3 minutes. Plunge them into cold water. Remove them from the water and cut off the ends before easily removing the stems.

BABY BACK RIBS WITH SAUERKRAUT

Serves 4

Serve with Italian
Beets (page 182)
to add color.

3 pounds baby back ribs
1 (32-ounce) container sauerkraut
3 cups shredded red cabbage
4 garlic cloves
1 (14½-ounce) can stewed
   tomatoes

2 tablespoons, plus 1 teaspoon
   paprika
1 teaspoon salt
1 teaspoon ground black
   pepper

1. Trim the ribs of excess fat. Drain and rinse the sauerkraut. Shred the red cabbage. Peel and mince the garlic.
2. Preheat oven to 375°.
3. In a medium-sized bowl, combine the sauerkraut, cabbage, garlic, tomatoes, and 1 teaspoon of the paprika; stir well to mix. Spread this mixture into the bottom of a large, oiled baking dish.
4. Arrange the ribs on top of the sauerkraut mixture, curved side up. Season with salt and pepper and the rest of the paprika. Bake in the oven, covered, for about 1 to 1½ hours or until the meat is tender. Uncover the pan, turn the ribs over, and bake uncovered for another 20 minutes. To serve, cut the ribs apart from the bones and serve over the sauerkraut.

Sauerkraut

Always thought of as a German creation, sauerkraut was eaten by Chinese laborers on the Great Wall of China more than 2,000 years ago. Chinese sauerkraut was made from shredded cabbage fermented in rice wine.

BALSAMIC-MARINATED BEEF TENDERLOIN

6 (10-ounce) beef tenderloin
   filets, 1-inch thick
½ cup extra-virgin olive oil,
   plus extra for grilling
½ cup, plus 2 tablespoons balsamic vinegar

2 tablespoons finely chopped
   fresh rosemary
1 teaspoon salt
1 teaspoon coarsely ground
   black pepper

Serves 6

Serve with
Champagne-Marinated
Summer Berries (page
189) for dessert.

---

1. Place the meat in a shallow casserole dish. Mix together the ½ cup olive oil, the 2 tablespoons balsamic vinegar, and the rosemary in a small bowl. Pour over the filets, turning the meat to ensure the steaks are evenly coated. Let marinate in the refrigerator, covered, for 2 hours. Turn after 1 hour.
2. Preheat grill to medium-high. Coat a grill pan or sauté pan lightly with oil and preheat until very hot, almost smoking. Turn down heat to medium.
3. Remove the filets from the marinade. Sprinkle salt and pepper on both sides. Place filets in preheated pan and cook for 3 to 4 minutes on each side for medium-rare.
4. Place the remaining balsamic vinegar in a small saucepan and cook over medium heat until reduced to about half. Let the filets sit for a few minutes after they are done cooking, then drizzle with a little of the reduced balsamic vinegar. Serve immediately.

Olive Oil

The difference between extra-virgin olive oil and other types of olive oil is mostly in the taste. Extra-virgin olive oil is from the first pressing of the olives. It is fruitier and more intense in flavor than other olive oils. It is best in vinaigrettes, chilled soups, or drizzled over any dish. Other olive oils are usually better to cook with because they have a higher smoking point.

SPICY COLD PEARS

Serves 4

Serve cold on a hot day with Spicy Chilled Shrimp (page 183).

4 fresh pears
1 teaspoon orange zest
1 teaspoon lemon zest
2 cups cranberry juice

2 tablespoons granulated sugar
½ teaspoon ground cinnamon
½ teaspoon ground cloves

1. Peel, core, and halve the pears lengthwise. Grate the rind of an orange and a lemon to create the zest.
2. In a medium-sized saucepan, combine all the ingredients. Bring to a boil, cover, and reduce heat to low; simmer until tender, about 15 minutes. Serve the pears warm or chilled.

ORANGE CUPS WITH LEMON CREAM

Serves 6

This dish must be served the same day it is prepared or the filling will start to separate.

4 large oranges
Zest of 1 lemon

⅓ cup whipping cream
½ cup vanilla yogurt

1. With a sharp knife, cut each orange in half crosswise. Remove the flesh (with a grapefruit spoon) and chop finely, then place the flesh in a bowl. Set the peels aside.
2. Mix the lemon zest with the chopped orange flesh. In a separate bowl, whip the cream until it is stiff. With a rubber spatula, fold the yogurt into the whipped cream. Add the cream mixture to the chopped oranges and stir gently to mix.
3. Very thinly slice off the bottom of each orange shell so they sit level on a plate. Fill all the shells with the orange mixture, then place on a serving plate. Refrigerate the filled shells until ready to serve.

CHAMPAGNE-MARINATED SUMMER BERRIES

1 cup fresh strawberries
1 cup fresh raspberries
½ cup red currants
½ cup fresh blueberries
2 tablespoons granulated sugar

⅛ cup fresh lemon juice,
* divided*
1 cup chilled champagne
1 bunch fresh mint sprigs

Serves 4

Serve as dessert for
Grilled Beef and
Onion Kebabs
(page 185).

1. Hull the strawberries and cut in half. Wash all the fruit in cold water.
2. Mix together all the fruit in a glass bowl and sprinkle with the sugar and the lemon juice. Set aside for 10 minutes.
3. To serve, spoon the fruit into glass dishes. At the table, pour the chilled champagne over the fruit and decorate with mint sprigs.

CHEERY CHERRY CRISPY

⅓ cup butter or margarine,
* divided*
2 pounds fresh cherries
⅓ cup water

⅔ packed cup brown sugar
½ cup quick-cooking oats
½ cup all-purpose flour
1 teaspoon cinnamon

Serves 8

This dish works
equally well with
blueberries or
raspberries.

1. Lightly grease a slow cooker with ½ teaspoon of the butter. Remove the stems and pits from the cherries and put the cherries in the slow cooker. Add the water.
2. In a bowl, mix together the brown sugar, oats, flour, and cinnamon. Cut in the remaining butter by using a fork and slicing the butter into small pieces. Continue doing this until the mixture is crumbly.
3. Sprinkle the crumbs over the cherries. Cook, uncovered, on low setting for 3 to 4 hours.

PLANTER'S PUNCH

Serves 1

Nothing says relaxation more than a Caribbean-style, rum and fruit drink.

2 ounces light rum
1 ounce dark rum
1 ounce lime juice
1 ounce lemon juice
2 ounces orange juice

1 ounce pineapple juice
Ice
1 dash Triple Sec
Grenadine
Fresh fruit, for garnish

1. Combine rums and juices in a shaker half-filled with ice. Shake well.
2. Pour into a highball glass nearly filled with ice. Top with Triple Sec and grenadine. Garish with slices of fresh fruit.

CARIBBEAN SUNSET

Serves 1

So tomorrow you have to go to work. Tonight you can pretend you live the life of leisure!

4 ounces red wine (such as Merlot)
2 teaspoons Cointreau

Dash bitters
Club soda
Lemon twist

Combine ingredients in a large wineglass. Stir. Add a lemon twist.

CHAPTER 14
FALL FAVORITES

FRUITED PORK LOIN CASSEROLE

Serves 4

For a change of pace, use small red potatoes sliced in half. Add some green grapes and dried pears to the recipe, too.

4 small Yukon Gold potatoes
2 (2-ounce) pieces pork loin
1 teaspoon olive oil
1 tablespoon grated Parmesan cheese
½ teaspoon salt
¼ teaspoon freshly ground black pepper
1 Red Delicious apple
2 fresh apricots
1 small red onion
⅛ cup apple cider

1. Preheat oven to 350°. Spread olive oil on the bottom and sides of a medium-sized casserole dish.
2. Peel the potatoes and slice thinly. Trim the pork loins and pound flat. Rub the olive oil over the entire surface of the loins. Sprinkle each side of the pork loins with the Parmesan cheese, salt, and pepper. Peel, core, and thinly slice the apple. Cut the apricots in half and remove the seeds. Peel the onion and chop into ⅛-inch pieces.
3. Layer ½ the potato slices across the bottom of the dish. Top with the first piece of flattened pork loin. Arrange the apple slices over the top of the loin and place the apricot halves on top of the apple. Sprinkle the red onion over the apricots and apples. Add the second flattened pork loin and layer the remaining potatoes atop the loin. Drizzle the apple cider over the top of the casserole.
4. Cover the casserole and bake for 45 to 60 minutes or until the potatoes are tender. Remove the casserole and keep it covered for 10 minutes.

Casseroles

Food placed in a deep casserole dish will take more time to cook than food placed in a shallow casserole dish. Try to match the size of the dish to the quantity of the food being placed in it.

ROASTED BUTTERNUT SQUASH PASTA

1 butternut squash
1 garlic clove
1 medium-sized red onion
4 teaspoons olive oil
2 teaspoons red wine vinegar

¼ teaspoon dried oregano
2 cups cooked linguine
½ teaspoon freshly ground
  black pepper

> **Serves 4**
>
> For added flavor, use roasted instead of raw garlic in this recipe. Roasting the garlic causes it to caramelize, adding a natural sweetness.

1. Preheat oven to 400°. Cut the squash in half and scoop out the seeds. Remove the skin from the garlic and mince finely. Remove the skin from the onion and chop into ¼-inch pieces.
2. Using nonstick spray, coat 1 side of each of 2 pieces of heavy-duty foil large enough to wrap the squash halves. Wrap the squash in the foil and place on a baking sheet. Bake for 1 hour or until tender.
3. Scoop out the baked squash flesh and discard the rind. Roughly chop the squash. Add the olive oil, garlic, and onion to a nonstick skillet and sauté until the onion is transparent.
4. Remove pan from heat and stir in the vinegar and oregano. Add the squash and stir to coat it in the onion mixture. Add the pasta and toss to mix. Season with freshly ground black pepper.

Stir Pasta Early

To prevent pasta from clumping and cooking unevenly, wait until water is boiling rapidly before adding dried pasta, and stir the pasta immediately to separate the pieces or strands. Pasta should boil vigorously in a large amount of water, uncovered.

WARM POTATO SALAD WITH BALSAMIC VINEGAR AND ONIONS

2 medium-sized yellow onions
1 pound small white "boiling" potatoes
2 tablespoons extra-virgin olive oil
3 sprigs fresh thyme leaves

½ teaspoon granulated sugar
1 tablespoon balsamic vinegar
½ teaspoon salt
¼ teaspoon pepper
Pinch of chopped fresh Italian parsley

1. Remove the skin from the onions and slice thinly. Halve the potatoes and boil in salted water until very tender. Drain water and discard.
2. Heat the olive oil on medium in a medium-sized skillet for 1 minute. Add the onions, thyme, and sugar. Cook slowly, stirring regularly with a wooden spoon until the onions are very soft and browned to the color of caramel, about 10 minutes.
3. Stir in the balsamic vinegar. Remove from heat. Toss gently with the warm cooked potatoes and season with salt and pepper. Allow to rest 10 minutes before serving, garnished with the chopped parsley.

Testing Potatoes for Doneness

To check a potato for doneness, poke the tip of a knife into the thickest part, then lift the knife up, handle first. If the potato falls off, it's done. If it hangs on, it needs more cooking time.

CARROT TIMBALES

2 cups fresh carrots
¼ cup shallots
½ cup chopped fresh tarragon
1 tablespoon unsalted butter,
  plus extra for buttering
2 tablespoons port wine
½ teaspoon salt

⅛ teaspoon freshly grated
  nutmeg
¼ teaspoon black pepper
1 cup cream
3 large eggs
¼ cup grated Parmesan cheese

Serves 4
Other vegetables may be substituted for carrots in this timbales recipe. Try cauliflower, broccoli, zucchini, or fresh sweet corn.

1. Peel and slice the carrots. Cook in boiling water until they can be easily cut with a butter knife but are not mushy. Drain off water and discard. Chop roughly in a food processor. Remove the peels from the shallots and chop finely. Chop the tarragon.

2. Preheat oven to 375°. Butter 4 6-ounce ramekins or custard cups.

3. In a small skillet over medium heat, melt the 1 tablespoon butter. Add the carrots and cook about 3 minutes. Add the shallots to the carrots, along with the Port, salt, nutmeg, and pepper. In a small saucepan, heat the cream until steaming but not boiling. Whisk the eggs into the vegetable mixture, then gradually whisk in the cream.

4. Divide the mixture into the prepared cups and line them up in a shallow casserole or roasting pan. Add enough hot tap water to come ⅔ of the way up the sides of the custard cups. Cover the pan with foil and bake in the center of the oven for 25 to 30 minutes or until almost set.

5. Open the oven door. Loosen but do not remove the foil and bake for 10 minutes more. Let rest at room temperature for 10 minutes before loosening with a knife, inverting, and unmolding. Garnish with the chopped tarragon and grated cheese.

WILD RICE WITH APPLES AND ALMONDS

Serves 8

This works equally well as a cold salad or a rice dish to accompany a main coarse. It also can be stuffed into zucchini boats.

½ cup uncooked wild rice
1 large white onion
1 Rome or Golden Delicious
   apple
½ cup almond slivers
¼ cup chopped parsley

1 tablespoon vegetable oil
¼ cup golden raisins
½ teaspoon salt
¼ teaspoon black pepper
1 tablespoon olive oil

1. Boil the rice in 2½ quarts salted water until tender, about 40 minutes. Drain, saving the cooking liquid. Set aside.
2. Remove the skin from the onion and chop into ¼-inch pieces. Peel the apple, remove the core, and dice into ¼-inch cubes. Toast the almond slivers in a small, dry skillet on medium heat until they are visibly shiny. Roughly chop the parsley.
3. Heat the oil in a large skillet over medium heat for 1 minute. Add the onions and cook until softened, about 5 minutes. Add the apples, raisins, and a splash of the rice cooking liquid. Cook for 5 more minutes until the apples are translucent.
4. Combine the cooked rice, the apple mixture, almonds, salt, and pepper. Stir in olive oil. Serve garnished with the parsley.

Preventing Boil-Over
A lump of butter or a few teaspoons of cooking oil added to water when boiling rice, noodles, macaroni, or spaghetti will prevent the liquid from boiling over.

VENISON WITH DRIED CRANBERRY VINEGAR SAUCE

½-pound venison roast
1 garlic clove
1 small red onion
2 tablespoons dried cranberries
1 tablespoon granulated sugar
3 tablespoons water
2 tablespoons white wine
   vinegar

2 teaspoons olive oil
2 tablespoons dry red wine
½ cup chicken broth
½ teaspoon cracked black
   pepper
1 teaspoon all-purpose flour
1 tablespoon water
2 teaspoons butter

Serves 4

This is excellent served with wild rice and roasted butternut squash.

---

1. Slice the meat thinly. Crush the garlic with the side of a large knife. Remove the skin from the red onion and cut into eighths.

2. Add the cranberries, sugar, water, and vinegar to a saucepan and bring to a boil. Reduce heat to a simmer for 5 minutes. Remove from heat and transfer to a food processor or blender. Process until the cranberries are chopped but not puréed. Set aside.

3. Pour the olive oil into nonstick skillet heated to medium-high. Add the garlic and onion, and sauté for 30 seconds. Deglaze the plan with the red wine, and cook, stirring occasionally, until the wine is reduced by half. Add the cranberry mixture and the chicken broth, and bring to a boil.

4. Reduce heat to medium-low, season with the pepper, and add the venison; simmer for 10 minutes, or until the meat is cooked. Remove the meat and set aside.

5. Whisk together the flour and water to form a smooth paste. Whisk the slurry into the sauce and simmer until the sauce thickens. Remove from the heat, add the butter, and whisk to incorporate the butter into the sauce. Drizzle the sauce over the meat before serving.

Slicing Meat
To slice meat thinly, freeze it first and let it thaw slightly. The meat will slice as easily as cheese when it is semi-thawed.

NEW ENGLAND BOILED DINNER

Serves 6

Serve with Apple Crisp (page 200) for dessert on a blustery fall day.

3-pound corned beef brisket
6 medium carrots
3 medium potatoes
3 medium parsnips
6 small yellow onions
½ medium head cabbage
1½ teaspoons whole black
  peppercorns

2 bay leaves
1½ cups milk
4 teaspoons cornstarch
2 tablespoons horseradish mustard

1. Trim excess fat from the meat. Peel the carrots and cut into chunks. Peel the potatoes and cut into quarters. Peel the parsnips and cut into chunks. Peel the onions and cut in half. Shred the cabbage.
2. Place the meat in a Dutch oven. Add the juices and spices from the package included with meat. Add enough water to cover the meat. Add the peppercorns and bay leaves. Bring to a boil. Reduce heat and simmer, covered, for 2 hours.
3. Add the carrots, potatoes, parsnips, and onions to the Dutch oven. Return to boiling. Reduce heat and simmer, covered, for 10 minutes. Add the cabbage and cook for 20 minutes or until the vegetables are tender.
4. Remove the meat and vegetables from the liquid. Discard the liquid and bay leaves. Slice the meat across the grain.
5. Make the mustard sauce by stirring together the milk and cornstarch in a small saucepan. Cook and stir until thickened and bubbly. Cook and stir for 2 minutes more. Stir in the mustard. Heat through.
6. Put the meat and vegetables on a platter and drizzle with the mustard sauce.

CHOCOLATE CHIP COOKIES

1 cup butter
¾ cup granulated sugar
*¾ packed cup light brown
  sugar*
1 teaspoon vanilla extract
2 large eggs

2½ cups all-purpose flour
1 teaspoon baking soda
1 teaspoon salt
*2 cups semisweet chocolate
  chips*

Makes 24

They might not be elegant, but they certainly are a comfort food. Who can imagine a family celebration that doesn't incorporate this all-time favorite?

1. Preheat oven to 375°. Soften the butter by leaving at room temperature for 1 to 2 hours or by microwaving for 10 seconds on high.
2. In a large mixing bowl, use a wooden spoon to cream together the butter, granulated sugar, brown sugar, and vanilla. Add the eggs 1 at a time, mixing until incorporated before adding the next egg.
3. In a separate mixing bowl, whisk together the flour, baking soda, and salt.
4. Add the flour mixture to the egg mixture in 3 additions, mixing just enough to incorporate after each addition. Stir in the chocolate chips.
5. Drop the dough in tablespoon-sized drops onto ungreased baking sheets. Bake until golden, about 10 minutes. Cool the pans for a few minutes before transferring the cookies to a wire rack to cool completely.

Warm Chocolate

Heat releases the flavor of chocolate and nutmeats. Try reheating chocolate chip cookies in your microwave or oven for a few seconds just before serving.

APPLE CRISP

4 medium-sized tart cooking apples such as Granny Smith
¾ packed cup light brown sugar
½ cup all-purpose flour
¾ teaspoon ground nutmeg
¾ teaspoon ground cinnamon
½ cup quick-cooking rolled oats
¾ cup margarine or butter

1. Preheat oven to 375°. Grease an 8-inch square baking pan.
2. Peel, core, and slice the apples thinly. Arrange the apples in the prepared pan.
3. In a medium-sized bowl, combine the sugar, flour, nutmeg, cinnamon, and oats; stir well. Add the butter and cut in with a pastry blender or 2 knives until crumbly. Sprinkle over the apples.
4. Bake for about 30 minutes or until the topping is golden brown and the apples are tender. Let cool slightly on a rack.

CARROT CAKE

3 cups grated carrots
½ cup chopped walnuts
3 cups all-purpose flour
2 teaspoons baking powder
2 teaspoons salt
1 teaspoon baking soda
2 teaspoons ground cinnamon
1½ cups vegetable oil
2 cups granulated sugar
2 eggs
1 cup raisins

1. Preheat oven to 350°. Peel, then grate the carrots. Chop the walnuts.
2. Sift together the flour, baking powder, salt, baking soda, and cinnamon in a medium-sized bowl. In a large bowl, mix together the carrots, oil, and sugar. Add the eggs 1 at a time, beating well after each addition.
3. Gradually beat the flour mixture into the carrot mixture, mixing well. Fold in the nuts and raisins. Pour into an ungreased 9-inch tube pan.
4. Bake for 1 hour or until a knife inserted into the center of the cake comes out clean. Let cool on a rack.

FRUITY CITRUS SPICE TEA

3-inch cinnamon stick

2 tablespoons fresh orange peel

6 whole cloves

¼ cup fresh cranberries

2 cups water

2 (1-serving) bags black tea

1 cup fresh orange juice

1 tablespoon brown sugar

Makes 4 servings

Create your own variations on this drink by adding raisins, apple chunks, or even fresh pineapple pieces.

1. Break the cinnamon stick into ¼-inch pieces. Cut the orange peel into ½-inch pieces.
2. In a medium-sized saucepan, combine the cinnamon stick, orange peel, cranberries, cloves, and water. Bring to a boil.
3. Remove from heat and add the tea bags. Let stand for 5 minutes.
4. Remove the tea bags. Stir in the orange juice and brown sugar. Heat through but do not boil. Pour the mixture through a strainer before serving.

Creating a Cheese Board

Cheese boards are an easy and elegant entertaining style. A cheese board should include a mix of goat, cow, and sheep's milk cheese. Use a variety of textures including soft cheeses such as Brie or Camembert; smoked cheeses such as mozzarella, Gouda, or provolone; hard cheeses such as manchego; and blue cheeses such as Roquefort or Gorgonzola.

CIDER PUNCH

2 quarts hard cider
6 ounces Drambuie
6 ounces dry sherry
¼ cup granulated sugar

2 ounces lemon juice
2 cups sparkling water
1 block of ice
4 apples

1. Add the liquid ingredients to a punch bowl with the block of ice.
2. Slice the apples and add to the punch bowl right before guests arrive.

NONALCOHOLIC MULLED CIDER PUNCH

2 gallons apple cider
2 lemons
2 oranges
5 cinnamon sticks

1 tablespoon cinnamon
1 tablespoon nutmeg
6 whole cloves

Combine all the ingredients in a large pot. Heat just to boiling. Reduce heat and serve warm.

Chapter 15
KIDS' CELEBRATIONS

SLOPPY JOES

Serves 12	

Add potato chips and carrot sticks to the plate and you have a true all-American lunch that is perfect for chilly outings or teen get-togethers.

1 medium-sized yellow onion
2 celery ribs
2 pounds extra-lean hamburger
½ cup canned tomato paste
¼ cup white vinegar
3 teaspoons Worcestershire
   sauce

2 tablespoons brown sugar
1 teaspoon garlic salt
½ teaspoon ground black
   pepper

1. Peel the onion and chop into ¼-inch pieces. Chop the celery into ¼-inch pieces.
2. Put the onion, celery, and hamburger in a medium-sized skillet on medium-high heat. Cook until the hamburger is brown and no pink remains. Drain off the grease.
3. Combine all the ingredients in a slow cooker. Cover and cook on low setting for 2 to 3 hours.

Mini-Bakery

Use a slow cooker as a mini-bakery for young children. Let them mix up a batch of chocolate chip cookies and watch through the glass lid as 1 or 2 cookies at a time bake right before their eyes.

PIZZA MEATBALLS

For the meatballs:
½ pound Swiss cheese
1 medium-sized yellow onion
½ green bell pepper
2 pounds extra-lean hamburger
2¾ cups bread crumbs
1 teaspoon salt
¼ teaspoon dried basil
¼ teaspoon ground black pepper
1 cup canned condensed vegetable soup
¼ cup skim milk

For the sauce:
1 garlic clove
1 medium-sized yellow onion
6 large ripe tomatoes
1 cup beef broth
½ cup (4 ounces) tomato paste
1 teaspoon salt
1 teaspoon dried oregano

> **Serves 8**
>
> Make these ahead of time and freeze them. They can be thawed in the microwave for those last-minute lunch demands or as an after-school snack.

1. To make the meatballs, cut the cheese into ¼-inch cubes. Peel and chop the onion into ¼-inch pieces. Remove the stem and seeds from the green pepper and chop the pepper into ¼-inch pieces.
2. Mix all the meatball ingredients together well and form into firm balls no larger than 2 inches in diameter. Lay the meatballs in the bottom of a slow cooker.
3. To make the sauce, peel the garlic and slice thinly with a paring knife. Peel and chop the onions into ½-inch pieces. Peel the tomatoes with a sharp paring knife, gently lifting the skin off; quarter the tomatoes, and mix in a blender on low speed for 2 minutes. Combine all the sauce ingredients and pour over the meatballs.
4. Cover and cook on low setting for 2 hours.

Replacing Fresh Tomatoes
You can substitute a 28-ounce can of peeled tomatoes for 3 fresh tomatoes in any slow-cooked recipe. Be sure to include the juice from the can when adding it to the recipe.

EASY CHILI

1 large yellow onion
2 celery ribs
1 pound lean ground beef
1½ teaspoons granulated sugar
½ teaspoon salt
¾ teaspoon garlic powder
1½ tablespoons chili powder

¾ teaspoon oregano leaves
¼ teaspoon pepper
1 (15-ounce) can tomato sauce
1 (6-ounce) can tomato paste
2½ cups water
1 (15½-ounce) can kidney
  beans

1. Peel and chop the onion into ¼-inch pieces. Chop the celery into ¼-inch pieces.
2. In a large, heavy skillet, cook the beef and onions until the beef is browned. Drain off the juices.
3. Add all the remaining ingredients *except* the kidney beans; mix well. Bring the mixture to a boil. Reduce heat and simmer, covered, for 30 minutes.
4. Drain the kidney beans and add them to the skillet; simmer, uncovered, for 10 minutes to heat the beans. Add more water if needed.

Cooking Beans

Any bean recipe gives you 2 options. Cook it longer and let the beans dissolve for a creamy texture. Serve it earlier in the cooking process, as soon as the beans are completely soft, for more distinct flavors in every bite.

MADHOUSE SPAGHETTI

2 medium-sized yellow onions
12 Spanish olives with
*   pimientos*
1 pound spaghetti
1 teaspoon salt

2 pounds lean ground beef
1 (28-ounce) can tomatoes
1 (6-ounce) can tomato paste
¼ cup grated Parmesan cheese

Serves 8

Serve with a lettuce salad and Strawberries in Butterscotch Sauce (page 211) for dessert.

---

1. Peel the onions and chop into ¼-inch pieces. Slice the olives. Boil the spaghetti noodles until al dente.
2. Sprinkle a Dutch oven with the salt. Add the beef and onions, and cook until the beef is browned. Pour off the fat.
3. Remove from heat and add the tomatoes and their liquid, chopping the tomatoes as you add them. Add the tomato paste and sliced olives. Return the mixture to the stovetop. Bring to a boil and reduce to a simmer. Simmer for 45 to 60 minutes, stirring occasionally.
4. Add the cooked spaghetti and mix well. Place in a large serving bowl. Sprinkle with the Parmesan cheese.

Buying Pasta
There are many types of exotic pastas on the market today, but once the sauce is added, you frequently can't taste the difference. Unless you are making plain buttered noodles, regular old pasta is the economical choice.

PARTY SNACK MIX

Serves 12

This nutritious, low-fat treat keeps for weeks in airtight containers, making it the ideal after-school snack.

½ teaspoon vegetable oil

4 tablespoons butter or margarine

1 teaspoon garlic salt

½ teaspoon onion salt

4 teaspoons Worcestershire sauce

3 cups Corn Chex cereal

3 cups Wheat Chex cereal

3 cups Rice Chex cereal

1 cup shelled, skinless peanuts

2 cups mini pretzel sticks

½ cup grated Parmesan cheese

1. Preheat oven to 250°. Put the vegetable oil on a paper towel and spread the oil over the bottom and sides of a large baking pan.
2. Combine the butter, garlic salt, onion salt, and Worcestershire sauce in the pan and place it in the oven until the butter is melted, about 5 minutes.
3. In the meantime, in a large bowl, combine the Corn Chex, Wheat Chex, Rice Chex, peanuts, and pretzel sticks. Add to the baking pan and stir until the mix is covered with the butter mixture.
4. Cook for 45 minutes, stirring after every 15 minutes. Spread the mixture on paper towels and lightly sprinkle with the Parmesan cheese.

No Breakfast?

If you have a child who doesn't like to eat breakfast, serve a snack mix such as this with a slice of cheese. Your child will get all the nutrition of a good breakfast and not even know it!

RED DEVIL CHOCOLATE CAKE

2 packed cups brown sugar, divided
1 cup milk, divided
3 squares (3 ounces) unsweetened chocolate
½ cup vegetable shortening
1 teaspoon vanilla
1 teaspoon red food coloring
3 eggs
2 cups sifted all-purpose flour
2 teaspoons baking soda
½ teaspoon salt

Serves 8

Serve with Minty Hot Chocolate (page 212).

1. Preheat oven to 350°. Line the bottom of 2 8-inch cake pans with wax paper and grease the sides.
2. In a small saucepan, combine 1 cup of the brown sugar, ½ cup of the milk, and the chocolate over very low heat until the chocolate melts. Remove from heat and let cool.
3. In a large bowl, stir the shortening to soften. Gradually add the remaining 1 cup brown sugar and cream until light and fluffy. Add the vanilla and red food coloring, mixing well. Beat in the eggs 1 at a time, beating well after each addition. Blend in the chocolate mixture.
4. In another bowl, sift together the flour, baking soda, and salt. Add the flour mixture to the creamed mixture alternately with the remaining ½ cup milk, beginning and ending with the flour mixture. Beat well after each addition. Pour into the prepared pans.
5. Bake for about 25 minutes, or until a knife inserted into the center of the cakes comes out clean. Cool on racks.

Try Different Flavors

The next time a recipe says vanilla extract, reach for a bottle of different flavored extract instead. In the grocery store, you will see almond extract as well as lemon, orange, mint, and even coconut.

OOEY, GOOEY S'MORES

Makes 8

For a different yet still scrumptious treat, use half of a chocolate bar with almonds or half of a Mounds bar instead of the half all-chocolate candy.

16 graham cracker squares
4 Hershey's chocolate bars
(without almonds)

4 large marshmallows

1. Preheat oven to 450°.
2. Place 8 graham cracker squares on a baking sheet. Top each with ½ of a chocolate bar. Top each with 1 marshmallow.
3. Cook for 10 minutes or until the chocolate is beginning to melt. Remove and add 1 graham cracker square to the top of each "sandwich." Press down until the chocolate and marshmallow begin to ooze out of the sandwich.

OLD-FASHIONED BAKED APPLES

Serves 4

Add raisins or dried cranberries to the filling ingredients for another tasty treat.

4 baking apples (Romes or
Cortlands are best)
8 whole cloves

2 ounces butter
⅓ cup light brown sugar
½ teaspoon ground cinnamon

1. Preheat oven to 350°.
2. Wash and dry the apples thoroughly. Using a small knife, cut a divot from the top of the apples, leaving the stem intact. This "cover" will be replaced when baking. Scoop out the seeds and core from the apples with a melonballer or small spoon. Drop 2 cloves into each apple.
3. Knead together the butter, brown sugar, and cinnamon. Divide equally into the apples, leaving enough space to replace the tops.
4. Place the apples in a 9" × 9" baking dish with ½ cup water in the bottom. Bake for 1 hour. Sprinkle with cinnamon or confectioners' sugar before serving.

STRAWBERRIES IN BUTTERSCOTCH SAUCE

¼ pound fresh strawberries
1 cup brown sugar
1 cup light corn syrup

½ cup heavy cream
4 drops vanilla extract

1. Wash and hull the strawberries.
2. Combine the sugar and corn syrup in a saucepan. Stir over low heat until the sugar dissolves. Cook for 5 minutes.
3. Remove from heat. Stir in the cream and vanilla. Beat for about 2 minutes, until the sauce is smooth. Pour the warm sauce over the strawberries.

Serves 4

This is the perfect dessert for any kids' party, whether you're serving Sloppy Joes (page 204) or Madhouse Spaghetti (page 207).

SPARKLING CITRUS PUNCH

1 (6-ounce) can tangerine juice concentrate
1 (6-ounce) can frozen grapefruit juice concentrate
1 pint fresh strawberries

2 cups cold water
1 liter sparkling water
Ice
Fresh mint sprigs

1. Thaw the tangerine and grapefruit juice concentrates. Wash and hull the strawberries, and cut them in half.
2. Mix together the tangerine juice, grapefruit juice, cold water, and sparkling water. Pour into a punch bowl and stir to mix. Add ice.
3. Add the strawberries and a few sprigs of mint.

Serves 12

Any fruit juices can be used to make this a special treat. Add blueberries or blackberries instead of strawberries when they are in season.

MINTY HOT CHOCOLATE

Serves 12

Use a soup ladle to let kids serve themselves right from the slow cooker.

12 cups whole milk
1 cup chocolate syrup

1 teaspoon peppermint extract

Combine all the ingredients in a slow cooker. Cook, uncovered, on high setting for 30 minutes, stirring every 5 minutes until the chocolate syrup is dissolved.

Little Slow Cookers

Pint-sized slow cookers are available at many household department stores. These are ideal for hot appetizers because they can keep them warm for an entire evening. If the appetizer starts to dry out, simply add a little water and stir.

CHAPTER 16
JEWISH HOLIDAYS

CARAWAY-RUBBED CHICKEN

Serves 4

Serve this Hanukkah meal with fresh green vegetables and yams.

2 tablespoons caraway seeds
¼ teaspoon whole black peppercorns
1 teaspoon finely shredded lemon peel

½ teaspoon salt
3–4 pound broiler-fryer chicken
2 tablespoons lemon juice
1 fresh lemon

1. Preheat oven to 375°.
2. With a mortar and pestle, slightly crush the caraway seeds and whole black pepper. Shred the lemon peel. Stir in the lemon peel and salt.
3. Rub the caraway mixture over the entire bird and under the skin of the breast.
4. Place the chicken, breast-side up, on a rack in a shallow pan. Roast, uncovered, for 1 to 2 hours or until the meat is no longer pink. Remove from oven, cover, and let stand for 10 minutes.
5. Drizzle the lemon juice over the chicken before carving. Cut the lemon into slices. Serve the chicken with the lemon slices.

Safe Chicken Handling

To prevent the transmission of salmonella and other bacteria from raw chicken, always wash your hands before and after handling raw chicken. Thoroughly wash all cutting boards and utensils you have used to prepare raw chicken. Also make sure chicken is cooked to at least 170°. If the chicken smells funny, throw it out.

YAM LATKES WITH
MUSTARD SEEDS AND CURRY

*2 packed cups coarsely grated,
    peeled yams*
*½ cup chopped red bell
    pepper*
*1 (15-ounce) can chickpeas
    (garbanzo beans)*
¼ cup chopped cilantro

3 tablespoons cornstarch
1 egg
2 teaspoons curry powder
1 teaspoon salt
2 teaspoons mustard seeds
8 tablespoons vegetable oil

Makes 12

This Hanukkah dish can
be served as a side
dish or entrée. Serve
with chutney or jam.

1. Peel and grate the yams. Chop the bell pepper into ¼-inch pieces.
   Drain the chickpeas. Chop the cilantro.
2. Place a baking sheet in the oven. Preheat oven to 325°.
3. Combine the yams and bell pepper in large bowl. Add the cornstarch.
   Toss to coat.
4. In a food processor, purée the chickpeas to coarse paste. Add the
   egg, curry powder, and salt; blend well. Transfer the mixture to a
   small bowl. Mix in the cilantro and mustard seeds. Stir the chickpea
   mixture into the yam mixture.
5. Heat 6 tablespoons oil in large skillet on medium. Working in batches,
   drop 1 heaping tablespoon batter per pancake into the hot oil. Using
   the back of a spoon, spread to 3-inch rounds. Cook until brown,
   about 3 minutes per side. Transfer to the baking sheet in the oven to
   keep warm before serving.

Toasting Seeds

*Toast seeds, from cumin to pumpkin, in a dry pan until they give
off a slight smoke and brown slightly, about 2 minutes over medium
heat. You can then pulverize them in a coffee grinder, if the recipe
calls for it.*

BRAISED LAMB IN POMEGRANATE SAUCE

Serves 8

This Hanukkah meal is wonderful served with Yam Latkes with Mustard Seeds and Curry (page 215).

7-pound lamb shoulder
2 medium-sized yellow onions
10 garlic cloves
¼ cup olive oil
1 tablespoon salt
½ tablespoon ground black
    pepper
2 cups, plus 1½ tablespoons
    all-purpose flour
2 cups chicken stock
1 cup dry red wine

1 cup unsweetened pome-
    granate juice
½ cup tomato paste
2 firmly packed tablespoons
    light brown sugar
1 tablespoon dried oregano
1 teaspoon ground cinnamon
¾ teaspoon ground allspice
1½ tablespoons margarine
1 bunch fresh parsley

1. Debone the lamb shoulder but reserve the bones. Trim excess fat from the meat. Roll the meat and tie it with butcher's twine. Peel the onions and chop into ¼-inch pieces. Peel the garlic and smash with the side of a large knife.

2. Position a rack in the lowest third of oven and preheat to 325°.

3. Heat the oil in heavy, large pot or Dutch oven over high heat. Add all the lamb bones and cook until brown, turning often, about 15 minutes.

4. Transfer the bones to a plate. Season the lamb meat with some of the salt and pepper, and dredge thoroughly in the 2 cups flour. Add to the pot and cook until brown on all sides, about 10 minutes. Transfer the lamb to the plate with the bones.

5. Add the onions and garlic to the pot and cook until the onions are just golden, about 5 minutes. Return the lamb meat to the pot. Arrange the bones around the lamb. Stir in the stock, red wine, pomegranate juice, tomato paste, brown sugar, oregano, cinnamon, and allspice. Bring to a boil. Baste the lamb with the stock mixture.

6. Cover and transfer to the oven. Bake, turning once, until the lamb is tender when pierced with long, sharp knife, about 2½ hours. Remove from oven and let cool. Cover and chill overnight.

7. Preheat oven to 325°.

8. Remove the fat from surface of the lamb and cooking liquid. Transfer the lamb to a platter. Remove the string from the lamb. Cut the meat into ½-inch-thick slices. Arrange in a shallow baking dish.

9. Bring the pan juices to a boil. Remove and discard the bones. Strain the pan juices, pressing hard on the solids to extract as much liquid as possible. Melt the margarine in the same pot over medium heat. Add the 1½ tablespoons flour and stir until the mixture begins to brown, about 2 minutes.

10. Whisk in the pan juices and boil until the sauce is reduced to 2 cups, about 15 minutes. Season with salt and pepper. Pour over the lamb. Cover with foil and bake until the lamb is heated through, about 25 minutes.

11. Arrange the lamb on a platter. Spoon the sauce over the top. Garnish with parsley.

If You Substitute Lamb or Veal . . .

Since lamb and veal are inherently tender meats, they need less cooking time than their grown-up counterparts. Decrease the time by half and add the meat later in the cooking cycle.

HUNGARIAN CABBAGE AND NOODLES

Serves 8

This unusual Purim recipe comes from Eastern Europe.

1 large cabbage
1 medium-sized yellow onion
1 teaspoon salt
3 tablespoons vegetable oil
1 tablespoon granulated sugar
1 teaspoon freshly ground
  black pepper
12 ounces egg noodles
1 tablespoon poppy seeds

1. Core the cabbage and thinly slice until you have about 8 cups. Peel the onion and chop into ¼-inch pieces.
2. Sprinkle the cabbage with the salt. Let stand for 30 minutes, then squeeze dry. Lay on paper towels to soak up excess moisture.
3. Heat the oil in a large skillet. Add the sugar and heat until the sugar browns. Add the onions and cook until they start to wilt. Stir in the cabbage. Sauté, stirring frequently, until the cabbage is tender, about 20 minutes. Season with the pepper. Transfer the cabbage and juices to a large bowl and keep warm.
4. Cook the noodles in boiling salted water until tender. Drain. Quickly toss the noodles with the cabbage mixture and the poppy seeds. Serve immediately.

Spicy Substitutions
Anytime a recipe calls for a basic spice, try substituting something more fun. In place of pepper flakes, for example, substitute toasted cumin seeds, fennel seeds, anise, or chopped fresh ginger.

PURIM RAVIOLI

For the pasta:
4 eggs
2½ cups all-purpose flour
½ teaspoon salt

For the filling:
2 pounds spinach
1 small yellow onion
1 small carrot

½ cooked chicken breast
3 tablespoons, plus 1 teaspoon
    and 1 pinch salt
2 tablespoons olive oil
1 teaspoon freshly ground
    black pepper
1 tablespoon unbleached flour
6 quarts water
3 cups prepared marinara sauce

Makes 8 dozen

Spinach ravioli is a traditional Purim treat.

1. Make the pasta by combining the eggs, flour, and salt; blend well.

2. Remove the stems from the spinach and rinse the leaves in cold water. Peel the onion and cut into quarters. Peel the carrot and chop coarsely. Cube the chicken breast.

3. Place the spinach in a pot with no water other than that retained from washing. Add a pinch of salt and cook, covered, for 5 minutes. Drain in a colander.

4. In a large skillet, combine the spinach, onion, carrot, chicken, and oil. Add 1 teaspoon of the salt and ⅛ teaspoon of the pepper; cook over moderate heat for 4 to 5 minutes or until most of the liquid has evaporated. Add the flour and stir for 1 minute. Remove from heat. Cool for 5 or 6 minutes, then very finely chop the mixture.

5. Roll half the pasta dough into a paper-thin sheet and place over a floured board. With a feather brush dipped in cold water, lightly brush the top to maintain moisture. Place mounds of the spinach mixture on the dough in straight lines about 2 inches apart.

6. Roll out the other half of the dough into a paper-thin sheet and place loosely over the sheet with the filling. With an Italian pastry wheel, press along the furrows, cutting and sealing at the same time.

7. Bring the water to a boil. Add the ravioli and the 3 tablespoons salt. Stir until boiling resumes. Cook for 4 to 5 minutes, uncovered. Drain and serve with the marinara sauce.

SALMON HASH

¾ pound fresh salmon fillet
½ teaspoon salt
½ teaspoon ground black pepper
2–3 medium-sized russet potatoes
¾ cup sliced yellow bell pepper
¾ cup sliced red bell pepper
1 large yellow onion
¾ cup sliced leeks (white part only)

1 tablespoon chopped Italian flat-leaf parsley
2 tablespoons fresh-squeezed lemon juice
2 cups cold water
6 tablespoons clarified butter
½ teaspoon chopped thyme
½ teaspoon minced savory
½ teaspoon minced tarragon
2 tablespoons unsalted butter

1. Remove the skin from the salmon fillet and cut the fish into 12 pieces. Season with salt and pepper, and refrigerate. Peel and shred the potatoes. Thinly slice the peppers, onion, and leek. Chop the parsley.

2. Combine the lemon juice and cold water in a large bowl. Place the potatoes in the lemon water. Just before frying, drain and squeeze out excess liquid from the potatoes.

3. In a large skillet, heat the clarified butter and spread the potatoes loosely and evenly on the bottom of the pan. Brown the potatoes and drain on paper towels. Set aside and keep warm.

4. Pour out all but 1 tablespoon of the butter from the pan. Add the bell peppers, onion, and leek. Sauté for 3 to 4 minutes or until the vegetables are softened. Stir in the herbs. Stir in the potatoes. Keep warm.

5. Melt the unsalted butter in a skillet over high heat and sauté the salmon until golden brown, about 2 minutes. Do not allow the pieces of salmon to touch or they will steam and not sear. Turn the salmon over and add the potato mixture to the skillet. Cook for an additional 1 to 2 minutes.

QUICHE IN A LOAF

½ cup minced scallions

½ cup minced green olives

½ cup minced sun-dried tomatoes

2 tablespoons minced flat-leaf
Italian parsley

2 teaspoons minced fresh dill

2 cups shredded white
Cheddar cheese

1 cup shredded Swiss cheese

¼ cup grated Parmesan cheese,
plus extra for garnish

6 eggs

1¾ cups all-purpose flour

1¾ teaspoons baking powder

¾ cup dry white wine

½ cup vegetable oil

½ cup light cream

1½ teaspoons salt

1 teaspoon garlic powder

¼ teaspoon pepper

1 teaspoon paprika, plus extra
for garnish

Serves 8
This Yom Kippur meal is great served with salsa or yogurt. It also can be served as an appetizer.

1. Mince the scallions, green olives, sun-dried tomatoes, parsley, and dill. Shred the cheeses. Lightly beat the eggs.
2. Preheat oven to 350°. Lightly grease a 9" × 5" loaf pan.
3. In a large bowl, blend the flour and baking powder. Make a well in the center of the dry ingredients and add the wine, the oil, cream, and eggs; stir to mix. Fold in the remaining ingredients. Pour or spoon the mixture into the prepared pan. Sprinkle the top with extra Parmesan cheese and dust with paprika.
4. Bake for 40 to 45 minutes, until set. Allow to cool before serving.

Break an Egg

Always break eggs 1 at a time into a small bowl before adding them to the pan or bowl. This way, if you get a bit of shell, a spoiled egg, or a broken egg for a dish calling for whole eggs, you won't ruin the entire item with 1 bad egg.

MOCK CHOPPED LIVER

Serves 8

Serve this Rosh Hashanah dish with matzo crackers and fresh vegetables.

2 shallots
1 pound button mushrooms
2 tablespoons unsalted margarine

½ teaspoon salt
½ teaspoon ground black pepper

1. Peel and finely chop the shallots. Clean the mushrooms and chop finely.
2. Melt the margarine in a large skillet over medium heat. Add the shallots and sauté until softened, about 2 minutes.
3. Add the mushrooms and sauté until the moisture is evaporated, about 10 minutes.
4. Purée the mushroom mixture in a blender or food processor. Season with the salt and pepper.

MOSCARDINI

Makes 30

This is a classic Purim recipe. Instead of almonds, try hazelnuts for a different flavor.

1¼ cups ground toasted almonds
1¼ cup granulated sugar
¼ cup unsweetened cocoa

¼ cup unbleached flour
⅓ teaspoon cinnamon
1 egg
1 egg yolk

1. Preheat oven to 350°.
2. Combine the ground almonds, sugar, cocoa, flour, and cinnamon in a small bowl. Add the egg and egg yolk, and mix well.
3. Place on an oiled and floured baking sheet, about 2½ inches apart. Flatten with a fork.
4. Bake for 10 minutes, then transfer to a cooling rack.

GORGONZOLA AND APPLE SALAD

1 tablespoon Dijon mustard
3 tablespoons balsamic vinegar
1 tablespoon lemon juice
1 tablespoon honey
½ cup olive oil
½ teaspoon salt

½ teaspoon ground black pepper
2 heads romaine lettuce
½ pound Gorgonzola cheese
2 Red Delicious apples
1 cup toasted pecans

Serves 8

This is perfect for Rosh Hashanah, but it is good any time of year.

1. Process the mustard, vinegar, lemon juice, and honey in a blender. Gradually add the olive oil until well blended. Season with salt and pepper. Cover and refrigerate for at least 1 hour.
2. Tear the lettuce into bite-sized pieces. Crumble the Gorgonzola cheese. Core the apples and slice thinly. (Do not peel the apples.) Chop the pecans.
3. Mix the lettuce and apples in a large bowl. Put large helpings on individual plates. Top with Gorgonzola and pecans. Drizzle the dressing on top.

Blanching Vegetables

Quickly parboiling green vegetables, or "blanching" them, locks in nutrition, flavor, and especially bright color. The key is to bring the vegetables immediately up to a boil, cook them only enough to tenderize them, and stop the cooking by plunging them immediately into ice-cold water, a step known as "shocking" the vegetables. Blanche only small amounts at a time so the water never stops boiling. Salt plays an important role in keeping green vegetables green, and it is recommended in both the blanching and shocking waters.

HAMANTASCHEN

Makes 30

This dish is a must for Purim. Try different fillings to see which your family likes best.

½ pound margarine
8 teaspoons granulated sugar
3¼ cups all-purpose flour
2 teaspoons baking powder
¼ teaspoon salt

2 eggs
3 teaspoons orange juice
2 teaspoons vanilla
1 jar jam or poppy seed filling

1. Cream together the margarine and sugar. Sift the dry ingredients and add to the margarine mixture; mix well. Add the eggs, orange juice, and vanilla. Knead until the dough forms and divide into 6 sections. Refrigerate until chilled, about 1 hour.
2. Preheat oven to 325°.
3. Roll out each section on a floured board. Use a glass as a cutter for forming circles for the hamantaschen shape. Place 1 teaspoon of filling into each circle and fold into a triangle by pinching the edges together. Bake on a baking sheet for 25 minutes.

How Many Carbs in Wine?

A bottle of wine will yield 4 to 5 servings. A 5-ounce serving of white wine contains 1.2 grams of carbohydrates; 5 ounces of red wine contains 2.4 grams of carbohydrates; and a 5-ounce glass of champagne contains 4.3 grams of carbohydrates.

HONEY CAKE LEKACH

2 tablespoons canola oil

½ cup plum/apple baby food

6 large eggs, at room temperature

1 cup honey

1½ firmly packed cups light brown sugar

3 cups all-purpose flour

1 teaspoon baking soda

2 teaspoons baking powder

⅛ teaspoon salt

2 teaspoons cinnamon

1 teaspoon ground nutmeg

½ cup finely chopped almonds

½ cup brewed coffee, at room temperature

¼ cup sliced almonds

Serves 20

These Rosh Hashanah cakes may be frozen for up to 3 months.

1. Preheat oven to 350° with a rack set in the lower third of the oven. Grease two 9" × 5" loaf pans. Separate egg whites from yolks.

2. Combine the oil, baby food, egg whites, honey, and brown sugar in a large mixing bowl. Beat with an electric mixer on medium speed for 3 minutes.

3. In a small mixing bowl, thoroughly mix together the flour, baking soda, baking powder, salt, cinnamon, nutmeg, and chopped almonds. Alternately, stir the flour mixture and the coffee into the sugar mixture, beginning and ending with the flour. *Do not overmix.* The batter will be very thin.

4. Pour the batter into the prepared pans. Rap the pans sharply on the counter several times to break any large bubbles. Sprinkle ⅛ cup of the sliced almonds on top of each loaf.

5. Place the cakes in the oven and bake for about 1 hour, until a toothpick inserted into the center of the cake comes out clean. Set the pans on a rack to cool. For best flavor, make the cakes 1 day ahead.

PURIM POPPY SEED CANDY

Makes 1½ pounds

This timeless Purim treat brings back memories for adults and will have children asking for more.

1 pound poppy seeds
2 cups chopped pecans
2 cups honey

½ cup granulated sugar
½ teaspoon powdered ginger

1. Grind the poppy seeds in a coffee grinder or with a mortar and pestle. Chop the pecans, if necessary.
2. In a medium-sized saucepan, cook the honey and sugar until syrupy. Stir in the poppy seeds and cook until the mixture is thick, about 20 minutes. Stir frequently. The mixture should not run when a small amount is dropped on a wet surface.
3. Stir in the nuts and ginger.
4. Moisten your hands with water and pat out the mixture onto a wet board or counter. It should be about ½-inch thick. Let cool for 5 minutes, then score into diamond shapes with a sharp knife. When cool, lift from the board with a spatula.

Sautéing Tip
For a light taste, sauté onions and garlic in extra-virgin olive oil, canola oil, or vegetable oil. For a richer flavor, use a darker olive oil or butter.

Chapter 17

FANCY FOODS FOR A DIABETIC DIET

CUCUMBER SLICES WITH SMOKED SALMON CREAM

Makes ½ cup

Use as an appetizer or substitute this for the salad course by adding fresh sliced carrots and celery to each plate.

2–3 medium cucumbers
1 ounce smoked salmon
8 ounces Neufchâtel cheese,
    at room temperature
½ tablespoon lemon juice
½ teaspoon freshly ground
    pepper
Chopped dill (optional)

1. Cut the cumbers into slices about ¼-inch thick. Place the slices on paper towels to drain while you prepare the salmon cream.
2. Combine the smoked salmon, Neufchâtel cheese, lemon juice, and pepper in a food processor; blend until smooth.
3. Fit a pasty bag with the tip of your choice and spoon the salmon cream into the bag. Pipe 1 teaspoon of the salmon cream atop each cucumber slice.
4. Garnish with dill, if desired.

WALNUT CHICKEN WITH PLUM SAUCE

Serves 4

This makes the perfect topping for a fancy salad. Or serve it with steamed vegetables and rice for a more traditional celebratory dinner.

¾ pound boneless, skinless
    chicken breast
1 teaspoon cooking sherry
1 egg white
2 teaspoons peanut oil
2 drops toasted sesame oil
    (optional)
⅓ cup ground walnuts

1. Preheat oven to 350°. Cut the chicken into bite-sized pieces and sprinkle with the sherry; set aside.
2. In a small bowl, beat the egg white and oils until frothy. Fold the chicken pieces into the egg mixture, then roll them individually in the chopped walnuts.
3. Spray a baking sheet with nonstick cooking spray. Arrange the chicken pieces on the baking sheet. Bake for 10 to 15 minutes or until the walnuts are lightly browned and the chicken juices run clear.

CHICKEN THIGHS CACCIATORE

½ cup chopped onion

2 garlic cloves

4 chicken thighs

1 (14½-ounce) can unsalted, diced tomatoes

2 teaspoons olive oil

½ cup dry red wine

1 teaspoon dried parsley

½ teaspoon dried oregano

¼ teaspoon ground black pepper

⅛ teaspoon granulated sugar

¼ cup grated Parmesan cheese

4 cups cooked spaghetti noodles

2 teaspoons extra-virgin olive oil

Serves 4

To add more flavor to this recipe, substitute beef broth for ½ of the red wine.

1. Remove the peel from the onion and chop into ¼-inch pieces. Peel and mince the garlic. Remove the skin from the chicken thighs. Drain the tomatoes.

2. Heat a deep, nonstick skillet over medium-high heat and add the 2 teaspoons olive oil. Add the onion and sauté until transparent. Add the garlic and chicken thighs. Sauté the chicken for 3 minutes on each side, or until lightly browned.

3. Remove the chicken from the pan and add the wine, tomatoes, parsley, oregano, pepper, and sugar. Stir well and bring to a boil.

4. Add the chicken back to the pan and sprinkle with the Parmesan cheese. Cover, reduce heat to low, and simmer for 10 minutes. Uncover and simmer for 10 more minutes.

5. Put 1 cup cooked pasta on each of 4 plates. Top each with a chicken thigh and then divide the sauce between the dishes. Drizzle ½ teaspoon olive oil over the top of each dish.

Fat-Free Flavor

To add the flavor of sautéed mushrooms or onions without the added fat of butter or oil, roast or grill them first. Thinly slice the mushrooms, then simply spread them on a baking sheet treated with nonstick spray. Bake for 5 minutes in a 350° oven.

CRAB CAKES WITH SESAME CRUST

Serves 5

Serve as an appetizer or make this a main dish and serve with fresh steamed vegetables, rice, and fresh fruit.

1 small scallion
1 pound lump crabmeat
1 large egg
1 tablespoon minced fresh ginger
1 tablespoon dry white cooking sherry
1 tablespoon freshly squeezed lemon juice

6 tablespoons mayonnaise
$\frac{1}{2}$ teaspoon sea salt
$\frac{1}{2}$ teaspoon ground white pepper
$\frac{1}{4}$ cup lightly toasted sesame seeds

1. Preheat oven to 375°. Treat a baking sheet with nonstick cooking spray. Remove the skin from the scallion and chop finely.
2. In a large bowl, mix together the scallion, crab, egg, ginger, sherry, lemon juice, mayonnaise, salt, and pepper.
3. Form the mixture into 10 equal cakes. Spread out the sesame seeds on a plate and dip both sides of the cakes in the seeds to coat the cakes evenly.
4. Arrange the cakes on the prepared baking sheet and bake for 8 to 10 minutes or until thoroughly warmed.

Proper Fish Handling

Always wash your hands after handling raw fish. Also wash all surfaces and utensils that the raw fish has touched.

MOCK STUFFED GRAPE LEAVES

1 cup cooked white rice
¾ cup golden raisins
½ cup apple jelly
⅛ teaspoon saffron
½ teaspoon salt
1 bunch fresh Swiss chard leaves

Makes about 24

Add a small dollop of apple jelly and a raisin on the top of each appetizer for a sweeter taste.

1. Combine the cooked white rice, ½ cup of the golden raisins, ¼ cup of the apple jelly, the saffron, and salt. Mix with a spoon until all the ingredients are evenly distributed.
2. Wash the Swiss chard leaves in cold water. Using a large melon scooper, place 1 scoop of the rice mixture in the center of each leaf. Fold in the ends and roll up tightly, as you would an egg roll. Place them in layers in a slow cooker.
3. Cover and cook on low setting for 2 to 4 hours.

FILLETS OF FISH WITH LIME AND CUMIN

12 fish fillets (such as haddock)
2 tablespoons lime juice
1 teaspoon ground cumin
¼ cup plain yogurt
½ teaspoon salt
½ teaspoon ground black pepper

Serves 4

Serve with whole-grain rice and Bananas Foster (page 234) for dessert.

1. Preheat oven to 350°.
2. Arrange the fish in a single layer in a baking dish. Combine the lime juice and cumin, and pour over the fish, turning to coat. Bake, uncovered, for 10 to 15 minutes or until the fish flakes easily when tested with a fork.
3. In a bowl, combine the yogurt with 1 tablespoon of the juice from the baking dish. Season with the salt and pepper and serve over the fish.

BROCCOLI AND CARROT CASSEROLE

Serves 6

Serve with Walnut Chicken with Plum Sauce (page 228).

1 cup fresh broccoli
3 medium carrots
1 small yellow onion
1/2 green bell pepper
1 cup unsalted tomato juice
1/8 teaspoon dried basil

1/8 teaspoon dried oregano
1/8 teaspoon dried parsley
1/4 teaspoon garlic powder
3 tablespoons grated Parmesan cheese, divided

1. Cut the broccoli into florets. Peel the carrots and slice into 1/4-inch rounds. Peel the onion and chop into 1/4-inch pieces. Chop the bell pepper into 1/4-inch pieces.
2. Preheat oven to 350°. Treat a large casserole dish with nonstick spray.
3. Layer the broccoli, carrots, onion, and pepper in the prepared casserole dish.
4. Mix together the tomato juice, seasonings, and 2 tablespoons of the Parmesan cheese; pour the mixture over the vegetables. Cover and bake for 1 hour.
5. Uncover, sprinkle with the remaining Parmesan cheese, and continue to bake for 10 minutes, or until the liquid thickens and the mixture bubbles.

Season First

When you ready vegetables for steaming, add fresh or dried herbs, spices, sliced onions, minced garlic, grated ginger, or just about any other seasoning you'd normally use. The seasonings will cook into the vegetables during steaming.

BERRY PUFF PANCAKES

2 large whole eggs
1 large egg white
½ cup skim milk
½ cup all-purpose flour
1 tablespoon granulated sugar

⅛ teaspoon sea salt
2 cups fresh berries of your
  choice
1 tablespoon confectioners' sugar

> **Serves 6**
>
> While perfect for breakfast or brunch, this also makes a wonderful dessert.

1. Preheat oven to 450°. Treat a 10-inch ovenproof skillet or deep pie pan with nonstick spray. Once the oven is heated, place the pan in the oven for a few minutes until it is hot.
2. In a medium-sized mixing bowl, beat the eggs and egg white until mixed. Whisk in the milk. Slowly whisk in the flour, sugar, and salt.
3. Remove the preheated pan from the oven and pour the batter into it. Bake for 15 minutes.
4. Reduce the heat to 350° and bake for an additional 10 minutes or until the batter is puffed and brown. Remove from the oven and slide the puffed pancake onto a serving plate.
5. Cover the pancake with the fruit and sift the confectioners' sugar over the top. Cut into 6 equal wedges, and serve.

Syrup Substitutes

Spreading 2 teaspoons of your favorite low-sugar jam or jelly on a waffle or pancake gives you a sweet topping while counting as a fruit for the day.

BANANAS FOSTER

Serves 4

Serve as dessert for
Chicken Thighs
Cacciatore
(page 229).

4 bananas
½ cup apple juice concentrate
Grated zest of 1 orange
¼ cup fresh orange juice

1 tablespoon ground cinnamon
12 ounces nonfat frozen vanilla
   yogurt

1. Slice the bananas about ¼-inch thick.
2. Combine all the ingredients *except* the yogurt in a nonstick skillet.
   Bring to a boil and cook until the bananas are tender.
3. Put 3 ounces of the yogurt in each dessert bowl or stemmed glass
   and spoon the heated banana sauce over the top.

Ripe Bananas

Overripe bananas are higher in sugar and therefore can adversely affect your blood glucose levels. You can freeze bananas in the skins until ready to use. Doing so makes them perfect additions for fruit smoothies or fruit cups. Remove them from the freezer and run a little water over the peel to remove any frost. Peel them using a paring knife and slice according to the recipe directions. Frozen bananas can be added directly to smoothies and other recipes.

CHAPTER 18

LOW-CARB CELEBRATIONS

CRABMEAT ON RED PEPPER STRIPS

<table>
<tr><td>

Makes about 16

Serve with white wine
as an appetizer
before a beef meal.

</td><td>

2 green onions
½ plum tomato
1 tablespoon chopped fresh
   parsley
1 tablespoon chopped fresh
   tarragon
2 large red bell peppers
⅓ cup mayonnaise
2 teaspoons fresh-squeezed
   lemon juice

</td><td>

½ teaspoon grated fresh lemon
   zest
⅛ teaspoon cayenne pepper
8 ounces flaked crabmeat
½ teaspoon salt
½ teaspoon ground black
   pepper
1 bunch fresh chervil sprigs

</td></tr>
</table>

1. Peel and finely chop the green onion. Seed and mince the tomato. Chop the fresh parsley and tarragon. Remove the stem and seeds from the red peppers and cut into 1-by-2-inch strips.
2. Mix together the green onions, tomato, parsley, tarragon, mayonnaise, lemon juice, lemon zest, and cayenne in a medium-sized bowl until blended.
3. Add the crabmeat and toss lightly to coat. Season with salt and pepper.
4. Spoon 1 or 2 teaspoons of the crab mixture onto each bell pepper strip. Garnish with chervil sprigs.

Fresh Seafood

While fresh seafood can be easier to find than ever before, small Midwestern towns still have trouble importing it in time. If you can't find fresh, look for seafood that has been flash frozen and thawed by the grocery.

PORK AND VEAL PÂTÉ

1¼ pounds pork shoulder or
rump
½ pound veal shoulder
½ pound salt pork
1 small yellow onion
1½ cups water

¼ teaspoon ground cloves
¼ teaspoon ground cinnamon
½ teaspoon salt
½ teaspoon freshly ground
black pepper

> ### Serves 6
>
> A French classic, this low-carb pâté has a crumbly texture because it is not weighted during the cooling and setting process.

1. If not available precut, cut the pork and veal into 1-inch cubes. Peel the onion and chop into ¼-inch pieces. Finely chop the salt pork.
2. With a sharp knife, finely chop the pork and veal pieces to the texture of ground meat. Put the pork and veal, onions, and water in a large pot. Cook over medium heat, uncovered, until the liquid has evaporated and the meat begins to brown, about 30 minutes.
3. Put the salt pork into a small saucepan. Cook, uncovered, over medium heat, stirring often, until the fat has been rendered and the pork is golden brown, about 30 minutes.
4. Add the salt pork and the rendered fat to the meat mixture along with the remaining ingredients. Transfer to a container with a cover and set aside to cool to room temperature. Cover and refrigerate for at least 3 hours before serving.

An Appetizer-Making Party

Consider asking some of your guests to assist in preparing appetizers for your party. People enjoy the chance to "do something" while they are getting to know everyone else. It also helps break the ice if many of your guests don't know each other. Most people gravitate to the kitchen to talk anyway, so put them to good use!

STILTON AND CHEDDAR CHEESE SOUP

Serves 8

Serve with Lobster
and Asparagus Salad
(page 240).

1 small white onion
1 medium carrot
1 celery rib
3 garlic cloves
2 tablespoons butter
3 cups chicken stock
½ cup crumbled Stilton cheese
½ cup diced Cheddar cheese
⅛ teaspoon baking soda

1 cup heavy cream
⅓ cup dry white wine
1 bay leaf
½ teaspoon salt
½ teaspoon freshly ground
   black pepper
¼ teaspoon cayenne pepper
¼ cup chopped fresh parsley,
   for garnish

1. Peel the onion and chop into ⅛-inch pieces. Peel the carrot and chop
   into ⅛-inch pieces. Chop the celery into ⅛-inch pieces. Peel and
   mince the garlic.
2. Melt the butter in a large saucepan over medium-high heat. Add the
   onion, carrot, celery, and garlic; sauté for about 8 minutes or until soft.
3. Add the stock, cheeses, baking soda, cream, wine, bay leaf, salt,
   pepper, and cayenne pepper; stir well to combine. Bring to a boil,
   reduce heat to low, and simmer for about 10 minutes. Remove and
   discard the bay leaf.
4. In a food processor or blender, purée the soup until smooth. Add
   milk to the soup if it is too thick. Garnish with fresh parsley.

Don't Eat Bay Leaves
*Remember, bay leaves add lots of flavor, but you should always
remove them before serving a dish. Bay leaves are sharp and
dangerous to eat.*

MUSTARD-GLAZED MONKFISH WRAPPED IN BACON

*12 slices apple-wood-smoked or
other high-quality bacon*
6 (6-ounce) monkfish fillets
½ teaspoon salt
½ teaspoon black pepper
⅔ cup Dijon mustard
2 tablespoons chopped tarragon

Serves 6
Serve with Refrigerator Pumpkin Pie with Macadamia Nut Crust for dessert (page 245).

1. Preheat oven to 350°.
2. Place the bacon on a nonstick baking sheet and precook for about 8 minutes. The bacon should be almost fully cooked but still pliable. Drain the bacon on paper towels. Discard the fat from the baking sheet.
3. Make sure the monkfish is trimmed of all membranes and dark spots. Season the monkfish with salt and pepper. Rub each fillet with 2 tablespoons of the mustard to coat completely.
4. Wrap each fillet with 2 slices of bacon, making sure the bacon doesn't overlap. Secure the bacon with toothpicks if necessary. Wrap each fillet tightly in plastic wrap, twisting the ends closed, and refrigerate for about 1 hour.
5. Preheat oven to 375°.
6. Unwrap the fish and place on an oiled baking sheet. Bake for about 20 to 25 minutes until the fish is almost cooked. Increase the oven temperature to low broil. To finish, place the fish under the broiler for just about 30 seconds to crisp the bacon.
7. Drizzle a bit of the natural pan juices over the fish and sprinkle with chopped tarragon. Serve immediately.

Poor Man's Lobster?

Monkfish has been described as the poor man's lobster even though it has no resemblance to lobster whatsoever. Cooked properly, it has the texture of shellfish and does not have the "flakiness" of most fish. Mild in flavor and moderately firm in texture, it is a hearty fish.

LOBSTER AND ASPARAGUS SALAD

Serves 2

Serve with Stilton and Cheddar Cheese Soup (page 238).

1 garlic clove
2 anchovies, well drained
1 tablespoon snipped fresh chives
1 tablespoon chopped fresh parsley
1 teaspoon chopped fresh tarragon
½ cup mayonnaise
1 teaspoon tarragon vinegar
½ teaspoon salt
½ teaspoon ground black pepper
2 tablespoons sour cream
1 pound (16–20 spears) asparagus spears
2 precooked lobsters, claw and tail meat removed, shells discarded
2 cups mixed salad leaves

1. Peel and crush the garlic clove. To make the dressing, combine the garlic, anchovies, and herbs in a food processor or blender; process until smooth. Add the mayonnaise; process to mix. Add the vinegar, salt, and pepper. Transfer to a bowl or other container, cover, and chill for at least 1 hour. Before serving, stir in the sour cream.
2. Trim off and discard the ends off the asparagus spears, making all the spears the same length. Use a vegetable peeler to peel off any tough outer layer on the stalks if necessary. Start about 1½ inches from the top when peeling. Cook the asparagus in a pan of salted, boiling water for 4 to 8 minutes, depending on the size, or until tender but still somewhat crisp and a vibrant green. Drain and rinse immediately under cold, running water, then drain again.
3. Slice the lobster tail meat into ½-inch rounds. Leave the claw meat intact. Arrange the asparagus spears and lobster meat on a bed of the salad leaves on a chilled salad plate. Spoon a little of the dressing over the salad and serve immediately.

Substituting Seafood

Most shellfish can readily be substituted for another in any recipe. Simply use the weight of the meat as the guide, not the weight with the shell on it. Remember that scallops and shrimp are shellfish, too.

SEAFOOD ROLL-UPS

8 ounces canned or fresh crab-
    meat and/or baby shrimp
¼ red bell pepper
2 tablespoons chopped fresh
    chives

1 (8-ounce) package cream
    cheese, softened
¼ cup mayonnaise
5 (9-inch) flour tortillas, at room
    temperature

Makes 24

For an extra treat,
serve with tomato
salsa as a dipping
sauce.

1. Chop the seafood into ¼-inch pieces. Chop the red pepper into ¼-inch pieces. Roughly chop the chives.
2. Combine the cream cheese and mayonnaise. Blend in the seafood.
3. Spread on the tortillas, dividing evenly. Sprinkle the red pepper and chives evenly over the tortillas.
4. Roll up each tortilla, tightly wrap with plastic wrap, and refrigerate at least 3 hours. Cut into ¾-inch pieces before serving.

RED SNAPPER WITH CAYENNE TOMATO SAUCE

1 tablespoon olive oil
5 ounces red snapper fillet, skin on
2 tablespoons sour cream
1 tablespoon minced chives
½ teaspoon sun-dried tomato paste

½ teaspoon cayenne pepper
1 teaspoon lemon juice
½ teaspoon salt
½ teaspoon ground white pepper

Serves 1

You can also heat the
sauce for a nice
touch.

1. Preheat oven to 375°. Add the olive oil to a small ovenproof nonstick sauté pan over medium-high heat. Place the snapper fillet, skin-side down, in the pan and cook until golden brown. Carefully flip the fillet and place in the oven. Bake the snapper for about 6 minutes or until cooked through. To check for doneness, insert a thin-bladed knife into the thickest part of the fillet. The flesh should be flaky with no translucence.
2. In a small bowl, mix together the sour cream, minced chives, tomato paste, cayenne pepper, and lemon juice. Season with salt and white pepper.
3. Serve the sauce over the snapper fillet.

PORTOBELLOS STUFFED WITH BASIL AND SALMON ON ARUGULA LEAVES

Serves 2

Serve as an appetizer before Sage- and Pancetta-Wrapped Shrimp (page 243).

2 large portobello mushroom caps
4 scallions
2 garlic cloves
¼ cup fresh basil leaves
½ pound salmon
10 ounces fresh arugula leaves
3 teaspoons light olive oil
½ teaspoon salt
½ teaspoon ground black pepper
3 tablespoons cream cheese

1. Preheat oven to 375°. Clean the mushroom caps by wiping with a damp cloth. Peel and mince the scallions and garlic cloves. Cut the basil leaves into julienne strips. Skin, debone, and chop the salmon into 1-inch cubes. Steam the arugula leaves until limp.

2. Brush the mushrooms with the oil and season with salt and pepper. Place the mushrooms on a foil-covered baking sheet, lightly oiled, stem-side up. Roast for about 20 to 30 minutes, until tender when pierced with a fork, but not shriveled.

3. Mix together the scallion, garlic, basil, and cream cheese in a small bowl. Split the salmon into 2 equal portions and place ½ on each mushroom cap. Top with the cream cheese mixture. Season with salt and freshly ground black pepper.

4. Bake the stuffed mushrooms, uncovered, for 20 to 25 minutes, until the cream cheese is bubbly and starting to brown on top and the salmon is cooked through. Serve each mushroom cap on a bed of arugula leaves.

Arugula

Arugula is also known as rocket. The tender baby leaves are best, featuring a peppery bite. The larger leaves are somewhat bitter. Fresh arugula contains a fair amount of grit, so the leaves should be rinsed several times before using. Arugula is a good source of iron as well as vitamins A and C.

SAGE- AND PANCETTA-WRAPPED SHRIMP

*1½ pounds uncooked large
    shrimp*
6 ounces thinly sliced pancetta

*28 fresh sage leaves (about
    2 bunches)*
½ cup sherry vinegar

> **Serves 4**
>
> This also makes an
> excellent appetizer
> when served just
> 1 per guest.

1. Remove the shells and tails from the shrimp. Devein the shrimp. Cut the slices of pancetta in half. Tear the sage leaves from the stems.
2. On a flat surface, lay out a half slice of pancetta. Place 1 large or 2 small leaves of sage on top, then place 1 shrimp across the pancetta and sage. Roll the pancetta around the shrimp and secure it closed with a toothpick, exposing the tail and head ends of the shrimp. Repeat with the rest of the shrimp.
3. Heat a medium-sized nonstick skillet on medium-high flame. Cook the rolled shrimp in 2 batches (to avoid overcrowding the pan) until the pancetta is light brown and crispy on each side. Place the shrimp on paper towels to drain, and cover to keep warm.
4. Immediately after all the shrimp have been cooked, keeping the pan on the flame, pour in the sherry vinegar and cook down to a syrup-like consistency. Place the shrimp on a platter and pour the hot reduced vinegar over the shrimp. Serve immediately.

What Size Shrimp?

Shrimp is sold in the following categories:

Colossal:	less than 10 pieces per pound
Jumbo:	11–15 pieces per pound
Extra-large:	16–20 pieces per pound
Large:	21–30 pieces per pound
Medium:	31–35 pieces per pound
Small:	36–45 pieces per pound
Miniature:	100 pieces per pound

CHICKEN WITH NECTARINE SALSA

Serves 4

Serve with a fresh green salad and a side of fresh fruit.

4 (4-ounce) boneless, skinless
  chicken breasts
1 tablespoon lime juice
1½ teaspoons ground cumin
½ teaspoon salt
½ teaspoon ground black
  pepper

1 fresh nectarine
1 jalapeño pepper
2 garlic cloves
2 tablespoons chopped fresh
  cilantro
½ cup chunky salsa
Lime wedges, for garnish

1. Preheat grill or broiler.
2. Rinse the chicken and pat dry. Brush the chicken with the lime juice and sprinkle evenly with the cumin, salt, and pepper. Grill the chicken on the rack of an uncovered grill directly over medium heat or broil for 12 to 15 minutes, until the chicken is tender and no longer pink, turning once.
3. Meanwhile, prepare the nectarine salsa: Chop the nectarine into ¼-inch pieces. Seed and finely chop the jalapeño pepper. Peel and mince the garlic. Chop the cilantro. Stir together the nectarine, jalapeño, garlic, cilantro, and salsa in a small bowl. Spoon over the chicken and serve with the lime wedges on the side for garnish.

Cooking Chicken

Chicken should be cooked to the following temperatures for safety:

Boneless chicken:	165°
Bone-in pieces:	170°
Ground chicken:	165°
Bone-in whole chicken:	180°

REFRIGERATOR PUMPKIN PIE WITH MACADAMIA NUT CRUST

1½ cups finely chopped
    macadamia nuts
16 packets sugar substitute
2 tablespoons butter, softened,
    plus extra for greasing
1 packet unflavored gelatin

¼ cup water
1 teaspoon pumpkin pie spice
1 (25-ounce) can pumpkin purée
2 teaspoons grated orange zest
1½ cups heavy cream
2 teaspoons vanilla extract

Serves 8

This medium-carbohydrate dish is excellent served as dessert for the very low-carb Mustard-Glazed Monkfish Wrapped in Bacon (page 239).

1. Heat oven to 400°. Butter the bottom and sides of a 9-inch spring-form pan.

2. In a medium-sized bowl, combine the macadamia nuts, 4 packets of the sugar substitute, and the butter; mix well. Press the mixture onto the bottom and 1 inch up the sides of the prepared pan. Bake for 10 minutes, until golden brown. Cool on a wire rack.

3. In a small bowl, sprinkle the gelatin over the water. Let sit for 5 minutes until the gelatin softens.

4. Heat a small skillet over medium heat and toast the pumpkin pie spice for 1 to 2 minutes, until fragrant, stirring frequently. Reduce heat to low, stir in the gelatin mixture, and cook for 1 to 2 minutes until the gelatin melts. Remove from heat and let cool to room temperature.

5. Place the pumpkin purée in a large bowl and mash with a fork to loosen. Mix in the orange zest. In another large bowl, using an electric mixer on high speed, beat the cream with the remaining 12 packets of sugar substitute and the vanilla until soft peaks form. With a rubber spatula, slowly fold in the gelatin mixture.

6. In 3 parts, gently fold the whipped cream mixture into the pumpkin purée. Pour the filling into the cooled pie shell and smooth the top. Refrigerate for at least 3 hours before serving.

CHAPTER 19
LOW-FAT CELEBRATIONS

PASTA AND SMOKED TROUT
WITH LEMON PESTO

Serves 4

Serve with fresh fruit
and freshly steamed
broccoli for a healthy,
festive meal.

2 garlic cloves
2 tightly packed cups fresh
   basil leaves
⅛ cup toasted pine nuts
2 teaspoons fresh-squeezed
   lemon juice
2 teaspoons water
5 teaspoons extra-virgin olive
   oil, divided

4 tablespoons grated Parmesan
   cheese, divided
4 ounces uncooked linguini
2 ounces boneless smoked
   trout
1 teaspoon freshly ground
   black pepper

1. Place the pasta in 1 quart boiling water and 1 teaspoon olive oil. Boil until the pasta is soft but firm. Drain and set aside.
2. Peel the garlic. In a food processor, pulse the garlic until finely chopped. Add the basil, pine nuts, lemon juice, and water; process until puréed. Add the remaining 4 teaspoons of the olive oil and 3 tablespoons of the Parmesan cheese; pulse until the pesto is smooth. Set aside.
3. Flake the smoked trout and add to the pesto mixture. Add the pasta and toss. Divide onto 4 plates and sprinkle each serving with Parmesan cheese.

Smoked Fish

Smoking is not just a way to add flavor to meat. Native Americans would smoke fish over their fires in the fall as a way to preserve it through the winter. Unlike other preservation methods, a well-smoked fish will remain flaky and tender for months.

BAKED RED SNAPPER ALMANDINE

1 pound red snapper fillets
1 teaspoon sea salt
½ teaspoon freshly ground
* white pepper*
4 teaspoons all-purpose flour

1 teaspoon olive oil
2 tablespoons raw almonds
1 teaspoon unsalted butter
1 tablespoon lemon juice

Serves 4

Serve with rice pilaf
and fresh fruit for a
festive yet light meal.

1. Preheat oven to 375°. Rinse the fish fillets and pat dry between layers of paper towels. Season with salt and pepper. Sprinkle the front and back of the fillets with the flour.
2. In an ovenproof, nonstick skillet on medium-high heat, sauté the fillets in the olive oil until they are nicely browned on both sides.
3. Finely grind the almonds and combine with the butter in a microwave-safe dish. Microwave on high for 30 seconds, or until the butter is melted. Stir.
4. Pour the almond-butter mixture and the lemon juice over the fillets.
5. Bake for 3 to 5 minutes, or until the almonds are nicely browned.

Lemon Juice at Hand
Squeeze juice from lemons when you have time or when lemons are on sale and freeze the juice so it's ready to use when you need it.

SALMON TORTELLINI SALAD

Serves 4

Serve with fresh fruit
and a green salad.

---

8 ounces frozen or fresh cheese
  tortellini
4 carrots
1 zucchini
1 red bell pepper
2 (6½-ounce) cans salmon

1 cup plain low-fat yogurt
¼ cup grated Parmesan cheese
¼ cup chopped parsley
1 tablespoon low-fat milk
1 teaspoon dried oregano

1. Cook the tortellini according to package directions. Drain, rinse under cold water, and drain again. Peel and slice the carrots thinly. Slice the zucchini. Remove the seeds and stem from bell pepper and cut into narrow strips. Drain the salmon and flake with a fork.
2. In medium-sized bowl, gently toss together the pasta, carrots, zucchini, and bell pepper. Add the salmon and mix.
3. In a small bowl, stir together the yogurt, cheese, parsley, milk, and oregano until well mixed. Add to the pasta mixture and toss gently to coat evenly.
4. Cover and refrigerate for several hours before serving.

Moldy Cheese

Chances are your mother probably told you that you just had to scrape off the mold before you ate cheese because cheese is just mold anyway. That is definitely an oversimplification. The mold on the outside of cheese comes from bacteria in the air and while it likely won't make you sick if you scrape it off, it is a sign that the cheese is not in perfect form.

FUSILLI WITH CHICKEN AND CORIANDER PESTO

2 whole chicken breasts, halved
1 pound fusilli pasta
4 garlic cloves
4 serrano chile peppers

½ cup slivered blanched almonds
3 ounces cilantro
2 tablespoons olive oil
1 cup low-fat mayonnaise

Serves 4

Serve with a green salad and fresh fruit for a traditional Italian dinner.

1. Preheat oven to 375°. Cook the pasta in boiling water until al dente.
2. Place the chicken breasts in a baking pan. Bake until cooked through and tender, 15 to 20 minutes. Remove from the oven and let cool. Remove and discard the skin and bones and shred the meat. Place the meat in a medium-sized bowl, cover, and chill.
3. Meanwhile, peel the garlic and cut into ¼-inch pieces. Remove the stems and seeds from the chili peppers. In a food processor or blender, combine the garlic, chilies, almonds, and cilantro; process until finely chopped. With the motor running, add the oil in a thin, steady stream, processing until the pesto is the consistency of a thick paste.
4. Place the pesto in a bowl. Whisk in the mayonnaise.
5. In a large bowl, combine the chilled pasta, shredded chicken, and the pesto; stir to mix well. Cover and chill for 1 hour before serving.

Releasing Garlic's Potential

Get the most out of garlic by "popping" the clove before adding it to a dish. Hold a large knife on its side and place the peeled clove under it. Push down until you hear the clove pop. You'll release all the wonderful oils without having to chop.

SAVORY PASTITSIO

2 teaspoons olive oil

1 large white onion, peeled and finely chopped

1½ pounds lean ground beef

1 cup water

¾ cup dry white whine

1 (6-ounce) can tomato paste

½ cup bulgur

¾ teaspoon cinnamon

¾ teaspoon nutmeg

¾ teaspoon allspice

1½ teaspoons salt

½ teaspoon ground black pepper

2 cups 1% cottage cheese

2 tablespoons all-purpose flour

1 cup fat-free chicken broth, divided

1 (12-ounce) can evaporated skim milk

¾ cup, plus 2 tablespoons freshly grated Parmesan cheese

1 pound elbow macaroni

2 tablespoons chopped fresh parsley

1. In a large nonstick skillet, heat 1 teaspoon of the oil over medium heat. Add the chopped onion and sauté until softened, about 5 minutes. Add the ground beef and cook, breaking it up with a wooden spoon, until no longer pink, about 5 minutes. Drain off fat.

2. Add the water, wine, tomato paste, bulgur, spices, 1 teaspoon of the salt, and the pepper. Simmer uncovered over low heat, stirring occasionally, until the bulgur is tender, about 20 minutes.

3. In a food processor or blender, purée the cottage cheese until completely smooth. Set aside.

4. In a small bowl, stir together the flour and ¼ cup of the chicken broth until smooth.

5. In a medium-sized heavy saucepan, combine the evaporated skim milk and the remaining chicken broth. Heat over medium heat until scalded (a thick film forms on top). Stir the flour mixture into the hot milk mixture and cook, stirring constantly, until thickened, about 2 minutes. Remove from the heat and whisk in the puréed cottage cheese and the ½ cup of grated cheese. Season with salt and pepper. To prevent

a skin from forming, place wax paper or plastic wrap directly over the surface and set aside.

6. In a large pot of boiling salted water, cook the macaroni until al dente, 8 to 10 minutes. Drain and return to the pot. Toss with ¼ cup of the grated cheese, the remaining 1 teaspoon oil, and ½ teaspoon of the salt.

7. Preheat oven to 350°. Spray a 9" × 13" baking dish with nonstick cooking spray.

8. Spread ½ of the pasta mixture over the bottom of the prepared dish. Top with ⅓ of the cream sauce. Spoon all of the meat sauce over the top, spreading evenly. Cover with another ⅓ of the cream sauce. Top with the remaining pasta mixture and cover with the remaining cream sauce. Sprinkle with the remaining 2 tablespoons of grated cheese.

9. Bake for 40 to 50 minutes, or until bubbling and golden. Sprinkle with parsley before serving.

Parsley Facts

While lots of dishes look nicer with a sprig of parsley, the problem is that you have to buy it in such big bunches. However, parsley will stay crisp and fresh for up to a week if you store it standing in a glass of ice water in the refrigerator. Change the water every couple of days. If you still haven't used it up, give it to the dog to help freshen his breath.

CHEESE COINS

24 coins

A perfect appetizer for Fusilli with Chicken and Coriander Pesto (page 251).

¼ cup reduced-fat margarine, at room temperature
2 cups shredded low-fat Cheddar cheese
½ teaspoon dry mustard
½ teaspoon seasoned salt

2 teaspoons minced canned green chili peppers
2 teaspoons minced pimientos
½ teaspoon Worcestershire sauce
1¼ cups all-purpose flour

1. Preheat oven to 350°.
2. In a bowl, using a mixer, beat together the margarine, cheese, mustard, seasoned salt, green chilies, pimientos, and Worcestershire sauce until blended.
3. Add the flour, beating it until a stiff dough forms. Shape into small balls (about ½ inch in diameter) and place well spaced on ungreased baking sheets. Press each ball lightly with the tines of a fork.
4. Bake until lightly browned, about 15 minutes. Remove from the oven and serve piping hot. Store in an airtight container at room temperature for up to 2 weeks.

Ovens

Even today's modern ovens can vary widely in temperature. Gas ovens are especially prone to variations. Before you begin using a new oven, buy an inexpensive food thermometer and determine the temperature your oven really cooks at when it's set at various temperatures.

ORECCHIETTE WITH SUMMER TOMATO SAUCE AND OLIVES

1½ pounds tomatoes
2 garlic cloves
2 tablespoons basil leaves
⅓ cup kalamata olives, pitted

3 tablespoons olive oil
½ teaspoon ground black pepper
1 pound orecchiette pasta

Serves 4

Serve with Lemon Blueberry Ice "Cream" (page 257) for dessert.

1. Peel, seed, and chop the tomatoes into ½-inch pieces. Peel and mince the garlic. Shred the basil leaves. Pit the olives, if necessary.
2. In a large bowl, combine the tomatoes, garlic, basil, oil, and pepper; stir to mix well. Set aside at room temperature for at least 30 minutes.
3. Cook the pasta in boiling salted water until al dente. Drain and place in a large warmed bowl.
4. Pour the tomato mixture into a food processor or blender and blend on medium speed until well mixed. Expect a few chunks of tomatoes to remain. (You likely will have to divide the mixture in half to do this.)
5. Put the tomato sauce in a large saucepan and heat on medium heat until it begins to bubble. Serve over pasta. Garnish with the olives.

Pitting Olives

Pitting olives is easy. The key is to use a tool that's as hard as the pits to get them out. Try the bottom of a small pot or pan. Put the olives on a cutting board in groups of 3 or 4 and put the bottom of the pan flat on top of them. With the heel of your hand, smash the olives between the pan and the board, using the curved edge of the pan for leverage. Once flattened, the olives will easily give up their pits.

PEARS IN ORANGE SAUCE

Serves 4

This is the perfect dessert for any Italian or fish dish.

2 Bartlett pears
1 cup water
⅔ cup orange juice
2 tablespoons lemon juice
1 tablespoon cornstarch

3 tablespoons honey
¼ teaspoon orange zest
¼ teaspoon salt
1 bunch fresh mint leaves

1. Halve the pears lengthwise and core.
2. In a medium-sized skillet, bring the water to boil. Add the pear halves, cover, and simmer gently over low heat until tender when pierced with a knife, about 10 minutes. Set aside.
3. In a small saucepan, mix together the orange juice, lemon juice, and cornstarch. Stir until the cornstarch is dissolved. Add the honey, orange zest, and salt; mix well.
4. Place over medium heat and cook until thickened and bubbly, about 10 minutes.
5. To serve, spoon the sauce over the pears and garnish with mint leaves.

Ripening Fruit

If you find you must buy unripe fruit, put it in a paper bag and store it in a cool place for a day or two. Before you know it, the fruit will ripen. This works for any kind of fruit, including berries and tomatoes.

LEMON BLUEBERRY ICE "CREAM"

1 pint fresh blueberries
½ cup granulated sugar, divided
1 tablespoon cornstarch
1 (12-ounce) can evaporated
   skim milk

2 egg whites
1 teaspoon lemon zest
2 tablespoons lemon juice
1 teaspoon pure vanilla extract

Serves 4

If you don't have an ice cream maker, take the mixture out of the refrigerator before it is solid and serve by scraping the top.

1. In a medium-sized saucepan, combine the blueberries with ¼ cup of the sugar. Place over medium heat, stirring constantly, until the sugar dissolves, about 5 minutes. Remove from heat.

2. Place a colander over a bowl and pour the blueberry mixture into the colander. Press the berries through the colander with the back of a spoon. Scrape the mashed berries from the outside of the colander into the bowl with the blueberry juice. Place the bowl in the refrigerator.

3. Add the remaining ¼ cup sugar and the cornstarch to the saucepan. Stir in about ⅔ of the evaporated milk. Place over medium heat and bring to a boil, stirring constantly. Cook the mixture until it is the consistency of pudding.

4. Remove from the heat and add the egg whites and the remaining evaporated milk, mixing well. Stir the milk mixture into the blueberry mixture. Add the lemon zest, lemon juice, and vanilla; stir until blended. Chill for 20 minutes.

5. Pour into an ice cream maker and freeze according to the manufacturer's instructions.

Add a Little Zest

Citrus goes great with seafood of all kinds. Try squeezing some lemon or lime on any of your favorite fish recipes.

CHAPTER 20
ETHNIC FAVORITES

SCANDINAVIAN BAKED COD
WITH SPICY PLUM SAUCE

Serves 4

Add fresh-steamed broccoli and carrots to create a colorful, wholesome meal.

1 garlic clove
1 medium Granny Smith apple
1 small red onion
1 pound cod fillets
1 teaspoon paprika
1 teaspoon grated fresh ginger
1 bay leaf
2 teaspoons soy sauce

1 teaspoon olive oil
¼ cup plum sauce
¼ teaspoon frozen unsweetened apple juice concentrate
¼ teaspoon dark molasses
¼ teaspoon Chinese five-spice powder
1⅓ cups cooked brown rice

1. Preheat oven to 400°. Treat a baking dish with nonstick spray. Crush the garlic clove with the side of a large knife and remove the skin. Peel, core, and chop the apple into ½-inch cubes. Remove the skin from the onion and chop into ¼-inch pieces.

2. Rinse the cod and pat dry between paper towels. Rub both sides of the fish with paprika and set in the prepared baking dish.

3. In a covered, microwave-safe bowl, mix together the garlic, apple, onion, ginger, bay leaf, and soy sauce in the oil and microwave on high for 3 minutes or until the apple is tender and the onion is transparent. Stir, discard the bay leaf, and top the fillets with the apple mixture. Bake, uncovered, for 10 to 15 minutes or until the fish is opaque.

4. While the fish bakes, add the plum sauce to a microwave-safe bowl. Add the apple juice concentrate, molasses, and five-spice powder. Microwave on high for 30 seconds. Stir, add a little water if needed to thin the mixture, and microwave for another 15 seconds. Cover until ready to serve.

5. To serve, equally divide the cooked rice among 4 serving plates. Top each with an equal amount of the baked fish mixture and plum sauce mixture, drizzling the sauce atop the fish.

CHRISTMAS PIGLET

1 (12- to 15-pound) piglet
1 teaspoon salt
½ cup sour cream

½ cup melted butter
¼ cup water

1. Preheat oven to 350°.
2. Scald the piglet and dry with paper towels. Rub the inside with salt and place, back-side up, on a baking sheet.
3. Brush the sides with the sour cream and pour the melted butter over the piglet. Pour the water on the baking sheet. Bake for 1½ hours, basting with the juice that drips onto the baking sheet.

> **Serves 8**
>
> For a traditional Russian meal, serve with baked apples and Roasted Garlic Mashed Potatoes (page 2).

COCONUT TURKEY CURRY

1 medium-sized yellow onion
1 garlic clove
5 cups cubed cooked turkey
½ teaspoon ground ginger
2 teaspoons curry powder
⅓ cup all-purpose flour

2 cups chicken or turkey broth, divided
1 teaspoon salt
1 teaspoon ground black pepper
1 (16-ounce) can coconut cream, unsweetened
1 cup skim milk

1. Peel the onion and garlic and cut into quarters. Cut the turkey into 1-inch cubes.
2. Purée the onions, garlic, ginger, curry powder, flour, and ½ cup of the broth until smooth.
3. In a large saucepan, combine the puréed mixture and all the remaining ingredients *except* the turkey. Cook, stirring often, until thickened. Add the meat and heat gently.

> **Serves 6**
>
> Serve with white rice and small dishes of raisins, peanuts, chutney, coconut, bacon, and green onions on the side.

VIETNAMESE CRAB AND PINEAPPLE SOUP

Serves 8

Be sure that you use fresh pineapple with this recipe. Canned pineapple will adversely affect the taste.

1 cooked Dungeness crab
15 medium-sized raw shrimp
15 medium-sized steamer clams
1 cup cubed fresh pineapple
½ small yellow onion
4 garlic cloves
½ pound ripe tomatoes
2 scallions
4 cilantro sprigs
5 basil leaves
3 dill sprigs
6 mint leaves

3 tablespoons olive oil
10 cups water
1 stalk lemongrass
3 tablespoons Vietnamese fish sauce
2 tablespoons granulated sugar
½ teaspoon chili sauce
1 teaspoon salt
2 tablespoons fresh-squeezed lime juice
⅛ teaspoon saffron
1 bay leaf

1. Remove the meat from the crab. Peel and devein the shrimp (leaving the tails on). Scrub the clamshells. Cut the pineapple into bite-sized chunks. Peel the onion and garlic, and chop into ¼-inch pieces. Seed and chop the tomatoes into ½-inch pieces. Chop the scallions, cilantro, basil leaves, dill, and mint.
2. Heat the oil in a soup pot. Add the onion and sauté on medium for 3 minutes. Add the garlic and tomatoes; cook for 3 more minutes. Add the pineapple, water, and lemongrass, bringing everything to a boil. Reduce to a simmer and cook for 20 minutes.
3. Add the fish sauce, sugar, chili sauce, salt, and lime juice. Bring to a boil. Add the crab, and the clams in their shells, cooking for about 5 minutes, until the clams are open.
4. Add the shrimp, scallions, cilantro, basil, dill, mint, saffron, and bay leaf; simmer for 2 to 3 more minutes, until the shrimp turn pink. Discard the bay leaf and lemongrass stalk, and serve.

BRAZILIAN PAELLA

½ pound spicy pork sausage
1 (2–3-pound) chicken
2 large yellow onions
1 pound canned tomatoes
½ teaspoon salt

½ teaspoon ground black pepper
1½ cups uncooked long-grain
    brown rice
3 chicken bouillon cubes
2 cups hot water

Serves 8

Serve with fresh-sliced oranges and bananas sprinkled with coconut to achieve a true Brazilian flavor.

---

1. Form the sausage into balls about the size of large marbles. Clean and cut the chicken into serving-sized pieces. Peel and chop the onions into ¼-inch pieces. Drain the tomatoes, retaining the liquid, and cut into 1-inch pieces.
2. Using a large skillet on medium-high heat, fry the sausage balls until they are well browned and crisp. Place them on paper towels to absorb the grease. Sprinkle the chicken with salt and pepper. Without emptying the grease from the skillet, fry the chicken pieces for about 10 minutes. Place the chicken on paper towels to absorb the grease.
3. Drain all but 3 tablespoons of grease from the skillet. Sauté the onions on medium heat in the skillet until translucent. Add the rice to the skillet and continue to sauté, stirring constantly for 10 minutes.
4. Place the sausage balls, chicken, onion and rice mixture, tomato juice, and tomatoes in a slow cooker. Mix the bouillon in the hot water. Add to the slow cooker. Cover and cook on low setting for 8 to 9 hours.

Freezing Cooked Rice
Cooked rice can be frozen up to 6 months. The next time you make some for a meal, make twice what you need and freeze the rest in an airtight container. It needs virtually no thawing when added to a casserole.

FRENCH COUNTRY MUSSELS

Serves 6

Serve with white rice and fresh-steamed asparagus.

1 large white onion
4 garlic cloves
1 (16-ounce) can peeled tomatoes
½ cup minced fresh parsley

4 pounds mussels
1 tablespoon olive oil
1 cup dry white wine
½ teaspoon ground black pepper

1. Peel the onion and chop into ¼-inch pieces. Peel and mince the garlic. Drain the tomatoes. Mince the parsley. Scrub and debeard the mussels.
2. In an 8-quart pot, heat the oil over medium heat. Add the onion and garlic, and sauté until browned, about 10 minutes.
3. Add the tomatoes, breaking them up with a wooden spoon. Add the parsley and pepper. Raise the heat to high and cook for about 2 minutes.
4. Add the wine and cook for another 2 minutes.
5. Add the mussels, tossing them to coat well with the tomato mixture. Cover and cook, stirring occasionally, until the mussels open, about 5 minutes. Discard any mussels that did not open. Serve immediately.

What Is Clarified Butter?

Clarified butter is also known as drawn butter. Clarifying butter separates the milk solids and evaporates the water, leaving a clear golden liquid. Clarified butter has a higher heating point before smoking and also has a longer shelf life than regular butter. Clarified butter is used to sauté where a high heating point is needed.

NORTH AFRICAN EGGPLANT

2 medium eggplants
3 tablespoons olive oil, divided
1 large ripe tomato
4 garlic cloves
1 tablespoon dried marjoram

1 teaspoon coriander seeds
¼ teaspoon salt
½ teaspoon crushed red pepper
1 tablespoon toasted pine nuts

> **Serves 6**
>
> This side dish is perfect with seafood or other light main dishes.

1. Preheat oven to 425°.
2. Peel the eggplants and cut into 1-inch cubes. Toss with half of the olive oil and place in a shallow roasting pan. Roast, uncovered, for 10 minutes, stirring once.
3. Meanwhile, chop the tomato. Peel and mince the garlic.
4. Heat the remaining oil in a large skillet. Cook the tomato, garlic, marjoram, coriander, salt, and red pepper until the tomato is soft. Add the eggplant and reduce heat to low.
5. Cook, covered, for 10 minutes. Stir in the pine nuts during the last 5 minutes of cooking.

What to Brown In

For browning and crispness, clarified butter achieves the best results. This may be because residual proteins in the butter caramelize on foods, or it may simply be the high temperatures that clarified butter can reach without burning. Start with a neutral oil, such as peanut oil, and add a nugget of whole butter to get a better brown.

NATIVE AMERICAN PUDDING

2 tablespoons butter, plus ¼
    tablespoon for greasing
3 cups 1% milk
½ cup cornmeal
½ teaspoon salt

3 large eggs, beaten
¼ packed cup light brown sugar
⅓ cup molasses
½ teaspoon allspice
½ teaspoon ginger

1. Lightly grease a 3- to 6-quart slow cooker with the ¼ tablespoon butter. Preheat the slow cooker on high for 15 minutes.
2. In a medium-sized saucepan, bring the milk, cornmeal, and salt to a boil. Boil, stirring constantly, for 5 minutes. Cover and simmer on low for 10 minutes.
3. In a large bowl, combine the remaining ingredients. Gradually whisk the cornmeal mixture into the combined ingredients until thoroughly mixed and smooth. Pour into slow cooker. Cover and cook on low setting for 4 to 5 hours.

Stocking Up on Ethnic Staples

If your local grocery store doesn't carry certain ethnic spices or ingredients, you may be able to find them on the Internet or at specialty shops. Just make sure to stock up on shelf-stable necessities so you can make these dishes whenever you like.

GERMAN COFFEE CAKE

½ cup butter
1¼ cups granulated sugar,
    divided
2 eggs
1 cup sour cream
1 teaspoon vanilla extract

1 teaspoon baking soda
1 teaspoon baking powder
½ teaspoon salt
2 cups all-purpose flour
½ cup chopped walnuts
1 teaspoon cinnamon

10 servings

This Bavarian treat often is served as a Sunday morning treat with strong black coffee.

1. Preheat oven to 350°. Grease a 13" × 9" baking pan.
2. Cream together the butter and 1 cup of the sugar thoroughly. Add the eggs, sour cream, vanilla, baking soda, baking powder, salt, and flour; beat well. Pour into the prepared baking pan.
3. Combine the remaining ¼ cup sugar, the nuts, and cinnamon to make the topping. Lightly stir 2 tablespoons of the topping into the batter. Pour patter into baking pan and sprinkle remaining topping on top.
4. Bake for 35 to 40 minutes.

Where'd They Get That Stuff?

Coffee, nuts, coconut, and cinnamon. Not exactly foods you think of being native to Germany, so how did these dishes become synonymous with this cool-weather country? Most likely, they were brought to Germany when Marco Polo followed Genghis Khan from eastern China through Russia and into Europe.

MINTED MIDDLE EASTERN BUTTERMILK SHAKE

Serves 1
Serve with red meat or chicken dishes.

Handful ice cubes
1 cup nonfat buttermilk
⅛ teaspoon salt

¼ cup fresh mint leaves, plus
*   extra for garnish*

Combine all of the ingredients in a blender. Cover and blend until the ice becomes blended. Pour into a tall mug and garnish with more mint leaves.

Fresh Mint

For the freshest mint, try growing your own. You can start them from seeds or from young seedlings that have already been started. Put them in an enclosed space or pots or they will spread. If you want to grow mint indoors, put it in a window that gets a lot of sunlight.

Appendices

Appendix A
Suggested Meals

Appendix B
U.S. to Metric Units Conversion

Appendix A: Suggested Meals

Thanksgiving
Roast Turkey with Fruit Stuffing / 3
Roasted Garlic Mashed Potatoes / 2
Oven-Roasted Asparagus / 7
Pecan Pie / 14
Spiced Cranberry Glogg / 14

Christmas
Holiday Goose with Cranberries / 21
Honey-Orange Beets / 24
Gingered Mashed Sweet Potatoes / 26
Oysters Rockefeller Soup / 28
Plum Pudding Pie / 38
Holiday Punch / 43

New Year's Eve Buffet
Stuffed Mushrooms / 48
Creamy Garlic and Red Pepper Dip / 50
Parmesan Crisps / 51
Artichoke Bottoms with Herbed Cheese / 51
Louisiana Hot Wings / 52
Fried Green Tomato Bruschetta / 55
Peanut Popcorn Fudge / 57
Champagne Mint drinks / 61

Valentine's Day
French Onion Soup / 70
Spinach-Wrapped Zucchini Flan / 69
Grilled Lobster with Lemon and Tarragon / 72
Caramel Rum Fondue / 74
Midori Mimosa drinks / 81

Easter
Apricot-Stuffed Pork Tenderloin / 88
Scented Escarole with Fennel / 86

Baked Pear Crisp / 91
Lemony Apple Drink / 97

Passover
Zucchini-Stuffed Chicken / 100
Spinach Fritatta / 108
Apple Haroset / 106
Chocolate Raspberry Torte / 109

Cinco de Mayo
Mexican Chicken Roll-Ups / 114
Baja Lobster Tails / 115
Margarita Pie / 120
Fruity Margaritas /124
Mexican Coffee / 122

Mother's Day
Mimosa / 141
Classic Waldorf Salad / 133
Figs with Brie and Port Wine Reduction / 129
Hot Dill Pasta with Scallops / 128
Cherries Jubilee / 140

Father's Day
Beer Soup / 129
Filet Southwestern / 132
Broccoli Florets with Lemon Butter Sauce / 127
Chocolate Mousse / 139

Memorial Day
Texas Caviar with chips / 144
London Broil with Mushrooms / 147
Green Beans in Lemon Honey / 145
Strawberry Sorbet / 153
Mint Julep / 154

Summer Picnics
Tricolor Pepper Salad / 161
Honey Dijon Tuna Salad / 158
Wild Blackberry Pie / 164
Cape Cod Punch / 165

Fourth of July
All-American Barbecued Chicken / 174
Jumbo Beer-Battered Onion Rings / 169
Barbecued Pork and Beans / 175
Three-Bean Salad / 170
Strawberry Pie / 178

Labor Day
Planter's Punch / 190
Sweet Corn Pudding / 182
Baby Back Ribs with Sauerkraut / 186
Cheery Cherry Crispy / 189

Fall Is in the Air Celebration
Nonalcoholic Mulled Cider Punch / 202
Venison with Dried Cranberry
Vinegar Sauce / 197
Roasted Butternut Squash Pasta / 193
Wild Rice with Apples and Almonds / 196
Apple Crisp / 200

Kid's Celebration
Sloppy Joes / 204
Red Devil Chocolate Cake / 209
Ooey, Gooey S'mores / 210
Minty Hot Chocolate / 212

Jewish Holidays
Caraway-Rubbed Chicken / 214
Yam Latkes with Mustard Seeds and Curry / 215
Purim Poppy Seed Candy / 226

Celebrate with Diabetes
Mock Stuffed Grape Leaves / 231
Cucumber Slices with
Smoked Salmon Cream / 228
Fillets of Fish with Lime and Cumin / 231
Bananas Foster / 234

Low-Carb Celebration
Crabmeat on Red Pepper Strips / 236
Stilton and Cheddar Cheese Soup / 238
Red Snapper with Cayenne Tomato Sauce / 241
Refrigerator Pumpkin Pie
with Macadamia Nut Crust / 245

Low-Fat Celebration
Cheese Coins / 254
Baked Red Snapper Almandine / 249
Pears in Orange Sauce / 256

International Celebration
Vietnamese Crab and Pineapple Soup / 262
Scandinavian Baked Cod
with Spicy Plum Sauce / 260
Minted Middle Eastern Buttermilk Shake / 268
German Coffee Cake / 267

Appendix B: U.S. to Metric Units Conversion

Volume

1 teaspoon	5 milliliters
1 tablespoon	15 milliliters
¼ cup	60 milliliters
⅓ cup	80 milliliters
½ cup	120 milliliters
1 cup	240 milliliters
1 pint (2 cups)	480 milliliters
1 quart (4 cups)	.95 liter
1 gallon (16 cups)	3.8 liters

Weight

1 ounce	28 grams
1 pound (16 ounces)	454 grams

Length

1 inch	2.54 centimeters
1 foot (12 inches)	30.48 centimeters

Temperature

32°F (freezing point of water)	0°C
300°F	150°C
350°F	175°C
400°F	200°C
450°F	230°C

Index

A

All-American Barbecued Chicken, 174

almonds
Almond Cookies, 96
Baked Red Snapper Almandine, 249
Crunchy Nut Treats, 58
Wild Rice with Apples and Almonds, 196

Amaretto Cake, 78

Anise Oval Cookies, 32

appetizers and dips
Artichoke Bottoms with Herbed Cheese, 51
Broccoli Dip, 50
Creamy Garlic and Red Pepper Dip, 50
Eggplant Caviar, 54
Fried Green Tomato Bruschetta, 55
Guacamole, 118
Herbed Clam Dip, 52
Hot Artichoke Dip, 56
Louisiana Hot Wings, 52
Parmesan Crisps, 51
Pears Wrapped in Prosciutto on a Bed of Mixed Greens, 53
Pepita Balls, 121
Spinach and Ricotta Dip, 56
Stuffed Mushrooms, 48
Vegetable Gado-Gado, 49

apples and apple juice
Apple Blossom, 15
Apple-Buttered Rum Pudding with Apple Topping, 79
Apple-Cinnamon Farfel Kugel, 107
Apple Crisp, 200
Apple Haroset, 106
Cheesy Golden Apple Omelet, 133
Classic Apple Pie, 179
Classic Waldorf Salad, 133
Fruited Pork Loin Casserole, 192

Gorgonzola and Apple Salad, 223
Lemony Apple Drink, 97
Mexican Christmas Eve Salad, 27
Old-Fashioned Baked Apples, 210
Roast Turkey with Fruit Stuffing, 3
Spinach Salad with Apple-Avocado Dressing, 158
Warm Sweet Potato and Apple Salad, 6
Wild Rice with Apples and Almonds, 196

apricots and apricot nectar
Apricot Sparkler, 98
Apricot-Stuffed Pork Tenderloin, 88
Fruited Pork Loin Casserole, 192

artichokes
about: how to eat, 64
Artichoke Bottoms with Herbed Cheese, 51
Artichokes in Court Bouillon with Lemon Butter, 64
Hot Artichoke Dip, 56
Pasta with Artichokes, 68
White Bean and Artichoke Salad, 105

arugula
about, 242
Portobellos Stuffed with Basil and Salmon on Arugula Leaves, 242

asparagus
about: freshness, 7
Lobster and Asparagus Salad, 240
Oven-Roasted Asparagus, 7

avocados
about: pitting of, 118
Avocado and Peach Salad, 157
California Garden Salad with Avocado and Sprouts, 162
Guacamole, 118

Orange-Avocado Slaw, 168
Spinach Salad with Apple-Avocado Dressing, 158
Texas Caviar, 144
Totopos, 113

B

Baby Back Ribs with Sauerkraut, 186

Baja Lobster Tails, 115

Baked Alaska, peppermint, 41

Baked Orange Roughy with Orange-Rice Dressing, 84

Baked Pear Crisp, 91

Baked Red Snapper Almandine, 249

Balsamic-Marinated Beef Tenderloin, 187

bananas
about: freezing, 234
Bananas Foster, 234
Polynesian Banana Salad, 159

Bar Harbor Fish Chowder, 135

bay leaves, 238

beans
about: cooking, 206
Barbecued Pork and Beans, 175
Enchiladas, 121
Green Beans in Lemon Honey, 145
Risotto with Fresh Summer Vegetables, 159
Scallops and Shrimp with White Bean Sauce, 65
Summer Vegetable Slaw, 163
Three-Bean Salad, 170
Totopos, 113
Vegetable Gado-Gado, 49
White Bean and Artichoke Salad, 105

beef
about: grades of, 151
Balsamic-Marinated Beef Tenderloin, 187

THE EVERYTHING SERIES!

BUSINESS

Everything® Business Planning Book
Everything® Coaching and Mentoring Book
Everything® Fundraising Book
Everything® Home-Based Business Book
Everything® Landlording Book
Everything® Leadership Book
Everything® Managing People Book
Everything® Negotiating Book
Everything® Network Marketing Book
Everything® Online Business Book
Everything® Project Management Book
Everything® Robert's Rules Book,
      $7.95($11.95 CAN)
Everything® Selling Book
Everything® Start Your Own Business Book
Everything® Time Management Book

COMPUTERS

Everything® Build Your Own Home Page Book
Everything® Computer Book

COOKBOOKS

Everything® Barbecue Cookbook
Everything® Bartender's Book, $9.95
      ($15.95 CAN)
Everything® Chinese Cookbook
Everything® Chocolate Cookbook
Everything® Cookbook
Everything® Dessert Cookbook
Everything® Diabetes Cookbook
Everything® Fondue Cookbook
Everything® Grilling Cookbook
Everything® Holiday Cookbook
Everything® Indian Cookbook
Everything® Low-Carb Cookbook
Everything® Low-Fat High-Flavor Cookbook
Everything® Low-Salt Cookbook
Everything® Mediterranean Cookbook
Everything® Mexican Cookbook
Everything® One-Pot Cookbook

Everything® Pasta Cookbook
Everything® Quick Meals Cookbook
Everything® Slow Cooker Cookbook
Everything® Soup Cookbook
Everything® Thai Cookbook
Everything® Vegetarian Cookbook
Everything® Wine Book

HEALTH

Everything® Alzheimer's Book
Everything® Anti-Aging Book
Everything® Diabetes Book
Everything® Dieting Book
Everything® Hypnosis Book
Everything® Low Cholesterol Book
Everything® Massage Book
Everything® Menopause Book
Everything® Nutrition Book
Everything® Reflexology Book
Everything® Reiki Book
Everything® Stress Management Book
Everything® Vitamins, Minerals, and
      Nutritional Supplements Book

HISTORY

Everything® American Government Book
Everything® American History Book
Everything® Civil War Book
Everything® Irish History & Heritage Book
Everything® Mafia Book
Everything® Middle East Book

HOBBIES & GAMES

Everything® Bridge Book
Everything® Candlemaking Book
Everything® Card Games Book
Everything® Cartooning Book
Everything® Casino Gambling Book, 2nd Ed.
Everything® Chess Basics Book
Everything® Collectibles Book
Everything® Crossword and Puzzle Book

Everything® Crossword Challenge Book
Everything® Drawing Book
Everything® Digital Photography Book
Everything® Easy Crosswords Book
Everything® Family Tree Book
Everything® Games Book
Everything® Knitting Book
Everything® Magic Book
Everything® Motorcycle Book
Everything® Online Genealogy Book
Everything® Photography Book
Everything® Poker Strategy Book
Everything® Pool & Billiards Book
Everything® Quilting Book
Everything® Scrapbooking Book
Everything® Sewing Book
Everything® Soapmaking Book

HOME IMPROVEMENT

Everything® Feng Shui Book
Everything® Feng Shui Decluttering Book,
      $9.95 ($15.95 CAN)
Everything® Fix-It Book
Everything® Homebuilding Book
Everything® Home Decorating Book
Everything® Landscaping Book
Everything® Lawn Care Book
Everything® Organize Your Home Book

EVERYTHING® KIDS' BOOKS

All titles are $6.95 ($10.95 Canada)
unless otherwise noted
Everything® Kids' Baseball Book, 3rd Ed.
Everything® Kids' Bible Trivia Book
Everything® Kids' Bugs Book
Everything® Kids' Christmas Puzzle
      & Activity Book
Everything® Kids' Cookbook
Everything® Kids' Halloween Puzzle
      & Activity Book ($9.95 CAN)

All Everything® books are priced at $12.95 or $14.95, unless otherwise stated. Prices subject to change without notice.
Canadian prices range from $11.95–$31.95, and are subject to change without notice.

Everything® Kids' Hidden Pictures Book
($9.95 CAN)
Everything® Kids' Joke Book
Everything® Kids' Knock Knock Book
($9.95 CAN)
Everything® Kids' Math Puzzles Book
Everything® Kids' Mazes Book
Everything® Kids' Money Book ($11.95 CAN)
Everything® Kids' Monsters Book
Everything® Kids' Nature Book ($11.95 CAN)
Everything® Kids' Puzzle Book
Everything® Kids' Riddles & Brain Teasers Book
Everything® Kids' Science Experiments Book
Everything® Kids' Soccer Book
Everything® Kids' Travel Activity Book

KIDS' STORY BOOKS

Everything® Bedtime Story Book
Everything® Bible Stories Book
Everything® Fairy Tales Book
Everything® Mother Goose Book

LANGUAGE

Everything® Conversational Japanese Book
(with CD), $19.95 ($31.95 CAN)
Everything® Inglés Book
Everything® French Phrase Book, $9.95
($15.95 CAN)
Everything® Learning French Book
Everything® Learning German Book
Everything® Learning Italian Book
Everything® Learning Latin Book
Everything® Learning Spanish Book
Everything® Sign Language Book
Everything® Spanish Phrase Book,
$9.95 ($15.95 CAN)
Everything® Spanish Verb Book,
$9.95 ($15.95 CAN)

MUSIC

Everything® Drums Book (with CD),
$19.95 ($31.95 CAN)
Everything® Guitar Book
Everything® Home Recording Book
Everything® Playing Piano and Keyboards Book
Everything® Rock & Blues Guitar Book
(with CD), $19.95 ($31.95 CAN)
Everything® Songwriting Book

NEW AGE

Everything® Astrology Book
Everything® Divining the Future Book
Everything® Dreams Book
Everything® Ghost Book
Everything® Love Signs Book,
$9.95 ($15.95 CAN)
Everything® Meditation Book
Everything® Numerology Book
Everything® Paganism Book
Everything® Palmistry Book
Everything® Psychic Book
Everything® Spells & Charms Book
Everything® Tarot Book
Everything® Wicca and Witchcraft Book

PARENTING

Everything® Baby Names Book
Everything® Baby Shower Book
Everything® Baby's First Food Book
Everything® Baby's First Year Book
Everything® Birthing Book
Everything® Breastfeeding Book
Everything® Father-to-Be Book
Everything® Get Ready for Baby Book
Everything® Getting Pregnant Book
Everything® Homeschooling Book
Everything® Parent's Guide to Children
with Asperger's Syndrome
Everything® Parent's Guide to Children
with Autism
Everything® Parent's Guide to Children
with Dyslexia
Everything® Parent's Guide to Positive Discipline
Everything® Parent's Guide to Raising a
Successful Child
Everything® Parenting a Teenager Book
Everything® Potty Training Book,
$9.95 ($15.95 CAN)
Everything® Pregnancy Book, 2nd Ed.
Everything® Pregnancy Fitness Book
Everything® Pregnancy Nutrition Book
Everything® Pregnancy Organizer,
$15.00 ($22.95 CAN)
Everything® Toddler Book
Everything® Tween Book

PERSONAL FINANCE

Everything® Budgeting Book
Everything® Get Out of Debt Book

Everything® Get Rich Book
Everything® Homebuying Book, 2nd Ed.
Everything® Homeselling Book
Everything® Investing Book
Everything® Money Book
Everything® Mutual Funds Book
Everything® Online Business Book
Everything® Personal Finance Book
Everything® Personal Finance in Your
20s & 30s Book
Everything® Real Estate Investing Book
Everything® Wills & Estate Planning Book

PETS

Everything® Cat Book
Everything® Dog Book
Everything® Dog Training and Tricks Book
Everything® Golden Retriever Book
Everything® Horse Book
Everything® Labrador Retriever Book
Everything® Poodle Book
Everything® Puppy Book
Everything® Rottweiler Book
Everything® Tropical Fish Book

REFERENCE

Everything® Astronomy Book
Everything® Car Care Book
Everything® Christmas Book,
$15.00 ($21.95 CAN)
Everything® Classical Mythology Book
Everything® Einstein Book
Everything® Etiquette Book
Everything® Great Thinkers Book
Everything® Philosophy Book
Everything® Psychology Book
Everything® Shakespeare Book
Everything® Tall Tales, Legends, & Other
Outrageous Lies Book
Everything® Toasts Book
Everything® Trivia Book
Everything® Weather Book

RELIGION

Everything® Angels Book
Everything® Bible Book
Everything® Buddhism Book
Everything® Catholicism Book
Everything® Christianity Book
Everything® Jewish History & Heritage Book

All Everything® books are priced at $12.95 or $14.95, unless otherwise stated. Prices subject to change without notice.
Canadian prices range from $11.95–$31.95, and are subject to change without notice.

Everything® Judaism Book
Everything® Koran Book
Everything® Prayer Book
Everything® Saints Book
Everything® Understanding Islam Book
Everything® World's Religions Book
Everything® Zen Book

SCHOOL & CAREERS

Everything® After College Book
Everything® Alternative Careers Book
Everything® College Survival Book
Everything® Cover Letter Book
Everything® Get-a-Job Book
Everything® Hot Careers Book
Everything® Job Interview Book
Everything® New Teacher Book
Everything® Online Job Search Book
Everything® Personal Finance Book
Everything® Practice Interview Book
Everything® Resume Book, 2nd Ed.
Everything® Study Book

SELF-HELP/ RELATIONSHIPS

Everything® Dating Book
Everything® Divorce Book
Everything® Great Marriage Book
Everything® Great Sex Book
Everything® Kama Sutra Book
Everything® Romance Book
Everything® Self-Esteem Book
Everything® Success Book

SPORTS & FITNESS

Everything® Body Shaping Book
Everything® Fishing Book
Everything® Fly-Fishing Book
Everything® Golf Book
Everything® Golf Instruction Book
Everything® Knots Book
Everything® Pilates Book
Everything® Running Book
Everything® Sailing Book, 2nd Ed.
Everything® T'ai Chi and QiGong Book
Everything® Total Fitness Book
Everything® Weight Training Book
Everything® Yoga Book

TRAVEL

Everything® Family Guide to Hawaii
Everything® Family Guide to New York City, 2nd Ed.
Everything® Family Guide to Washington D.C., 2nd Ed.
Everything® Family Guide to the Walt Disney World Resort®, Universal Studios®, and Greater Orlando, 4th Ed.
Everything® Guide to Las Vegas
Everything® Guide to New England
Everything® Travel Guide to the Disneyland Resort®, California Adventure®, Universal Studios®, and the Anaheim Area

WEDDINGS

Everything® Bachelorette Party Book, $9.95 ($15.95 CAN)

Everything® Bridesmaid Book, $9.95 ($15.95 CAN)
Everything® Creative Wedding Ideas Book
Everything® Elopement Book, $9.95 ($15.95 CAN)
Everything® Father of the Bride Book, $9.95 ($15.95 CAN)
Everything® Groom Book, $9.95 ($15.95 CAN)
Everything® Jewish Wedding Book
Everything® Mother of the Bride Book, $9.95 ($15.95)
Everything® Wedding Book, 3rd Ed.
Everything® Wedding Checklist, $7.95 ($12.95 CAN)
Everything® Wedding Etiquette Book, $7.95 ($12.95 CAN)
Everything® Wedding Organizer, $15.00 ($22.95 CAN)
Everything® Wedding Shower Book, $7.95 ($12.95 CAN)
Everything® Wedding Vows Book, $7.95 ($12.95 CAN)
Everything® Weddings on a Budget Book, $9.95 ($15.95 CAN)

WRITING

Everything® Creative Writing Book
Everything® Get Published Book
Everything® Grammar and Style Book
Everything® Grant Writing Book
Everything® Guide to Writing a Novel
Everything® Guide to Writing Children's Books
Everything® Screenwriting Book
Everything® Writing Well Book

....

Introducing an exceptional new line of beginner craft books from the *Everything®* series!

All titles are $14.95 ($22.95 CAN)

Everything® Crafts—Create Your Own Greeting Cards
1-59337-226-4
Everything® Crafts—Polymer Clay for Beginners
1-59337-230-2

Everything® Crafts—Rubberstamping Made Easy
1-59337-229-9
Everything® Crafts—Wedding Decorations and Keepsakes
1-59337-227-2

Available wherever books are sold!
To order, call 800-872-5627, or visit us at *www.everything.com*
Everything® and everything.com® are registered trademarks of F+W Publications, Inc.